Guide to
Adirondack Trails:

EASTERN
REGION

Second Edition
The Forest Preserve Series (2nd ed.), Volume VI

By Carl Heilman II
Series Editor, Neal Burdick

The Adirondack Mountain Club, Inc.

First edition, 1987
Second edition, 1994

Library of Congress Cataloging-in-Publication Data

Heilman, Carl, 1954–
    Guide to Adirondack Trails: Eastern Region / by Carl Heilman II.
        —2nd ed.
            p. cm.—(The Forest preserve series. ; v. 6)
            Rev. ed. of: Guide to Adirondack Trails: Eastern Region / Betsy Tisdale.
        ©1987.
    Includes index.
    ISBN 0-935272-74-7 : $16.95   ISBN 0-935272-64-x (set)
        1. Hiking – New York (State)—Adirondack Mountains – Guidebooks.
2. Trails— New York (State)—Adirondack Mountains Guidebooks.
3. Adirondack Park (N.Y.)—Guidebooks   I. Tisdale, Betsy, 1947–
Guide to Adirondack Trails: Eastern Region.   II. Title.
III. Series : Forest preserve series (2nd ed.) ; v. 6.
GV199.42.N652A3474   1994
796. .5'1'097475—dc20

94-28835
CIP

Printed and bound in the
United States of America

Dedication

To all those who cherish and protect the wilderness.

CARL E. HEILMAN II

Eastern Region

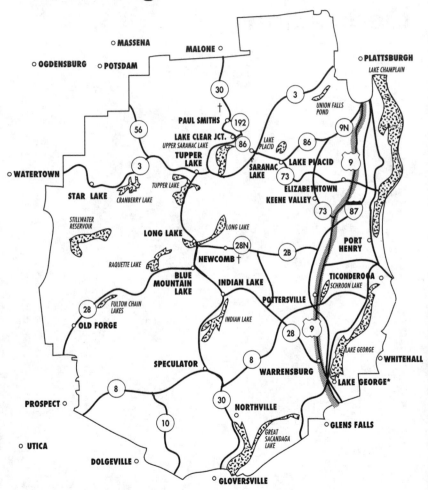

* Adirondack Mountain Club Information Center & Headquarters
† Visitor Interpretive Center

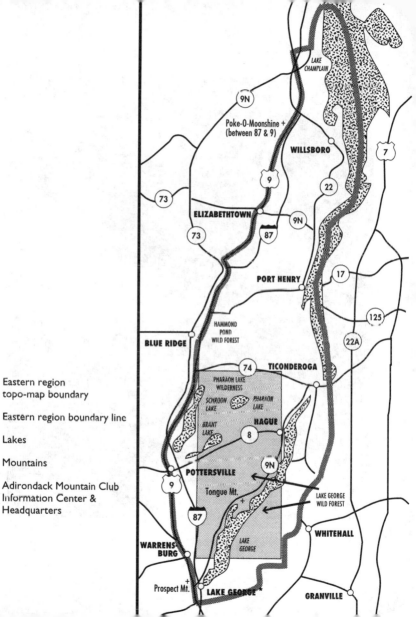

Eastern region
topo-map boundary

Eastern region boundary line

Lakes

+ Mountains

* Adirondack Mountain Club
Information Center &
Headquarters

LAKE CHAMPLAIN

9N

Poke-O-Moonshine +
(between 87 & 9)

WILLSBORO

7

9

22

73

ELIZABETHTOWN

9N

73

87

PORT HENRY

17

125

22A

HAMMOND POND WILD FOREST

BLUE RIDGE

74

TICONDEROGA

PHARAOH LAKE WILDERNESS

SCHROON LAKE

PHARAOH LAKE

BRANT LAKE

HAGUE

8

9N

POTTERSVILLE

Tongue Mt.

LAKE GEORGE WILD FOREST

9

87

WHITEHALL

WARRENSBURG

LAKE GEORGE

Prospect Mt. +

LAKE GEORGE *

GRANVILLE

Pharaoh Lake and the Pharaoh Lake Wilderness from Treadway Mt.

Preface to the Second Edition

Each region of the Adirondacks has its own distinct appeal and the Eastern Region is no exception. Bordered by Lake Champlain on the east, the High Peaks, Hoffman Notch Wilderness and Schroon Lake on the west, and containing the Lake George area in the south, this region is characterized by rolling mountains and foothills, numerous isolated ponds and some beautiful lakes. Scenery varies from subtle and serene shoreline views to spectacular vistas from lookouts and mountaintops. Many of the trails in the region lead to or connect bodies of water. So, while walking the trails is enjoyable in itself, hiking the trails with a small ultralight canoe such as Hornbeck's Rushton design Lost Pond boat adds a whole new dimension to exploring the eastern Adirondacks.

This second edition of *Guide to Adirondack Trails: Eastern Region* is a complete revision of the first. Not only have there been a number of changes in the trails themselves, but also the whole format of the guidebook has been changed. The book has been divided into sections containing integral geographic units with emphasis placed on the trails within each. These geographic units conform to guidelines set by DEC (New York State Department of Environmental Conservation) to help tie in with their overall master plan for the Park.

Changes in format include the numbering of all trails with corresponding numbers on the map to make both map and guidebook use easier. The map is also marked with grid coordinates that correspond to each trail description. In addition, there are now descriptions of potential winter uses of each trail for both ski touring and snowshoeing where appropriate. The list of trails includes only those trails either on public lands or those with public right-of-way, to help avoid problems with private land being closed in the future and potential conflicts with private landowners.

In revising this book, I have used a number of Betsy Tisdale's trail descriptions from the first edition and want to express my thanks for all she did to put together that edition, and for her help with this edition. Also, many thanks to those folks who have helped with various information along the way, including Todd Earl, Rick Stevens, DEC foresters Rick Fenton and James Papero, Warrensburg DEC operations director John Stevens, and forest rangers William Houck and Ed Russell. Thanks also to Bill Brown, Tim Barnett and Tom Duffus of the Adirondack Nature Conservancy and Adirondack Land Trust, and to Mike Carr of the Lake George Basin Land Conservancy for their help with information regarding conservancy projects as well as other trail descriptions. And a special thanks to series editor Neal Burdick for picking up on on all the details and smoothing out the text, and to Andrea Masters, ADK publications director, for her guidance and patience throughout the whole project.

In rewriting this guide, I have not included most of the many fine bushwhacks in the region. There are no towering high peaks in the eastern region, but there are many fine lookouts and open rock knobs with spectacular views of the High Peaks, Lake Champlain and Vermont, and the rolling hills of the eastern Adirondacks. I feel that one of the appeals of these isolated unmarked lookouts is the challenge of exploring the region and finding them on your own. The purpose of this guidebook is to help people safely traverse the marked and maintained trails throughout the region and to introduce people to its beauty, not to stake out every unknown lookout and untracked pond. As pressures continue to mount on the wild regions of the Earth, my hope is that there will always be some uncharted wilderness for the backcountry adventurer.

The Pharaoh Lake Wilderness, the only wilderness region within the scope of this guidebook, sees a lot of use throughout the summer season. Some parts of this region suffer from considerable overuse, while trails a short distance away are seldom used. To help maintain the character of wilderness, consider seeking out the lesser-used trails, or visit some of the other areas in the region. Although Pharaoh is the only designated Wilderness Area in the eastern section, some of the trails in the Wild Forest regions are just as isolated, wild and beautiful as any found in the Adirondack Park. Our own use of these sensitive areas determines the quality of every other person's wilderness experience. It is only through our own proper actions (or inactions) that the character of these regions will be maintained for the future.

CARL HEILMAN II
Brant Lake, New York
August 1994

Attention All Hikers, Backpackers and Canoeists!

Because trail and waterway conditions change, and new boundaries and easements are established, we revise and update our guidebooks regularly. If you have come across an error, discrepancy, or need for an update in this guidebook (be sure you are using the latest edition), we want to hear about it so a change can be made in the next edition.

Please address your comments to the publications director of the Adirondack Mountain Club, citing guidebook title, year of edition, section or trail described, page number, and date of your observation. Thanks for your help.

Note: ADK makes every effort to keep its guidebooks up to date. However, each printing can only be as current as the last press date; thus, use of this information is at the sole risk of the user.

Contents

Page Maps

Introduction

The Adirondack Mountain Club Forest Preserve Series

The Forest Preserve Series of Guides to Adirondack and Catskill Trails covers all hiking opportunities on the approximately 2.75 million acres of public Forest Preserve land located within the Adirondack and Catskill parks. The Adirondack Mountain Club (ADK) published the first guidebook in this series over sixty years ago with the idea that hiking guides would eventually cover all Forest Preserve lands; it is appropriate that the completion of this series coincided with the decade-long centennial celebration of the enactment of the Forest Preserve legislation. Each guide in this series, listed below, has been written or revised within the last few years.

The public lands that constitute the Adirondack Forest Preserve are unique among all other wild public lands in the United States because they enjoy constitutional protection against sale or development. The story of this unique protection begins with the earliest history of the Adirondacks as recounted below, and it continues today as groups such as the Adirondack Mountain Club strive to guard this constitutional protection. The protection of many of the scenic and aesthetic resources of the Forest Preserve also rests with the individual hiker, who has the responsibility not to degrade these resources in any way while enjoying their wonders. The Forest Preserve Series of trail guides seeks not only to show hikers where to hike but also to interpret the area's natural and social history and offer guidelines whereby users can minimize their impact on the land.

The Adirondacks

The Adirondack region of northern New York is unique in many ways. It contains the only mountains in the eastern U.S. that are not geologically Appalachian. In the late 1800s it was the first forested area in the nation to benefit from enlightened conservation measures. At roughly the same time it was also the most prestigious resort area in the country. In the 20th century, the Adirondacks became the only place in the Western Hemisphere to host two winter Olympiads. In the 1970s the region was the first of significant size in the nation to experience comprehensive land use controls. The Adirondack Forest Preserve (see below) is part of the only wild lands preserve in the nation whose fate lies in the hands of the voters of the entire state in which it is located.

Geologically, the Adirondacks are part of the Canadian Shield, a vast terrane of ancient Precambrian igneous and metamorphic rock that underlies about half of Canada and constitutes the nucleus of the North American continent. In the U.S. the Shield bedrock mostly lies concealed under younger Paleozoic sedimentary rock strata, but it is well exposed in a few regions, among them the Adirondacks. The Adirondacks are visibly connected across the

Thousand Islands to the Grenville Province of the eastern side of the Shield, which is around one billion years old. Upward doming of the Adirondack mass in the past few million years—a process that is still going on—is responsible for the erosional stripping of the younger rock cover and exposure of the ancient bedrock. The rocks here are mainly gneisses of a wide range of composition. One of the more interesting and geologically puzzling rocks is the enormous anorthosite mass that makes up nearly all of the High Peaks region. A nearly monomineralic rock composed of plagioclase feldspar, this particular rock was apparently formed at depths of up to 15 miles below the surface. It is nearly identical to some of the rock brought back from the moon.

The present Adirondack landscape is geologically young, a product of erosion initiated by the ongoing doming. The stream-carved topography has been extensively modified by the sculpturing of glaciers which, on at least four widely separated occasions during the Ice Age, completely covered the mountains.

Ecologically, the Adirondacks are part of a vegetation transition zone, with the northern, largely coniferous boreal forest (from the Greek god Boreas, owner of the north wind, whose name can be found on a mountain peak and series of ponds in the High Peaks region) and the southern deciduous forest, exemplified by beech/maple stands, intermingling to present a pleasing array of forest tree species. Different vegetation zones are also encountered as one ascends the higher mountains in the Adirondacks; the tops of the highest peaks are truly arctic, with mosses and lichens that are common hundreds of miles to the north.

A rugged and heavily forested region, the Adirondacks were generally not hospitable to native Americans, who used the region principally for hunting and occasionally for fighting. Remnants of ancient campgrounds have been found in some locations. The native legacy survives principally in such place names as Indian Carry, on the Raquette River–Saranac Lakes canoe route, and the Oswegatchie River in the northwest Adirondacks.

The first white man to see the Adirondacks was likely the French explorer Jacques Cartier, who on his first trip up the St. Lawrence River in 1535 stood on top of Mont Royal (now within the city of Montreal) and discerned high ground to the south. Closer looks were had by Samuel de Champlain and Henry Hudson, who came from the north and south, respectively, by coincidence within a few weeks of each other in 1609.

For the next two centuries the Champlain Valley to the east of the Adirondacks was a battleground. Iroquois, Algonquin, French, British and eventually American fighters struggled for control over the valley and with it supremacy over the continent. Settlers slowly filled the St. Lawrence Valley to the north, the Mohawk Valley to the south, and somewhat later the Black River Valley to the west. Meanwhile the vast, rolling forests of the interior slumbered in virtual anonymity, disturbed only by an occasional hunter, timber cruiser or wanderer.

With the coming of the 19th century, people discovered the Adirondacks. Virtually unknown as late as the 1830s (the source of the Nile River was located before the source of the Hudson), by 1850 the Adirondacks made New York the leading timber producing state in the nation. This distinction did not last for long, though, as the supply of timber was quickly brought close to extinction. Meanwhile, mineral resources, particularly iron, were being exploited.

After the Civil War, people began to look toward the Adirondacks for recreation as well as for financial gain. An economic boom, increasing acceptability of leisure time, and the publication of a single book, *Adventures in the Wilderness* by the Rev. William H. H. Murray in 1869, combined to create a veritable flood of vacationers descending upon the Adirondacks. To serve them, a new industry, characterized by grand hotels and rustic guides, sprang up. Simultancously, thanks to the pioneering work of Dr. Edward Livingston Trudeau, the Adirondacks, particularly the Saranac Lake area, became known far and wide as a mecca for tubercular patients.

In the decades following the Civil War the idea of conservation began to take on some legitimacy, thanks in large part to the book *Man and Nature* written by George Perkins Marsh in 1864. In this remarkably influential book, which noted historian Lewis Mumford once called "the fountainhead of the American conservation movement," Marsh called for the implementation of such practices as reforestation and watershed protection, and suggested that the Adirondacks were a good laboratory for testing these ideas.

Another trend in the middle decades of the 19th century was an increasing acceptance of wilderness. This was brought about partly through the work of poets such as William Cullen Bryant, writers such as Henry David Thoreau, and artists such as Frederick Church. Also contributing to this trend was the fact that, as the frontier moved steadily westward, the wilderness was no longer seen as a physical threat, at least not in the more populous, affluent East.

Vacationers, tubercular patients, conservationists, wilderness devotees—all of these people wanted to see the resources of the Adirondacks preserved. This was partially achieved in 1885, when, after much political wrangling, the New York State legislature created the Adirondack Forest Preserve and directed that "the lands now or hereafter constituting the Forest Preserve shall be forever kept as wild forest lands." This action marked the first time a state government had set aside a significant piece of wilderness for reasons other than its scenic uniqueness.

In 1892, the legislature created the Adirondack Park, consisting of Adirondack Forest Preserve land plus all privately owned land within a somewhat arbitrary boundary surrounding the Adirondacks, known as the "blue line" because it was drawn in blue on a large state map when it was first established. In 1894, in response to continuing abuses of the Forest Preserve law, the state's voters approved the inclusion of the "forever wild" portion of that law in the constitution of New York State, thus creating the only preserve in the nation that has constitutional protection. Today the Forest Preserve consists of 2.5 million acres, being those lands owned by the people of the State of New York that are within the 6-million-acre Adirondack State Park, which is the largest park in the nation outside of Alaska.

In the first decade of the 20th century, raging fires consumed hundreds of thousands of acres of prime Adirondack forest lands; the scars from these fires can still be seen in many locations, both in exposed rock and in vegetation patterns. After World War I, tourism gradually took over as the primary industry in the Adirondacks. The arrival of the automobile, the invention of theme parks (some of the very first of which were in the Adirondacks), the development of winter sports facilities (with Lake Placid hosting the Winter Olympics in 1932), the increasing popularity of camping and hiking, and the growth of the second-home industry all brought such pressures to bear on the region that in 1968 Governor Nelson Rockefeller created a Temporary Study Commission on the Future of the Adirondacks. This commission made 181 recommendations, chief among them that a comprehensive land use plan, covering both public and private lands, be put in place and administered. This was accomplished by 1973, with the creation of the land use plans and the Adirondack Park Agency to manage them. While the plans and the agency have remained controversial, they are indicative of the need to address the issues facing the Adirondacks boldly and innovatively.

In 1990, there were 130,000 permanent residents and 100,000 seasonal residents in the 9375-square-mile Adirondack Park, which is roughly the size of Vermont. Recreation, forestry, mining and agriculture are the principal industries in the park.

The Eastern Region

The trails in this book are all in the eastern Adirondacks, an area roughly 100 miles long and 20 to 30 miles wide, from Valcour Island on the north to the village of Lake George on the south, "the Northway" (I-87) on the west and Vermont on the east. This area includes the villages of Keeseville, Willsboro, Essex, Lewis, Westport, Moriah, Crown Point, Ticonderoga, North Hudson, Schroon Lake, Adirondack, Brant Lake, Hague, Bolton Landing, Lake George and West Fort Ann. The principal highways are the Northway, US 9, NY 22, NY 8, NY 74 and Warren County Route 149.

The eastern region of the Adirondacks is less travelled by the hiker than the High Peaks region. An unusual combination of large lakes, Lake Champlain and Lake George, smaller lakes like Brant Lake and Pharaoh Lake, dozens of small ponds, old roadways and trails through lowlands and over mountains make this region spectacularly beautiful, as well as accessible to the hiker.

Using This Guidebook

Like all the books in the Adirondack Mountain Club Forest Preserve Series of Guides to Adirondack and Catskill Trails, this book is intended to be both a reference tool for planning trips and field guide to carry on the trail. All introductory material should be read carefully, for it contains important information regarding the use of this book, as well as numerous suggestions for safe and proper travel by foot in the Adirondacks. For campers, there is an important section on the relevant rules and regulations for camping in the Adirondacks.

Listed in this book are more than 200 miles of old roadways, marked trails, and a few miles of faintly marked or unmarked trails. Be sure to read carefully the introduction to each section as well as the descriptions of any trails you intend to follow.

If you find discrepancies, inaccuracies, or other changes from what is described here, please write the Publications Director, Adirondack Mountain Club, RR 3, Box 3055, Lake George, NY 12845-9522.

Maps

The map enclosed in the back of this book is a composite of U.S. Geological Survey quadrangles with updated overlays of trails, shelters and private land lines. The map is especially valuable because of the combination of contour lines from the original base maps and recent trail information, updated with each printing of this guide. It covers most of the terrain described in this guidebook, but a few isolated trails not conveniently shown on it are shown on individual page maps within the text. Extra copies of the Eastern map are available from many retailers or directly from the Adirondack Mountain Club, RR 3, Box 3055, Lake George, NY 12845.

The USGS maps covering this area include the 15-minute series for Plattsburgh, Keeseville, Willsboro, Elizabethtown, Port Henry, Paradox Lake and Bolton Landing. More recent metric maps include Lewis, Willsboro and Witherbee. "The Adirondacks—Lake George Region" map by Adirondack Maps Inc. (formely Plinth, Quoin and Cornice Associates) is extremely useful. The DEC Adirondack Land Map, 1985 Centennial Edition, shows boundaries of public and private land. Road maps for Essex, Warren and Washington counties are helpful. County base maps published in 1993 by the New York State Department of Transportation (DOT) and the DOT 7.5-minute quadrangle series accurately show roads and state land boundaries for Warren and Washington counties. These are available from:

NYS Department of Transportation
Map Information Unit
State Office Campus, Bldg. 4, Room 105, Albany, NY 12232
(518) 457-3555

Trail Signs and Markers

The routes described in this guidebook vary from wide, well-marked DEC trails to narrow unmaintained footpaths that have become established through long use by hunters and anglers. With normal alertness and careful preparation the hiker should have few problems in land navigation. Nevertheless, careful map study and route planning are fundamental necessities. The eastern Adirondack region has some large tracts of wild lands. Many routes are isolated and some trails may be travelled by few other people. Consequently the hiker should never expect immediate help should an emergency occur. This is especially true in winter when there even fewer people using the woods.

In addition to a map, all hikers should carry a compass and know at least the basics of how to use it properly. If unfamiliar with the area you are heading into, take compass bearings before leaving the trailhead and check your route along the way. A compass is an indispensable aid in the event you lose your way.

Marked and maintained DEC trails can be hiking, cross-country skiing, snowmobile, or horse trails. Route descriptions include the color and type of marker. Blue markers generally indicate N–S trails; red markers generally indicate E–W trails; yellow markers generally run at diagonal compass bearings.

One other type of marker is becoming more common. A large disk with a teepee on it indicates a designated camping area (see p. 18). A similar disk with an X through the teepee means one cannot camp at the location.

Snowmobile trail markers have larger disks than do hiking and ski trails. In recent years, the number of snowmobiles seen on the trails has diminished and skiers may frequently use them, especially in light-use midweek periods. It should be remembered that ski and snowmobile trails often follow marsh and river channels and may be unsuitable for hiking in warmer months of the year.

The hiker should not be overly skeptical about following unmaintained trails. Often hunters and anglers maintain them. An "unmaintained" trail means that DEC is not officially maintaining the trail. Because most routes follow streams up open deciduous valleys, or along a lake shore, the route is often obvious. It is only when crossing a divide or when beaver activity obliterates a section of a trail that careful attention is necessary.

Should a trail become temporarily unclear, leave one person at the last known point on the trail and send other hikers out in a fan pattern in all directions until a trail is relocated. All people must stay within sight and/or hearing distance of each other. Minor blowdowns and beaver activity are most often the cause of such circumstances.

The routes described in this book are normally not difficult to follow in summer months. Winter travelers will need route-finding skills unless following well-marked trails. Well-used, marked trails normally have trail signs located at the trailhead and all major trail junctions. These trail signs give the distance to named locations on the trail. Distances given on the signs may or may not conform to the accuracy of the guidebook distance.

Finally, it should go without saying that one should never remove any sign or marker. Hikers noticing damaged or missing signs should report this fact to the proper DEC offices at the addresses given below:

Warren County: Lands and Forest Headquarters
                 Department of Environmental Conservation
                 Hudson St. Extension
                 P.O. Box 220
                 Warrensburg, NY 12885
Essex County: Lands and Forests Headquarters
                 Department of Environmental Conservation
                 Ray Brook, NY 12977

Distance and Time

All trails in this guidebook have been measured with a professional surveyor's wheel.

At the start of each section of this guide is a list of trails in the region, the mileage unique to the trail, and the number of the page on which the trail description is located. All mileage distances given in the trail description are cumulative, the beginning of the trail being the 0.0 mi. point. A distance summary is given at the end of each description, with a total distance expressed in kilometers as well as in miles. If a trail has climbed significantly over its course, its total ascent in both feet and meters is provided. To the inexperienced hiker, these distances will seem longer on the trail, but he or she will quickly learn that there is a great difference between "sidewalk" miles and "trail" miles.

The distances given in this guide are often at odds with the distances given on the DEC trail signs. The DEC has used a variety of measuring methods over the years and has not always updated every sign after every change of distance caused by rerouting, etc. In all cases where there is a disagreement, the guidebook distance can be assumed to be correct; the DEC is currently in the process of revising all of its sign distances based on the wheel measurements found in this guide.

No attempt has been made to estimate travel times on these trails. A conservative rule to follow is to allow an hour for every 1.5 mi. plus one-half hour for each 1000 ft. of ascent, with experience soon indicating how close each hiker is to this standard. Most day hikers will probably hike faster than this, but backpackers will probably find they go more slowly. Some time will usually be saved on the descent, but on a rough trail the descent may take nearly as long as the ascent, especially with heavy packs.

Abbreviations and Conventions

In each of the books in the Forest Preserve Series, R and L, with periods omitted, are used for right and left. The R and L banks of a stream are determined by looking downstream. Likewise, the R fork of a stream is on the R when one faces downstream. N, S, E and W, again without periods, are used for north, south, east and west. Compass directions are given in degrees, figuring from true N, with E as 90 degrees, etc. The following abbreviations are used in the text and on the maps:

ADK	Adirondack Mountain Club
DEC	New York State Department of Environmental Conservation
USGS	United States Geological Survey
ft.	feet
jct.	junction
km	kilometer or kilometers
m	meter or meters
mi.	mile or miles
yds.	yards

Hiking with Children

Most hikers with children want to start them hiking as early as possible, but one needs to be aware that children can have very different perceptions of what it means to go on a hike. Given the range of physical abilities and mental outlooks, there is no one "right" way to introduce a child to the concept of struggling up a steep hill only to turn around and return to the starting point. The guidelines below may help avoid a few of the common pitfalls. Also, see Appendix III for a table of short hikes in the region.

Attitude:

Having a positive experience is more important than reaching one's destination. At least at first, children are not goal-oriented, so that the promise of reaching the view at the top does not have the same motivation factor it has for adults. Be prepared to stop short of the original goal; as one experienced father put it, "You are where you are." Make an adventure out of the tough spots ("we're almost to the 'mountain goat pitch' ") and a game out of boring spots ("how many trail markers can you see?"). Be prepared to stop and look at anything of interest, whether it is you or the child who notices the plant, frog, moss, stick, leaf or whatever. A lady-slipper along the trail may be an adult's greatest treat, but a child will take even greater pleasure in finding a stick that looks vaguely like a dinosaur.

Make sure to reward the child for completing a hike. Make it a special occasion, perhaps a reason for a call to the grandparents or a favorite dessert with dinner. You may want to keep a chart or map of hikes done to show progress. Show the child the day's trip on a map, and get it out again to plan the next one. Over time, most children will come to appreciate the satisfaction of a fun hike, and will want to do more.

Distance and Destination:

Three-year-olds (and even strong two-year-olds) can hike as much as a mile, and a mile will get you to the top of some small mountains. Walking uphill can be a problem, however, and many children are just as excited to hike a flat route to a stream where they can throw rocks and sticks. Four- to six-year-olds are more likely to be able to focus on making an ascent of over a mile to a summit—but again, too much steep going can prove discouraging.

Time:

At least double your own time for a particular hike. Children not only walk more slowly but also want to take frequent breaks. Have an open-ended time schedule so that you don't become impatient with slower-than-expected progress. Adult hikers know that a steady pace with fewer stops is usually the most efficient, but children need to take "mental" breaks as well as physical rests. While actually hiking, however, encourage steady progress as opposed to the "20 running steps followed by a complete stop" type of pace that many children will try at first.

Equipment and Supplies:

Even small children should be encouraged to carry at least some of their own gear, but be prepared to take it if the pack seems to be the only thing causing an unpleasant time. Bring plenty of water and food and don't feel that your goal is to instill toughness by forcing the march to the summit before the first sip of water can be had. On a hot day, freeze a few plastic water bottles beforehand. Not only will you have cool water, but watching the ice melt and telling others about a "special hiking trick" will add to the hike in ways an adult could never understand. Likewise, avoid using food (i.e. candy) as a bribe too often, but I doubt if there are many parents who can claim never to have promised a treat for just a little more effort. Bring insect repellent; a cap can be very helpful in keeping the bugs off the back of the head.

Hiking boots are the preferred footwear, but running shoes are fine as long as they are sturdy enough to offer protection from sharp rocks underneath and sticks above. Make sure the child wears socks and has a sweater and raincoat at all times. Add a wool hat and mittens if it is at all cold because a summit can be much colder.

Long pants offer protection from twigs and brambles as well as reducing the exposed skin area for insect bites, but don't push it if the child prefers shorts.

Most importantly, double-check that every needed item is indeed packed. One forgotten cookie can ruin the whole trip.

Safety:

Children have very little judgment and, at first, virtually no ability to stay on even an "obvious" trail. Let them lead but keep them in sight, and be ready to take the lead near any cliffs, bridges or other dangerous areas. Be especially careful on top of ledges and keep them from throwing anything over the edge of a cliff. Not only is it very easy for a child to throw himself off as well, but there may be others below. Children love to hike with the family dog, but large, rambunctious dogs pose the danger of knocking a child down or even off the trail as they race back and forth checking on everyone or chasing sticks.

Above all, keep the group together and never solve the problem of a reluctant hiker by sending him back down the trail alone. The above list of safety concerns is hardly complete, but it may alert parents to a few of the potential problems unique to hiking.

Hiking with the Physically Impaired

Everyone should have the opportunity to share the beauties of nature and the joy of testing one's skills in the outdoors. Physically impaired individuals have completed the 132-mi. Northville–Lake Placid Trail, paddled the Fulton Chain, camped in winter snows and participated in practically any outdoor activity that can be named. However, we all have limitations, and it is necessary to stay within these parameters if we are to have a safe and enjoyable experience. It is important that each individual and each trip leader know the limitations of the members of the group. Therefore, while there really are no trails that are off limits for *some* physically impaired individuals, each physically impaired person must realistically determine his or her limitations.

Trip Leader:

Before taking a physically impaired person on a particular trail, it is essential that the trip leader be extremely familiar with that trail and that he or she has taken into account the necessary actions that will be required to safely negotiate any rough spots with the physically impaired person. This person should be informed of the difficulties to be met along the way and the expected demands.

The trip leader must also take into account the other members on the trip. Is the trip especially designed for the physically impaired person or does it just happen to have a physically impaired person in the group? Will the rate of travel and general situation be a surprise to the others in the group, completely changing the expected nature of the hike, or will the rate and situation be essentially as it would be in the absence of the physically impaired person? If the former is the case, then the other members of the group should be so notified prior to the day of the trip.

The Senses:

Part of the enjoyment of nature is the exposure to heightened experiences of the senses. Take this into account when designing trips for the physically impaired. If the person has lost some senses, plan activities that will increase use of other senses. Night or pond sounds, the murmuring of brooks, star-gazing, the smells of balsam fir, swimming, the movement or sounds of birds, the feel and sound or rain and snow, the wind and many more sensations can have particular meaning if they are new to the person or infrequently experienced.

Attitude:

The physically impaired person, assisting leader, and friends should have a clear and mutual understanding of what outcomes are expected on trips. No desired activity should be considered impossible until detailed thought has taken place. Outings become failures only when problems have not been anticipated, when difficulties are not looked upon as desired challenges, and when the limitations of the trip have not been accepted so that the possibilities can be fully enjoyed. A "can do" attitude will result in many things being done.

Appendix III, at the end of this book, lists several outings of various types that physically impaired people may find interesting. The hiker can adapt these to the needs of the individual.

Wilderness Camping

It is not the purpose of this series to teach one how to camp in the woods. There are many good books available on that subject which are more comprehensive and useful than any explanation that could be given in the space available here. The information below should, however, serve to make hikers aware of the differences and peculiarities of the Adirondacks while giving strong emphasis to currently recommended procedures to reduce environmental damage—particularly in heavily used areas.

There are lean-tos at many convenient locations along the trails, and there are also many possibilities for tenting along the way. The regulations regarding tenting and the use of these shelters are simple and unrestrictive when compared to those of other popular backpacking areas in the country; but it is important that every backpacker know and obey the restrictions that do exist, since they are designed to promote the long-term enjoyment for the greatest number of people.

General Camping Guidelines:

Except for groups of ten or more, or smaller groups planning to stay in one place for more than three nights (see "Groups" below), no camping or fire permits are required in the Adirondacks, but campers must obey all DEC regulations regarding camping. Listed below are some of the most important regulations. Complete regulations are available from the DEC and are usually posted at most access points.

1) No camping within 150 ft. of a stream, other water source, or trail except at a designated campsite. Most areas near an existing lean-to are considered designated campsites; other areas are designated with the following symbol:

2) Except in an emergency, no camping is permitted above 4000 ft. in elevation. (This rule does not apply from December 15 to April 30.)

3) All washing of dishes must be done at least 150 ft. from any stream, pond, or other water source. No soap, even so-called "biodegradeable" soap, should ever get into the water, so use a pot to carry water at least 150 ft. away from your water source and wash

items and dispose of water there. One can also take a surprisingly effective bath by taking a quick dip and then using a pot for soaping and rinsing away from the stream or pond.

4) All human excrement must be buried under at least four inches of dirt at a spot at least 150 ft. away from any water source. All toilet paper should be similarly buried. Use established privies or latrines when available.

5) No wood, except *dead and down* timber, may be used for fire building. Good wood is often scarce at popular campsites, so a portable stove for cooking is highly recommended.

6) No fire should be built near any flammable material. Much of the forest cover in the Adirondacks is composed of recently rotted twigs, leaves, or needles and is highly flammable. Build a fire at an established fireplace, on rocks, or on sand. Never leave a fire unattended. Before leaving, be sure the fire is extinguished and that all traces of any fireplace you built have been destroyed. Again, a portable stove is preferable to an open fire.

7) Paper or wooden refuse can be burned or carried out of the woods. Do not bury refuse. Be sure that no packaging to be burned contains metal foil—it will not burn no matter how hot the fire. Remember—if you carried it in, you can carry it out!

8) In general, leave no trace of your presence when leaving a campsite, and help by carrying out any litter left by those less thoughtful than you.

Lean-tos:

Lean-tos are available on a first-come, first-served basis up to the capacity of the shelter—usually about seven persons. A small party cannot therefore claim exclusive use of a shelter and must allow later arrivals equal use. Most lean-tos have a fireplace in front (sometimes with a primitive grill) and sanitary facilities. Most are located near some source of water, but each camper must use his own judgment as to whether or not the water supply needs water purification before drinking.

It is in very poor taste—and is illegal—to carve or write one's initials in a shelter. Please try to keep these rustic shelters in good condition and appearance.

Since reservations cannot be made for any of these shelters, it is essential to carry a tent or other alternate shelter. Many shelters away from the standard routes, however, are rarely used, and a small party can often find a shelter open in the more remote areas.

The following regulations and suggestions apply specifically to lean-tos, in addition to the general camping regulations listed above:

1) No plastic should be used to close off the front of a shelter.

2) No nails or other permanent fastener may be used to affix a tarp in a lean-to, but it is permissible to use rope to tie canvas or nylon tarps across the front.

3) No tent may be pitched inside a lean-to.

Groups:

Any group of ten or more persons, or smaller groups planning to stay in one place for more than three nights, must obtain a permit *before* camping on state land. This system is designed to prevent overuse of certain critical sites and to encourage groups to split into smaller parties more in keeping with the natural environment. Permits can be obtained from the DEC forest ranger closest to the actual starting point of one's proposed trip. The local forest ranger can be contacted by writing to him or her directly; if in doubt about whom to write, send a letter to the Department of Environmental Conservation, Ray Brook, NY 12977. They will forward the letter, but allow at least a week for the letter to reach the appropriate forest ranger.

One can also make the initial contact with the forest ranger by telephone, but keep in mind that rangers' schedules during the busy summer season are unpredictable. Forest rangers are listed in the white pages of local telephone books under "New York, State of; Environmental Conservation, Dept. of; Forest Ranger." Remember when calling that most rangers operate out of their private homes. Observe normal courtesy, please. Contact by letter is much preferred, and, as one must realize, camping with a large group requires careful planning several weeks before the trip.

Regulations regarding group sizes reflect the need to minimize environmental impact and are designed to enhance everyone's experience in the wilderness.

Drinking Water

For many years, hikers could trust practically any water source in the Adirondacks to be pure and safe to drink. Unfortunately, as in many other mountain areas, some water sources have become contaminated with a parasite known as *Giardia lamblia*. This intestinal parasite causes a disease known as *giardiasis*—often called "Beaver Fever." It can be spread by any warm-blooded mammal when infected feces wash into the water; beavers are prime agents in transferring this parasite because they spend so much of their time near water. Hikers themselves have also become primary agents in spreading this disease since some individuals appear to be unaffected carriers of the disease, and other recently infected individuals may inadvertently spread the parasite before their symptoms become apparent.

Prevention: Follow the guidelines for the disposal of human excrement as stated in the "Wilderness Camping" section (above). Equally important, make sure every member of your group is aware of the problem and follows the guidelines as well. The health of a fellow hiker may depend on your consideration.

Choosing a Water Source: While no water source can be guaranteed to be safe, smaller streams high in the mountains which have no possibility of a beaver dam or temporary human presence upstream are usually safe to drink. If, however, there is any doubt, treat the water before drinking.

Treatment: Boil all water for 2-3 minutes, or administer an iodine-based chemical purifier (available at camping supply stores and some drug and department stores), or use a commercial filter designed specifically for giardiasis prevention. If after returning from a trip you experience recurrent intestinal problems, consult your physician and explain your potential problem.

Forest Safety

The eastern Adirondack region is primarily rolling terrain covered with open deciduous forest. In summer the day hiker need not be overly concerned about the ruggedness of the land. Factors of safety, however, include confidence, knowledge, physical condition, awareness and weather as much as the element of topography. Leaders of outings should consider each of these factors in relation to each member of the group. Limits of activity should be set that are within the ability of all participants.

There are times and places when judgement must be sound. Although there are no towering high peaks in the eastern region, there are some rather difficult trails and ascents. Vertical elevation gain, as well as trail distances, needs to be carefully considered before starting on a hike.

Be sure to observe proper precautions for wildlife whenever you hike and camp. Remember you are entering into the natural habitat of many different animal species, and it is important to show respect for their environment. In the Tongue Mt. area along Lake George and the Split Rock Mt. area along Lake Champlain it is particularly important to observe the proper precautions listed in each section so as not to disturb the protected eastern timber rattlesnake. The snakes are rarely seen, but caution is always needed.

Winter trips, especially, must be carefully planned. Travel over ice on cross-country skiing trips must be done with caution. The possibility of freezing rain, snow and cold temperatures should always be considered from early September until late May. True winter conditions can commence as early as November and last into April. The lower elevations usually have more mild conditions than the upper reaches of summits. However, it is surprising how long deep snow can linger each year in the deeper shaded valleys, where the low-angled sunlight of spring doesn't penetrate. It is highly recommended that hikers travel in parties of at least four people, be outfitted properly, rest when the need arises, and drink plenty of water. Leave trip plans with someone at home and then keep to your itinerary. For more information on winter travel, refer to the Adirondack Mountain Club publication *Winterwise* by John Dunn.

Hunting Seasons

Hikers should be aware that, unlike the national park system, sport hunting is permitted on all public lands within the Adirondack and Catskill parks. There are separate rules and seasons for each type of hunting (small game, waterfowl, and big game); but it is the big game seasons, i.e. deer and bear, that are most likely to cause concern for hikers.

For those hikers who might be concerned, the following is a list of all big game hunting seasons—running from approximately mid-September through early December.

Early Bear Season: Begins the first Saturday after the second Monday in September and continues for four weeks.

Archery Season (deer and bear): September 27 to opening of the regular season.

Muzzle-loading Season (deer and bear): The seven days prior to the opening of regular season.

Regular Season: Next-to-last Saturday in October through the first Sunday in December.

Because of its topography, the eastern region sees a lot of use by hunters during the hunting season. The most hunters are in the woods during opening week, and it is best to avoid hiking during that period. The rest of the season, care should be exercised. Wear at least one piece of orange or red clothing—don't wear anything brownish-gray or white.

The Adirondack Mountain Club does not promote hunting as one of its organized activities; but it does recognize that sport hunting, when carried out in compliance with the game laws administered by the DEC, is a legitimate and necessary method of managing game populations. The harassment of hunters engaged in the legitimate pursuit of their sport is illegal and inappropriate. Suspected violations of the game laws should be reported to the nearest DEC forest ranger or conservation officer.

Off-Trail Hiking

There are many unmarked and unmaintained trails and old roads throughout the eastern Adirondack region on both state land and private land. It is important when traveling these trails to leave them in the same condition you found them and to respect all the rights of the private land owners. Failure of hikers to recognize restrictions on private lands currently open to hiking may result in these lands being added to those already closed to public access.

Hiking and climbing without maintained trails calls for leadership by people experienced in map reading and use of compass along with possessing a feel for route-finding in forested mountain terrain. Fog, rain and snow can complicate staying on course, and dealing with injuries and illness is obviously more difficult away from trails.

Know the vicinity of all trails in the region, and know the mountain peaks and be able to recognize them from any viewpoint. Before you take your trip, learn about topographic map and compass use. Carry a guidebook, USGS topographic map, compass, flashlight with extra batteries and bulb, first-aid kit, insect repellent, matches, a whistle and mirror for signalling, extra food and clothing (not cotton), and raingear designed to keep you as dry and warm as possible in case unexpected inclement weather forces you to spend a night out.

Off-trail hikers have a special obligation not to climb alone, to sign in as well as out at all DEC registers encountered, and to let other responsible people know of their planned route. Such consideration is due the people who may have to participate in a rescue party.

For those who desire greater challenges in the mountains, there are many trailless peaks and backcountry ponds in the eastern Adirondacks. By obtaining and studying detailed topo maps you will realize the almost limitless possibilities for true exploration in the region.

Emergency Procedures

An ounce of prevention is always worth a pound of cure, but if one is in need of emergency assistance in the woods, the DEC is the first place to contact for help. Make sure that the person going for help has the following phone numbers plus a complete *written* description of the type and exact location of the accident. A location marked on a map can be very important. Make plans to meet with a forest ranger and stick to them so contact can be made.

The first call for help should be to DEC at Ray Brook. **Call (518) 897-1300 Monday–Friday from 8 a.m.–4:30 p.m. All other times call (518) 891-0235.** This is an emergency dispatch number which, if still state funded, will get you help or provide a necessary referral. If for some reason neither of these numbers can be reached, call (518) 897-2000, which is a regional emergency dispatch number for the NYS Police. If all else fails, dial O and ask the operator for the New York State Police.

The Adirondack Mountain Club

The Adirondack Mountain Club (or ADK, the initials AMC having been claimed by the previously formed Appalachian Mountain Club) was organized in 1922 for the purpose of bringing together in a working unit a large number of people interested in the mountains, trails, camping, and forest conservation. A permanent club headquarters was established, and with increasing membership, club chapters were organized. The chapters are as follows:

Adirondak Loj (North Elba), Albany, Algonquin (Plattsburgh), Black River (Watertown), Cold River (Long Lake), Connecticut Valley (Hartford), Finger Lakes (Ithaca–Elmira), Genesee Valley (Rochester), Glens Falls, Hurricane Mt. (Keene), Iroquois (Utica), Keene Valley, Knickerbocker (New York City and vicinity), Lake Placid, Laurentian (Canton–Potsdam), Long Island, Mid-Hudson (Poughkeepsie), Mohican (Westchester and Putnam counties, NY, and Fairfield County, CT), New York (metropolitan area), Niagara Frontier (Buffalo), North Jersey (Bergen County), North Woods (Saranac Lake–Tupper Lake), Onondaga (Syracuse), Penn's Woods (Harrisburg, PA), Ramapo (Rockland and Orange counties), Schenectady, Shatagee Woods (Malone), and Susquehanna (Oneonta). In addition, there is an extensive membership-at-large.

Most chapters do not have qualifying requirements: a note to the Membership Director, Adirondack Mountain Club, RR 3, Box 3055, Lake George, NY 12845-9522, will bring you information on membership in a local chapter (e.g., names and addresses of persons to be contacted) or details on membership-at-large. Persons joining a chapter, upon payment of their chapter dues, *ipso facto* become members of the club. Membership dues include a subscription to *Adirondac*, a bimonthly magazine; ADK's semiannual newsletter; and discounts on ADK books and at ADK lodges. An application for membership is in the back of this book.

Members of the Adirondack Mountain Club have formulated the following creed, which reflects the theme of the club and its membership:

> We, the Adirondack Mountain Club, believe that the lands of the State constituting the Forest Preserve should be forever kept as wild forest lands in accordance with Article XIV, Section 1, of the New York State Constitution. We favor a program under the administration of the Department of Environmental Conservation (in the Adirondacks, pursuant to the Adirondack Park Agency policy) that will provide ample opportunities for outdoor recreation in a manner consistent with the wild forest character of the Preserve. We favor acquisition of additional wild lands to meet the goals of the State Land Master Plans for watershed and wildlife protection and for recreation needs, and we support protection of the open-space character of appropriate private lands within the Adirondack and Catskill parks. We believe an informed public is essential to the well-being of the Preserve and the parks. We seek to accomplish measures that are consistent with this policy, and we oppose measures that are contrary thereto.

In the 1990s, approximately 19,000 "ADKers" enjoy the full spectrum of outdoor activities, including hiking, backpacking, canoeing (from floating on a pond to whitewater racing), rock climbing, cross-country skiing and snowshoeing. Most chapters have an active year-round outings schedule as well as regular meetings, sometimes including a meal, and programs featuring individuals ranging from chapter members to local and state officials. Many ADKers are also active in service work ranging from participation in search-and-rescue organizations to involvement in the ongoing debate over the best use of our natural resources and forest or wilderness lands, not only in the Adirondacks but also in their immediate localities.

ADK Information Center & Headquarters:

At the southeastern corner of the Park is the long log cabin that serves as the ADK Information Center and Headquarters. The building, located just 0.2 mi. S of exit 21 of I-87 ("the Northway"), is open year-round. Hours: June 15 to Columbus Day, Monday–Saturday, 8:30 a.m.–5 p.m.; Tuesday after Columbus Day–June 14, Monday–Friday, 8:30 a.m.–4:30 p.m.

ADK staff at this facility provide information about hiking, canoeing, cross-country skiing, climbing and camping in the Adirondack Park. In addition, they host lectures, workshops and exhibits; sell publications and ADK logo items; and provide membership information. For further information, call or write ADK, RR 3, Box 3055, Lake George, NY 12845-9522 (telephone: 518-668-4447). For information about ADK accommodations, see below.

High Peaks Information Center:

Located on the Heart Lake property near Lake Placid, the Club's

High Peaks Information Center (HPIC) offers backcountry and general Adirondack information, educational displays, publications, some outdoor equipment and trail snacks.

Adirondack Mountain Club Lodges:

The Adirondack Mountain Club, Inc., owns and operates two lodges for overnight guests in the High Peaks Region near Lake Placid. Johns Brook Lodge is accessible only by foot, whereas Adirondak Loj can be reached by car. For further details and reservation information about these and other ADK facilities, write the Manager, Adirondak Loj, P.O. Box 867, Lake Placid, NY 12946 (telephone: 518/523-3441).

NEAL BURDICK, Forest Preserve Series Editor
CARL HEILMAN II

On Poke-O-Moonshine Mt., Lake Champlain in distance

Northern Section

This section encompasses a large area north of a line from Elizabethtown to Mineville and Port Henry, with Lake Champlain on the east and a western boundary of US 9 and the High Peaks region. While much of this area is owned by private landowners and timber companies, there are a number of fine trails with great diversity in terrain. From Valcour Island in the extreme NE corner of the Adirondack Park, to the Split Rock Mt. area which contains the longest undeveloped shoreline on Lake Champlain, this area offers some unusual Adirondack experiences.

While trails are well suited for the beginning hiker, the veteran hiker may find exploring some of the trailless rocky crags and outlooks an unexpected challenge. There are also two wildlife management areas just north of Port Kent: the Ausable Marsh State Wildlife Management Area, and Wickham Marsh Wildlife Management Area. There is both hiking and canoeing in these two regions.

Trails in winter: In a good snow year, most trails in the region's northern section are suitable for snowshoeing and skiing. However, since most of these trails are at lower elevations and many are near Lake Champlain, snow conditions will deteriorate more quickly than in the rest of the Adirondacks. It is advisable to carry instep crampons in case of icy conditions. These suggestions are for all trails in the region unless otherwise noted

Short Hike:

Belfry Mt.—*0.4 mi. A short, easy walk to an open summit and fire tower with views of Mineville, the Adirondacks and the Green Mts. in Vermont.*

Moderate Hike:

Valcour Island Perimeter Trail—*5.7 mi. Spectacular views on all sides as you circle this historic island. There are several ways to shorten this loop using interior trails.*

(1) Valcour Island Perimeter Trail   Page Map

Valcour Island is a jewel in Lake Champlain. The island itself is varied and fascinating, with coves that offer good anchorage for boaters and pleasant, easy trails that often give the hiker spectacular views of the Adirondacks and Vermont's Green Mountains. Rocky shelves provide excellent seats to watch crashing waves on the east

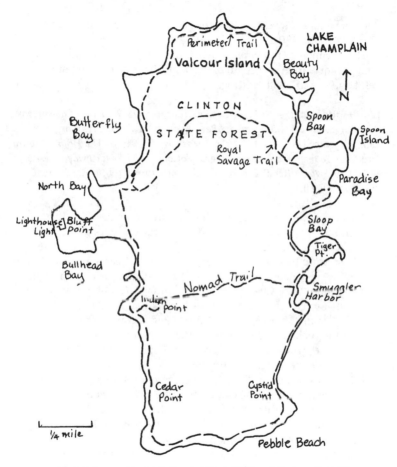

Valcour Island Perimeter Trail (1), Nomad Trail (2), Royal Savage Trail (3)
Based on Plattsburgh and Keeseville quadrangles, 7.5-min. series, 1966.

side, as well as a lovely, quiet sandy beach on the west side. The island is about 980 acres.

The Perimeter Trail circles the island in 5.7 mi.; two interior trails combine for a total of 7.8 mi. of trails on the island. Campsites are well kept and in idyllic settings.

Trailhead: *From the Air Force Base entrance on US 9, just S of downtown Plattsburgh, drive S 4.5 mi. to the Peru Boat Launch. Coming from the S, from the jct. of US 9 and NY 22 in Keeseville, drive N on US 9 8.8 mi to the Peru Boat Launch. From Exit 35 (Peru–Valcour) on the Northway take Route 422 (Bear Swamp Road) E 3 mi. to US 9, and turn L (N). It is 3.3 mi. to Peru Boat Lunch.*

There is a parking lot and public bathroom at the Peru Boat Launch site. On a summer Saturday a parade of cars and trucks back trailers down the ramp to unload motorboats. Many of these people seem to be families headed to Butterfly Beach for picnics and swimming on Valcour (which means "almost one rock" in French).

A warning: Lake Champlain's deep waters are notorious for being cold. Huge waves can sweep across the lake on rough days. Do not use a canoe in cold weather or if the water is rough. Hypothermia can set in quickly. Late summer is the best time for a canoe crossing. In winter when the lake is frozen it is possible to ski across, observing proper safety precautions.

It is almost exactly 1.0 mi. E from the boat launch to Bullhead Bay, a pleasant, grassy place just S of the old lighthouse where hikers can pull up their boats and find the Perimeter Trail almost immediately. Or they can go NE around the point to Butterfly Bay and pull up on the sandy beach.

The DEC officer who patrols the island from a boat gives out maps of the island that show the hiking trails, names of bays, campsites and rules. Those planning to camp on the island must register with him upon landing, or on his rounds.

The following describes a hike around the island on the Perimeter Trail (1) starting S from Bullhead Bay. From Bullhead Bay (0.0 mi.) walk inland from the beach about 50 ft. through the woods to the Perimeter Trail. Turn R, heading S. Soon you will come into an open meadow, then to a small foot bridge. Then, from poplars and poison ivy (lots of it on the island) the trail enters cedar woods, reaching a trail jct. at 0.3 mi. with signs indicating Indian Point (R) and the Nomad Trail (2) to Smuggler's Harbor (L).

A short trail to the R leads to a large, open clearing with a new fireplace, privy and good campsite above lovely Indian Point. The stone shelves are excellent for picnicking, swimming and play. Campsites 2, 3 and 4 are also here, offering good views of the Adirondacks. In August, purple loosestrife grows between the cracks in the shelving rock. Numerous light yellow butterflies attend to business among these flowers.

Continuing S, the Perimeter Trail enters cool, deep woods of white cedar, white and red pine, maple, oak, ash, spruce, wild grapes and giant poison ivy. At 0.5 mi. is a large spruce tree with a sign, "American Revolution, Battle of Valcour, October 11, 1776." On that date a small American fleet led by General Benedict Arnold hid behind the west side of the island and surprised a larger British fleet heading S down the lake, led by Captain Thomas Pringle. The British fleet chased the Americans for two days S to Ticonderoga and destroyed Arnold's brash brigade of boats. Despite this loss, Benedict Arnold won a tactical victory by delaying the British, forcing them to return to Canada for the winter. This extra time gave the American troops at Saratoga a chance to build up men and supplies, which resulted in their victory there on October 17, 1777. History buffs revel in the imagined sight of Arnold's tiny, gusty fleet rounding the southern tip of Valcour to destroy what Pringle thought would be an unchallenged trip down Lake Champlain.

It is about 50 ft. R to a grassy overlook on a cliff with an excellent view of Whiteface Mt. and of interesting fissures in the shoreline rock into a stand of cedars and out into a meadow. The trail crosses a footbridge at a little over 0.6 mi. and at 0.7 mi. reaches campsite 1 (with privy) on Cedar Point. This is a smooth rocky promontory.

The trail onward is over a broad, solid rock incline going into cedar, hemlock and birch woods. A long elbow-shaped cement dock comes into view on the R through trees. At 0.8 mi. a beautiful old stone house with slate roof offers a path from its front R corner to a pumphouse, dock and point. You may walk on the dock, or picnic, but are not permitted to moor a boat here.

Rejoining the Perimeter Trail and walking S to 1.0 mi., turn R off the trail to a faint track that leads to high cliffs with spectacular S and E views of Lake Champlain, the Green Mountains and the Adirondacks. There is loose gravel here, so stay away from the edge and find a firm footing. This is not a recommended spot for acrophobics.

The Perimeter Trail continues around the S side of the island through deep, cool cedar woods with chickadees. At 1.4 mi. it curves L (N) along the E side of the island. At about 1.5 mi. there is a sign to Pebble Beach on the R, a steep trail descending to a cozy beach surrounded by fantastic metamorphic cliffs on either side. Beach stones are rounded and smooth from wave action. This is the closest view of Garden Island.

The Perimeter Trail continues through oak, ash and maple woods. At 1.7 mi. there is a turn R off the trail to a SE promontory, and at 1.8 mi. there is a 20-ft. cliff facing E to Vermont.

The trail now curves W along the shore around a wide cove with shelving rock. There is a good view here of Grand Isle in Vermont. At 1.9 mi. the trail reaches small but spectacular Cystid Point, with campsite 18 (cement fireplace, table and privy). At 2.0 mi. there is a wooden walkway, then a rocky shelf beach, excellent for swimming.

At 2.4 mi. a small foot trail leads R to a rocky overlook above a small cove that offers a good mooring. Just N, at 2.6 mi., there is another campsite, where you cross a wooden walkway to a fenced area around a large beach rock in memory of the captain of the ship *Nomad*, Gerald Walker Birks, "who sailed these waters many years and found safe harbour in this cove" and to "four members of the crew who fought with Canadian and Imperial Forces 1914–1918."

At 2.7 mi., at a trail jct., turn R to Smuggler's Harbor in a few hundred yds., or L to return to Indian Point on the W side of the island. This is the Nomad Trail (trail 2), 0.8 mi. Campsites 15, 16 and 17 are along Smuggler's Harbor. You may continue along the Perimeter Trail to the next jct. for Tiger Point (0.1 mi.), or take a more interesting route 0.2 mi. from campsite 15 N along the shore to Tiger Point and back inland to the Perimeter Trail. The strange shape of Tiger Point makes interesting exploring.

From the Tiger Point jct., the Perimeter Trail goes around Sloop Cove for 0.4 mi. There are two privies at Sloop Cove.

At 3.2 mi., at another trail jct., you may go 0.1 mi. straight ahead on a spur to Paradise Bay. Down this spur to Paradise Bay are an old fireplace and chimney and campsite 13. A larger, more beautiful stone fireplace and chimney on the point suggest that this must have been a site for a house. Campsite 14 overlooks the lake to Spoon Island.

Soon after the Paradise Bay turn-off, the Perimeter Trail descends through cool cedar woods to a jct. at 3.4 mi. Turn R to Spoon Bay, which is reached in a few hundred feet, or go L on the Royal Savage Trail (3) 1.3 mi. across the interior of the island to Butterfly Bay.

Continuing N, the Perimeter Trail, which has merged with the Royal Savage Trail (3) for about 250 ft., reaches another jct. The Royal Savage Trail turns L (W) to cross the interior of the island. The Perimeter Trail veers R to continue N, going uphill through hemlocks, then levelling out at 3.7 mi. overlooking Spoon Bay.

At 3.8 mi. there is an overlook over Beauty Bay. The trail turns L over a wooden bridge through giant hemlocks to another wooden bridge, then reaches campsites 10 and 11.

Now the trail goes through giant white pines, and at 4.1 mi. reaches a sandy beach on the N edge of the island. Crab Island is straight N. On a mainland bluff to the W is North Country Community College. Just before 4.4 mi. there are five more campsites: 5, 6, 7, 8 and 9. This is Island's End.

The trail heads S. At 4.8 mi. there is a giant white oak, then a large overgrown pasture, then at 4.9 mi. a privy. Now the trail turns L under a huge canopy hedge to a "Pioneer Farm Orchard" sign in a pasture and a pioneer farm site at 5.0 mi. This is now a huge open pasture with raspberries and goldfinches in summer. From the edge of the pasture one can see the Peru Boat Launch with Whiteface Mt. directly behind.

At 5.2 mi., the trail crosses a wooden bridge surrounded by poison ivy. At 5.3 mi. there is another well-built wooden bridge, then at 5.4 mi. a sign, "Island's End," pointing N.

Now the trail enters a lovely mown clearing with shade trees and ten fireplaces and picnic tables on the N edge of the beach on Butterfly Bay. Turn L (E) to find the trail again. The Royal Savage interior trail (3) to Spoon Bay (1.3 mi.) starts behind the privy on the E side of the clearing. Continuing on the Perimeter Trail S from this jct., it is another 0.3 mi. S to the starting point at Bullhead Bay at 5.7 mi.

Please note: There is no trail S from Butterfly Beach and W to the point with the lighthouse (built in 1874) because until recently this was private land. This last private in-holding has been purchased by the state. At some time in the future, a trail to the point may be marked.

Distances: *Peru Boat Launch to Bullhead Bay via boat, 1.0 mi. Bullhead Bay* to stone house, 0.8 mi.; to Pebble Beach trail, 1.5 mi.; to Nomad Trail jct., 2.7 mi.; to Royal Savage Trail jct., 3.4 mi.; to Island's End, 4.1 mi.; to pioneer farm site, 5.0 mi.; to Bullhead Bay, 5.7 mi. (9.5 km).

(2) Valcour Island Nomad Trail

Map: p. 33

The two interior trails add up to another 2.1 miles. The shorter trail, on the S, is the Nomad Trail (0.8 mi.), which connects Indian Point on the W and Smugglers Harbor on the E. This is a beautiful deep-woods trail with gigantic white and red pine, cedar, hemlock, maple, birch and oak.

From the Indian Point jct., the trail goes E 0.6 mi. to a wooden walkway, at 0.7 mi. crosses another wooden walkway, and at 0.8 mi. reaches a jct. with the Perimeter Trail (1) on the E side of the island. Straight ahead is Smuggler's Harbor, R (S) is Cystid Point and L (N) is Sloop Cove.

There is a small side trail to Tiger Point from the S side of Sloop Cove. It is 0.2 mi. from the turn-off R to a campsite (unnumbered) with table, fireplace and crude camping shack, a low divide, then a point crested with cedars. There are excellent N–S views of Garden Island, Spoon Island and Crab Island. This is a fantastic spot.

From the trail jct. 0.5 mi. N of Smuggler's Harbor go straight 0.1 mi. on the Perimeter Trail to Paradise Bay where the trail dead-ends, or L 0.3 mi. to the jct. of the Royal Savage interior trail (3) with the Perimeter Trail. Heading NW the trail goes through beautiful cedar woods, descending a short distance to the next jct., where R leads to a dead-end at Spoon Bay, and L to another jct. in a few hundred yds. where the trail divides again R to the N side of Spoon Bay.

Distance: Indian Point to Smuggler's Harbor, 0.8 mi. (1.3 km).

(3) Valcour Island
Royal Savage Trail

Map: p. 33

The trail to the L at 3.4 mi. on the Perimeter Trail is the Royal Savage Trail, which goes 1.3 mi. W through the northern interior of the island to Butterfly Bay. At first it passes through deep woods, then through an open field filled with Queen Anne's lace in summer, then across a wooden walkway into mature white pine, cedar, birch and hemlock. After a second wooden bridge, the trail emerges into an open area with wild fruit trees, then sumac, then into deep woods again, then into another overgrown sunny field. After passing through a grassy tree-shaded picnic area, it reaches a jct., with the W Perimeter Trail (1) at Butterfly Bay. A loop using both interior trails equals 3.5 mi.

Distance: Royal Savage Trail, 1.3 mi. (2 km).

(4) Poke-O-Moonshine Mt.

Page Map

This fire tower peak is extremely popular because of its tremendous view of Lake Champlain and of the high peaks in the distance to the SW. Its unusual name appears to be a combination of two Algonquin Indian words, "Pohqui" and "Moosie," which mean, respectively, "broken" and "smooth." The name then, later corrupted by the early settlers, seems to refer to the smooth rocks of the summit or the prominent slab on the SE side and the broken rocks of the impressive cliff on the E side.

Trailhead: The trail starts at the state campground on Rt. 9, 9.3 mi. N of the jct. of the road from Lewis to exit 32 on the Adirondack Northway and 3.0 mi. S of exit 33. There is a parking fee charged at this state facility (and all similar facilities), and parking on the highway in front of the campground

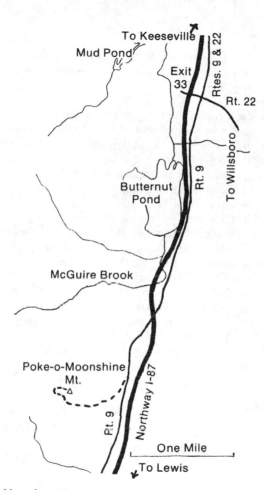

Poke-O-Moonshine (4)
Based on Ausable Forks and Willsboro Bay quadrangle, both 15-min. series, 1969.

is prohibited. This presents no problem in the off-season, but hikers should either be prepared to pay this fee or to walk a few hundred yds. extra from outside the "no parking" zone.

Starting from the S end of the campground (0.0 mi.), the red-marked trail enters the woods and immediately begins climbing, steeply at times, to the base of a cliff at 0.28 mi. Skirting the cliff on the L, the trail switchbacks R to a good lookout on the R at 0.33 mi. The grade now eases somewhat but remains steady to a saddle S of the summit at 0.82 mi. Here are the remains of the fire observer's cabin with a lean-to approximately 65 yds. to the L.

From this saddle there are two trails leading up to the R. The L trail is now marked as the official route; it leads up past a lookout on the L and along a shelf before turning R and up to the summit plateau. Turning R again, the trail goes through open woods to the summit and tower at 1.2 mi. (The R trail leading up from the observer's cabin is the old route, now badly eroded, which leads past an old spring house and then up steeply through a slot in the summit cliffs. It joins the current trail 0.1 mi. below the summit.)

Distances: *Campground to summit of Poke-O-Moonshine, 1.2 mi. (1.9 km). Ascent, 1280 ft. (390 m). Elevation, 2180 ft. (664 m).*

(5) Lyon Mt.

Page Map

Lyon Mt., while located within the boundaries of ADK's Northern Region guidebook by Peter O'Shea, is a fine hike not too far from the Eastern Region boundary. This description is taken from the Northern book.

This trail climbs a massive isolated peak in the far NE area of the Adirondack Park to offer what few mountains in the Adirondacks can—a truly international view. Red-marked, it is the

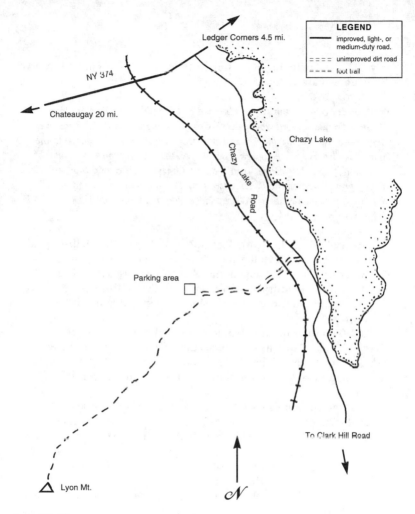

LEGEND
improved, light-, or medium-duty road.
==== unimproved dirt road
- - - - foot trail

Ledger Corners 4.5 mi.

NY 374

Chateaugay 20 mi.

Chazy Lake

Chazy Lake Road

Parking area

To Clark Hill Road

𝒩

Lyon Mt.

Lyon Mt. (5)
Based on Moffitsville quadrangle, 7.5-min. series, 1968.

only DEC-designated trail in the scattered patches of Forest Preserve in the immediate vicinity.

Trailhead: *Access to this trail is obtained by taking NY 374 W from Interstate 87 (the Adirondack Northway) exit 38N at Plattsburgh approx. 23.2 mi. over Dannemora Mt. and around Chazy Lake, above which Lyon Mt. looms, to the Chazy Lake Rd. For those coming from the W, this intersection is 3.7 mi. E of the center of Lyon Mt. village. Turn S on the Chazy Lake Rd. and proceed 1.8 mi. to a gravel road on the R. Take this gravel road 0.9 mi. to its end at the white ruins of the Lowenberg Ski Area lodge. Park here; the trail begins to the L of the lodge ruins.*

The trail starts its steady, strenuous ascent to the 3820-ft. peak of Lyon Mt. by initially following an old jeep road through a second-growth forest of aspen and cherry. This area was clear-cut about a quarter century ago for a ski trail. Before this, the forest was cut over heavily to furnish charcoal for iron smelting in the last century.

At 1.0 mi. balsam fir starts to come in heavily. Shortly thereafter, at 1.1 mi., at an intersection the trail keeps L; the R fork goes to the top of the old ski slope. White birch begins to appear at 1.2 mi. and at 1.3 mi. the remains of the old fire observer's cabin are seen.

The trail continues rising steeply, keeping R at another fork where the telephone wire path goes to the L. The forest is now composed of mature white birch with an undergrowth of spruce and fir. The spruce and fir indicate the composition of the future forest here, while the white birch attest to the severe forest fires that occurred at the turn of the century.

At 1.8 mi. balsam fir becomes the dominant tree in the canopy as the winds begin to pick up somewhat. Deer come up to this zone in the summer to use the increased wind velocity to escape the biting flies down below.

At 2.5 mi., after an extra steep pitch, the summit is attained. The fire tower has been abandoned, but was still standing in 1992. The summit is covered with scrubby conifers and mountain ash, as is also the case on the summits of DeBar and St. Regis mts. These reflect the poor soil and harsh climatic conditions on the exposed tops of these mountains. The craggy slopes of Ellenburg and Johnson mts. can be seen nearby, while the distant High Peaks may be seen to the S on a clear day. That same clear day can provide, in addition, a view of the skyscrapers in Montreal. Closer by, both the St. Lawrence River and Lake Champlain can be seen, with the Green Mountains of Vermont clearly outlined to the E.

Trail in winter: *Not suitable for cross-country skiing.*

Distances: *Parking area to fork, 1.1 mi.; to remains of cabin, 1.3 mi.; to fire tower, 2.5 mi. (4.0 km).*

Split Rock Mt. Area

The Split Rock Mt. area N of Westport on Lake Champlain is a beautiful but little-used region. As of August 1994 there are no state-marked trails, but a system of old tote roads leads out from a parking lot on state land. A management plan is being developed for the region, so it's likely that a state trail system will be marked out in the near future. Some flagging has been placed on the main trails in the region, and new trails will be added, including a trail that traverses the rock ledges over the top of Split Rock Mt. It has the potential of being one of the more spectacular trails in the region.

For those interested in viewing wildlife, just NW across the Lake Shore Rd. is Webb Royce Swamp. There are no trails here, but the area is not far from the road and is inhabited by a variety of wildlife.

While parts of this region were at one time developed and logged, there are few remnants in the southern half of this tract of that period except for the old logging roads and stonework from the old granite mine. The northern half (from the current trail access N to the private land boundary) has seen more timber activities. It's this complexity of logging roads that will form the backbone of the future trail system. This area was also worked for both granite and iron ore over a century ago, and there are remnants of these activities in a couple of places.

The forest is characterized by the lower-elevation flora of an open hardwood forest, with oaks and juniper trees on the rocky bluffs and hemlocks growing densely along the cool, moist streambeds. This area is within the historic range of the timber rattlesnake, so it may be wise to use caution when traveling over open rocky areas just in case there are snakes still calling this area home. Never tease or corner a rattler. If you give them a wide berth and leave them alone, they'll leave you alone. Eastern timber rattlesnakes are protected under New York State law. It is illegal to kill, take, or possess this species without a special DEC permit.

Trailhead: *From exit 31 on the Northway, head E on NY 9N to the intersection of NY 22 in 4.2 mi. Turn L (N) onto NY 22 (0 mi.) and in 0.4 mi. turn R (NE) onto Lake Shore Rd. At 0.9 mi. bear R (E) at the Y with Sherman Rd. Continue on (N) past Halds Rd. and Ainger Hill Rd. on the L (W), reaching the parking lot on the R with a Forest Preserve sign at 4.7 mi. from NY 9N.*

Trails 6, 7 and 8 are proposed trails within the vicinity. These trails will be added in future updates of the Eastern guide as the trailwork is completed.

(9) Snake Den Bay Lookout Trail   Page Map

The main access trail leads E into the woods from the parking lot (see above), heading gradually uphill on an old rutted road. At 0.1 mi. another road cuts off to the R (S). (This road to the R is a slightly longer route that rejoins the main road at 0.8 mi.) The main road continues on straight ahead and uphill. At 0.3 mi. there is another jct. with a road cutting off to the L (N).

Continuing straight ahead, the mostly level trail meanders through a mixed coniferous and deciduous forest, crossing over a couple of streams. At 0.75 mi. a wet area with a water hole on the L is passed and the trail soon climbs gradually and swings around to the L. After it levels off again, another road soon comes in from the R at a Y at 0.8 mi. The trail gradually begins descending and at 1.0 mi. the cutoff to the Barn Rock Trail (10) is on the R (S).

The trail continues straight ahead following a series of hemlock-covered ledges on the L with a number of sturdy old grapevines hanging from the trees along the trail. After dropping steadily for a while, the trail soon levels and Lake Champlain can be seen shining through the trees in the distance. At 1.45 mi. a T intersection is reached. The Bay Trail spur (9A) heads off to the L. Bearing R, in a short distance the Lookout Trail turns L onto a small ridge and fades to a small footpath at the height of the ridge at 1.6 mi. From there it is a short scramble down to a nice outlook through the junipers down to the Palisades on Lake Champlain with the shimmering waters of Snake Den Bay about 300 ft. below.

(9A) Bay Trail   Page Map

This side trail leads down to a small bay on the shoreline of Lake Champlain, from the intersection at 1.45 mi. with the Lookout Trail (9). It's a pretty view looking N along the rocky, wild shoreline

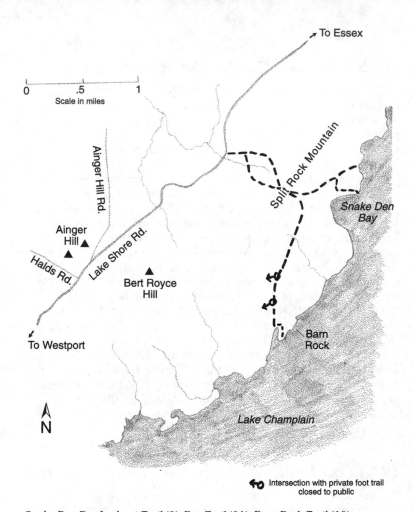

🔗 Intersection with private foot trail closed to public

Snake Den Bay Lookout Trail (9), Bay Trail (9A), Barn Rock Trail (10)
Based on Westport quadrangle, 15-min. series, 1980.

across Louis Clearing Bay to Orc Bed Point and beyond.

Leaving the jct. on the Snake Den Lookout Trail (0.0 mi., 1.45 mi. from the parking lot), the trail heads N then E down a moderately steep grade. The trail is rocky and a bit wet in a couple of places along its descent to the rocky bay, which is reached at 0.3 mi. after the path crosses a small flow of water. There are great views to the N, S and E across the lake to Vermont.

Distances: *Parking lot to Barn Rock (trail 10), 1.0 mi.; to intersection with Bay Trail spur (trail 9A), 1.5 mi.; to lookout at height of the ridge, 1.6 mi. (2.56 km). The trail ascends and then descends approx. 200 ft. (61 m) to get to the lookout.*

Bay Trail: From 1.4-mi. point on Snake Den Lookout Trail to lakeshore, 0.3 mi. (0.5 km). Total distance from parking lot, 1.8 mi. (2.9 km). Descent from Lookout Trail, approx. 300 ft. (91 m). Total ascent from Lake Champlain back to the parking lot is about 465 ft. (142 m).

(10) Barn Rock Trail

Map: p. 48

This trail travels through a nice forest of mixed woods, descending to the shore of Lake Champlain and a quite unique viewpoint over the lake. It is at present unmarked and unmaintained, and is quite wet in some spots as it follows what appears to be an old carriage road to the shore of Lake Champlain. If following the overgrown trail near the end proves to be too much of a problem, following the stream will bring you down to the small isolated bay beside Barn Rock.

The trail begins at a sharp R turn off the Lookout Trail (trail 9) at the head of a small ravine. The trail soon veers L and climbs gradually up the side of the slope. At 0.2 mi. the trail levels off, turns and heads in a S and SE direction, then gradually begins descending to a level area at 0.6 mi. The road is level with a couple of wet areas until at 0.9 mi. it begins descending again. At 1.0 mi. a Y is reached. The L (S) fork goes to Barn Rock; the R trail leads to private property.

Dropping fairly steeply at first over rocks, the trail soon changes to a more moderate descent. At 1.1 mi. a beautiful old stone bridge crosses over the stream to the R, eventually leading again to private property.

The trail on the L stream bank is faint here, but follows down along some interesting rock work in the stream bed, crossing over the stream at 1.25 mi. Soon a rock wall is passed on the R, and the bay is visible through the trees with Barn Rock just beyond jutting out into Lake Champlain. A herd path cuts down the steep bank to the L and heads across the sandy shore of the small bay, while the trail itself continues on for a short distance, ending at 1.5 mi. at a small stream by some beaver work.

If Barn Rock is the only goal, then the herd path down the steep bank would be the shortest route. Going to the end of the trail, however, gives a nice perspective of Barn Rock and the beaver work in the area, and it's a nice short walk back along the shoreline to the herd path up to Barn Rock. Follow the cobbled shoreline back a short distance and then cross the short gravelly section at the mouth of the bay. Head R (E) along the shoreline toward Barn Rock to a small gully on the L. This is the easiest herd path ascent up to the top of the ridge. Follow up the L side of the gully and then turn R along the herd path along the center of the ridge. The main path soon heads over to the R side, then back to the center again before arriving at the end of Barn Rock, with beautiful views along and across Lake Champlain. Keep an eye out for Champ, the famous Lake Champlain monster! Distance from the trail at the bay is approx. 0.4 mi., or 1.9 mi. from the Lookout Trail (9).

Distances: *From Lookout Trail to first cutoff to L, 1.0 mi.; to the L fork at the stone bridge, 1.1 mi.; to the end of the trail along the shore, 1.5 mi.; and to the end of Barn Rock., about 1.9 mi. (2.9 mi. from the parking lot). Descent to the lake from the highest point on the trail, approx. 510 ft.*

Coon Mt. (bushwhack)   Page Map

The Coon Mt. Preserve is a 246-acre property located in the Adirondack Land Trust's Champlain Valley Farm and Forest Project area. The mountain includes many steep rock faces, small wetlands and several streams, and the mixed hardwood forest supports a variety of wildlife. From the top are fine views of Lake Champlain, the Green Mountains, and the Adirondack High Peaks rising beyond the farmlands in the valley. At present (August 1994) there is a route for a trail under consideration, but it's only in the preliminary stages. The preserve contains most of the higher part of the mountain, and is bordered on all sides by private lands, so be sure to keep your bearings straight to avoid becoming lost and wandering onto private property.

This is a preserve. No camping, fires or littering are allowed, nor the destruction or removal of any plants. For more up-to-date information please call the Adirondack Nature Conservancy and Adirondack Land Trust at 518-576-2082.

Proposed Trailhead: *Heading E on 9N from exit 31 on the Northway, in a short distance take the L (N) turn onto Youngs Rd. (0.0 mi.) The town of Wadhams and the intersection with NY 22 is reached at 2.6 mi. Continue L (N and E) on 22, taking the R turn (SE) onto Morrison Rd. at 3.7 mi. In another mile cross the bridge over the Boquet. Bear R, then cross the road that parallels the river onto Halds Rd., which soon enters a wooded area. There is a small parking lot by the road on the L (N) side at 5.5 mi., by the Adirondack Land Trust signs.*

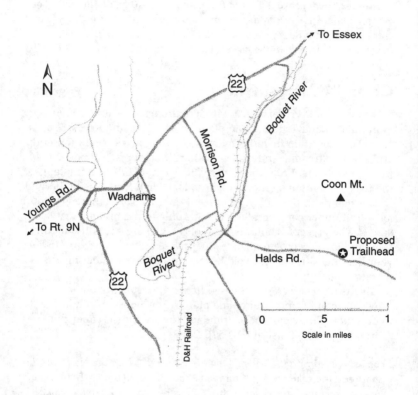

Coon Mt.
Based on Westport quadrangle, 15-min. series, 1980.

It is easiest to climb to the upper ledges by following the old log road to near the east boundary of the property, then working your way up across some fairly steep terrain to the summit plateau. This is the same area in which the trail is planned, and there might be some surveyor's tape on the trees in this area that you can follow. Once on top, head in a NW then W direction for a short distance, dropping into a small sag before climbing up onto a small ridge. Heading S along the ridge brings you to the top of a rock outcrop and a fine 240-degree panorama. It's best to head back down the same way you came. Some of what look like short easy routes down quickly become steep and difficult.

Trail in winter: *In winter this route would be a nice snowshoe trip, albeit steep in one section, but it is definitely not a ski route.*

Four Ponds (Lincoln Pond–Mineville Area)

While there are a couple of short trails in and around these ponds, these were added to round out the experience in this region. A day in the area might include some canoeing and swimming or fishing on the ponds and a short hike up Belfry Mt. for some fine views.

Trailhead: *Just E of exit 30 on the Northway, take the first L onto the Mineville Rd. (Essex Co. Rt. 6) and follow this to the first intersection in Witherbee. Turn L (0.0 mi.) onto Essex Co. Rt. 7C toward Belfry Mt. and Lincoln Pond. At 1.3 mi. Essex 7 rejoins at a Y. Continue on to the L and in a short distance at 1.6 mi. there is a dirt road to the R (N) which leads to both Tanaher (12) and Mill (13) ponds. In another 0.2 mi., at 1.8 mi., is another dirt road to the R (N). This leads to the W end of Mill Pond (14) and is near Murrey Pond (14). In just another 0.2 mi. on the R (N) at 2.0 mi. is the*

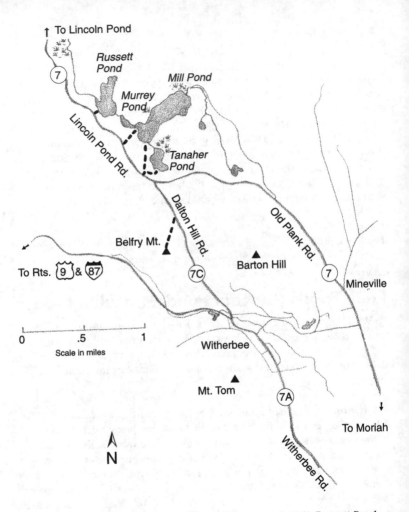

Tanaher Pond (12), Mill Pond (13), Mill and Murrey ponds (14), Russett Pond (15), Belfry Mt. (16). Based on Witherbee quadrangle, 15-min. series, 1978.

footpath to Russett Pond (15), the last in this series of ponds. From this point it's about 2.25 mi. to the Lincoln Pond state campsite farther N on Essex Co. Rt. 7.

(12) Tanaher Pond   Page Map

This is a pretty pond, ringed with a boggy shoreline. From the road (see trailhead description above) drive downhill to a Y at 0.07 mi. Bear R (E) for a short distance to a pulloff at 0.1 mi. From there the pond is visible and there's a short wet path (N) leading to the edge of the pond at 0.2 mi.

(13) Mill Pond   Page Map

The trail starts at the same access as for Tanaher Pond (12). Heading downhill on the dirt road to the Y at 0.07 mi., bear L (W). The road soon dissipates to an unmarked footpath that wanders over a couple of knolls, and down to a small access at the shoreline of Mill Pond at 0.2 mi.

(14) Mill and Murrey Ponds   Page Map

This is a short, moderately steep access to both the SW corner of Mill Pond and to Murrey Pond. From the road (see trailhead above), there is a dirt road that leads a short distance down the hill, with a couple of footpaths leading to the water at 0.1 mi.

(15) Russett Pond   Page Map

This is the closest pond to the road. It's only about 150 ft. along the footpath to the pond from the parking along the shoulder of the road by the Forest Preserve sign (see trailhead above).

(16) Belfry Mt.

Map: p. 54

This is a real treat: a short walk and a fantastic view, the lazy hiker's heaven. High Peaks Audubon members come up here to watch hawks fly low over this peak during their fall and spring migrations. At other times it is possible to see a few hawks soaring, so bring your binoculars.

Trailhead: In Mineville, turn L between the Rexall drug store and Citgo gas station. Drive 1.0 mi. to a yield sign. Turn R at a green sign which says "Elizabethtown 11, Lincoln Pond 4." Go 1.1 mi. steadily uphill. Park on the shoulder of the road on the R, across from a bright yellow steel gate on the L (0 mi.).

From the top of the hill by the gate it is 3.5 mi. W to the Lincoln Pond state campsite and day-use area.

The route follows the ranger access road behind the gate 0.2 mi. to a cabin and radio tower, then at 0.3 mi. reaches a clearing and two sheds. The fire tower is in sight. Just under 0.4 mi. the summit is reached.

From the fire tower there are good views of Lake Champlain, Vermont to the E, the Dix Range to the W, the Great Range, Whiteface to the NW, Rocky Peak Ridge, Giant and Hurricane Mt. to the N. Mineville and the slag heaps left over from the days of the iron mines can be seen below.

Distance: Road to summit on ranger road, 0.4 mi. (0.7 km). Ascent, 120 ft. (36.6 m). Summit elevation, 1820 ft. (557.6 m).

(17) Morehouse Bridge to Boquet

Page Map

This is a pleasant and easy walk along an old road which starts in the town of Willsboro and ends in the town of Essex. Take along a picnic and eat lunch on the ledges of the Boquet River before making your return trip. This road is also an excellent cross-country ski route.

Trailhead: *From Essex, go W on NY 22 1.5 mi. to the Middle Road. Turn R (N) and go 1.8 mi. to Coonrod Road. Turn L (W) and go 1.7 mi. to Morehouse Bridge over the Boquet River. Cross the bridge and at 1.8 mi. turn L onto a dirt road which ends at the McAuliffe farm. Ask Mr. McAuliffe for permission to park. If he is not there, be sure to park on the grass beyond the barn where you are not blocking the road because he often takes his tractor out to the fields.*

The hike starts from the farm, straight ahead through fields on the abandoned road. At 0.1 mi. the road passes a pond down to the L, then starts going gently uphill, at 0.3 mi. gently downhill, then uphill again. At 0.4 mi. the road enters woods; soon there is an old clearing on the R and a junked refrigerator. The road descends.

At 0.5 mi. the road curves L high over a stream, then uphill and into a sunny field on the R. North Boquet Mt. is visible across the field. At 0.6 mi. the road reenters woods and at 0.7 mi. reaches the end of the field, seen through the trees. Now the road goes gradually downhill. At 0.8 mi. the river can be heard down to the L.

The road goes gently uphill and then down again. At 1.0 mi. there is a rock ledge on the R, then an overgrown field and at 1.1 mi. the abandoned clubhouse of the Boquet Snowdrifters, a snowmobile club, at the Willsboro–Essex town line.

At 1.2 mi. the road crosses a stream. A side track L leads to the

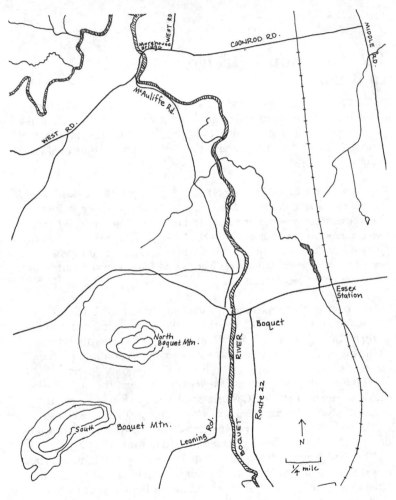

Morehouse Bridge to Boquet (17)
Based on Willsboro, New York/Vermont quadrangle, 15-min. series, 1980.

river. Now the road goes uphill past a huge rock ledge on the L, covered with ferns and mosses.

At 1.3 mi. there is a turn-out on the L above the river, from which the river can be seen and heard down the steep hill on the L. At 1.5 mi. a paved road goes up Crooked S Hill. A walk downhill L to another track on the L in 200 ft. leads to an easy path to the shelving ledges and waterfall at 1.6 mi., below the green iron bridge over the river. Across the river are the remains of a stone mill, one of several that were here in the little hamlet of Boquet more than 100 years ago. Now this is a popular local picnic, fishing and swimming spot.

Distances: *McAuliffe farm to Crooked S Hill, 1.5 mi.; to Boquet River ledges, 1.6 mi. (2.6 km).*

Pharaoh Lake

Hammond Pond Wild Forest, Crown Point, Moriah Section

This section is centrally located within the eastern Adirondack region. It's bordered by Elizabethtown, Mineville, and Port Henry on the north, and NY 74 from exit 28 on the Northway to Ticonderoga on the south. The eastern side is a pretty landscape of farmlands along Lake Champlain, while the western side is the extensive Hammond Pond Wild Forest area that's bounded by US 9 on the W. This region underwent extensive review in the late 1980s and most of the suggested improvements have taken place. At present this area sees little use, especially when compared to the Pharaoh Lake Wilderness just to the S. While a trail system connects some of the most popular destinations, there are several trailless mountains and isolated ponds that are waiting to be explored. The Hammond Pond Wild Forest area is perfect for an ultralight "Lost Pond" boat.

Trails in winter: Most of the marked trails in this region are over low rolling terrain and are perfect for skiing and snowshoeing. Other recommendations for specific trails are listed with the trail descriptions.

Suggested hikes in the region include:

Short Hike:

Arnold Pond—*0.3 mi. A short but steep hike to a pretty pond tucked in at the base of a rock slide on Skiff Mt.*

Moderate Hike:

Peaked Hill—*2.2 mi. plus canoe. This is a fun summer route, canoeing across Paradox Lake and then hiking a moderate route to Peaked Hill Pond followed by the steeper climb up Peaked Hill.*

Trail Described	Total Miles (one way)	Page
(18) Sunrise Trail to Mt. Gilligan	1.1	63
(19) Bald Peak	3.9	63
Split Rock Falls (unmarked footpaths)		66
(21) Proposed trail		
(22) Crowfoot Pond	3.0	67
(23) Sharp Bridge Campground to Round Pond & E Mill Flow	5.2	69
(24) Howard & Munson ponds	1.2	72
(25) Bass Lake Trail	3.2	73
(26) Challis Pond	0.6	75
(27) Berrymill Flow and Moose Mt. Pond	3.5	77
(28) Hammond & Bloody ponds	3.0	78
(29) Peaked Hill & Peaked Hill Pond	2.2	80
(30) Arnold Pond	0.3	83
(31) Old Ironville Road	2.3	84
(32) Sherman Lake and Cubtown roads	4.6	87
(33) Lindsay Brook Access to Dix Wilderness	0.9	90
(34) West Mill Access to Dix Wilderness	1.1	90
(35) Walker Brook Access to Dix Wilderness	0.7	92

(18) Sunrise Trail to Mt. Gilligan Page Map

Formerly known as Sunrise Mt., this little peak rises directly above the Boquet River and offers views of Pleasant Valley, Rocky Peak Ridge and the Dixes from the summit and the several lookouts along the way.

Trailhead: The trail starts from Rt. 9, 3.6 mi. N of its jct. with NY 73 and 2.6 mi. S of the New Russia Post Office. A dirt road leads to a bridge over the river, with an informal parking lot just before the bridge. Park here (0.0 mi.), cross the bridge, and turn L off the road after 150 yds. just before reaching a house on the L. Marked with ADK markers, the trail proceeds on the flat for a few hundred yds. before climbing to a higher shelf up to the R and then, after some more flat going, climbs steeply up to the first lookout at 0.3 mi., with a good view of Dix.

Continuing on, the trail dips briefly and then climbs steadily to another lookout at 0.6 mi. Now the grade is easier along the top of the ridge before it dips down and crosses an old lumber road in a small col at 0.8 mi. Climbing past an interesting overhung rock, the trail reaches a broad open area at 0.86 mi., with good views of Rocky Peak Ridge and the Dix Range. Just after this ledge, the trail joins and briefly follows an old lumber road before branching L and up to the final lookout at 1.1 mi. at the end of the trail. The wooded summit of Gilligan Mt. is about 100 yds. beyond.

Distances: Parking area near Rt. 9 to lookout below summit of Mt. Gilligan, 1.1 mi. (1.8 km). Ascent, 670 ft. (204 m). Elevation, 1420 ft. (433 m).

(19) Bald Peak Page Map

This is a rewarding climb that is technically part of the High

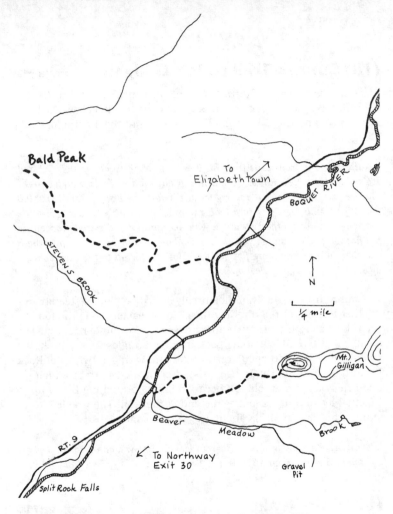

Sunrise to Mt. Gilligan (18), Bald Peak (19), Split Rock Falls (20)
Based on Elizabethtown quadrangle, 15-min. series, 1978.

Peaks region and part of the much longer Rocky Peak Ridge trail. Much of the trail is in the open, and there are views all along the way. Be sure, though, to bring plenty of water on a hot summer day, and crampons in the winter for the exposed upper reaches of Bald Peak. On a cool fall day with Adirondack fall colors at their peak, this is a spectacular hike.

Except for a small stand of first-growth hemlock near the start of the trail, this entire route is through smaller second growth. This is a result of the great fire of 1913, which burned all of Rocky Peak and much of Giant. Nearly all of the views along this route are a result of this last major fire in the Adirondacks.

Trailhead: *The trail begins at a parking lot on Rt 9, 4.9 mi. N of the junction with NY 73 and 1.3 mi. S of the New Russia post office.*

From the parking lot the trail crosses a nearly grown-up field, begins to climb an old tote road, and comes to the L bank of a small stream at 0.7 mi. Following up the L bank, the trail enters a flat notch at the far end of which it swings L and climbs to the first view on the L at 1.6 mi. A second view is just off the trail to the R at 1.8 mi.

Continuing up, the trail comes to the first lookout on Blueberry Cobbles on the L at 1.9 mi. and then comes to a jct. at 2.0 mi. with a red trail leading R that bypasses the top of Blueberry Cobbles. (In season there is no doubt that Blueberry Cobbles is appropriately named.) The yellow trail L leads past many other views of the Boquet Valley and the Dix Range before turning sharp R and down at 2.3 to Mason Notch, where the red bypass trail rejoins it. The trail climbs over the slightly wooded summit of Mason Mt. (2330 ft.) at 2.8 mi. before descending to Hedgehog Notch at the base of Bald Peak. Now the trail begins to climb steeply over mostly bare rock to the summit of Bald Peak (3060 ft.) at 3.9 mi., where there are good views in all directions. From the summit one can look out over most all of the eastern Adirondack region, as well as some of the High Peaks region. Further hiking possibilities in the High Peaks region are described in ADK's High Peaks guide.

Trail in winter: *This trail is not a skiing route, but makes a great snowshoeing trail. With poor snow conditions, crampons (full or instep) are a must for the steeper exposed sections.*

Distances: *Parking lot to Blueberry Cobbles, 1.9 mi.; to top of Bald Peak, 3.9 mi. Ascent, 2447 ft. (746 m). Elevation, 3060 ft. (933 m).*

Split Rock Falls   Map: p. 64

Currently there is no marked trail system in the Split Rock Falls area, but several herd paths lead around the falls, along the river, and to the base of the falls, a popular swimming spot on a hot summer day. With the addition of a parcel of land surrounding the falls to the Forest Preserve there is potential for marked trails in the region in the future.

Trailhead: *The parking lot is along the E side of Rt. 9, 2.3 mi. N of NY 73 and 3.8 mi. S of the New Russia post office. The parking lot is small and there are No Parking signs along both sides of the road for some distance beyond the parking lot, so on a hot summer day it may be necessary to walk some distance to get to the falls.*

A couple of herd paths lead E from the parking lot along the edge of the ravine, with a couple more heading down into the steep-sided ravine to the Boquet River and the base of the falls. It can be fun to explore downstream along the river as well. Another footpath leads along the river from the S side of the bridge across the Boquet. This also leads downstream along the falls and to the river. The falls is a very pretty spot, as is the area downstream, where the steep rocky sides narrow in along the riverbanks.

Trail 21 is a proposed trail within the vicinity. This trail will be added in future updates of the Eastern guide.

(22) Crowfoot Pond   Page Map

Trailhead: At Northway exit 30 drive E on US 9 and make an immediate turn L onto Tracy Road, just after the northbound Northway entrance ramp. Go 1.8 mi. down this curving road to a track forking off to the R (0 mi.). This used to be a town road. Park on the shoulder of Tracy Road.

(An end-to-end trip can be made by spotting a car at Crowfoot Pond. Drive to Moriah Center and then W 1.2 mi. on county Rt. 4 to the dirt road on the R which leads another mile to the pond. Be careful not to park by the private camps.)

This would be an excellent cross-country ski run. Most of the bridges across Crowfoot Brook are ramped for snowmobiles. It might be good to inquire locally about the frequency of snowmobile use since it is a snowmobile trail. This old road is a very pleasant walk in the fall. The trees are spectacular and the brook becomes an old friend as you cross and recross it before reaching the pond.

There are yellow and red DEC snowmobile trail signs on a dead tree 50 ft. down the old road. The road follows Crowfoot Brook on the R, past a Forest Preserve sign on a tree on the R, and at 0.1 mi. crosses a bridge over Crowfoot Brook. After the bridge, the trail turns L and climbs gently through hemlocks and birches. The road

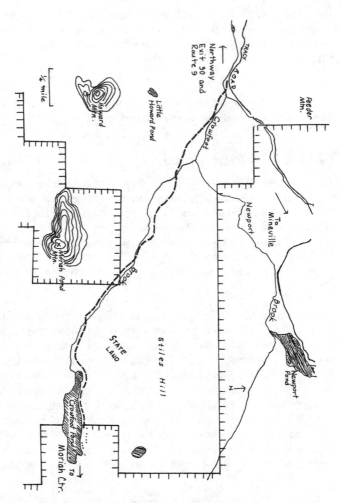

Crowfoot Pond (22)
Based on Witherbee quadrangle, 15-min. series, 1978.

now traverses a hill high above the brook.

At 0.3 mi. the road crosses a rotting corduroy at a spring. At 0.4 mi. there is a wooden town line marker between North Hudson and Moriah (which is ahead) on the R. The woods now are more deciduous with many ferns along the path.

At 0.5 mi. the trail bends L and R again around a fern-lined small streambed. Then it enters darker woods with more hemlocks. At 0.7 mi. there is another town line marker on the L.

At 0.8 mi. there is a log bridge over the brook. The road now climbs steadily upward. At 1.1 mi. the road begins to descend, and at 1.3 mi. crosses another log bridge. At 1.6 mi. there is a "Private Lands" sign. At 1.7 mi. the road crosses a rocky streambed, then a smaller streambed, then at 2.0 mi. a rotten, broken bridge (it might be better to cross on stones). Just after the bridge a Forest Preserve sign is on the L, and 20 ft. beyond it a town line marker in a rock cairn.

At 2.3 mi. the road divides in a small clearing. Continue straight through the clearing, not on the R track. At 2.5 mi. the W end of Crowfoot Pond comes into view. At 2.7 mi. there is a log cabin camp on a hillside on the L, then another camp, then about 10 more camps at the E end of the pond. At 3.0 mi. the road reaches the furthest eastern end of the pond. The road runs along the pond edge, with a lovely view of the wooded hill across the long narrow pond.

Distance: *Tracy Road to Crowfoot Pond, 3.0 mi. (5 km).*

(23) Sharp Bridge Campground to Round Pond and East Mill Flow   Page Map

This trail is a relatively flat and pleasant walk through some fine woods, giving access to picturesque Round Pond as well as the

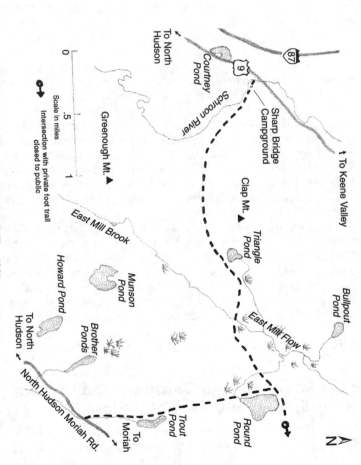

Sharp Bridge Campground to Round Pond and East Mill Flow (23)
Based on Witherbee quadrangle, 15-min. series, 1978.

beautiful and unique open area known as East Mill Flow. This trail was cut out a few years ago but has not been well maintained recently. It is still quite passable, though; one only needs to be careful not to lose it in the alders at a few of the stream crossings.

Trailhead: *The start is at Sharp Bridge Campground on Rt. 9, 7.1 mi. N of the village of North Hudson and 2.9 mi. S of exit 30 on the Adirondack Northway. Parking is at the gravel turnout just outside the gate.*

From the parking area (0 mi.), the trail goes to the far end of the large, flat field near the Schroon River and then along the L bank of the river on an old road. Crossing several small brooks, the trail comes to an old bridge abutment at 0.8 mi. This apparently was the original crossing point used as early as the 1830s both by the predecessor of US 9 and by a road leading W from Port Henry to Tahawus and beyond. Turning sharp L at this point, the trail follows this old road for several miles.

The trail climbs briefly, drops to cross a small brook, and then begins a steady climb to a height of land at 1.5 mi. Dropping down the other side in two short pitches, the trail continues mostly on the level through several magnificent stands of white pine to the R bank of East Mill Brook at 2.7 mi., at the S end of East Mill Flow. Swinging R, the trail drops down and makes a somewhat difficult crossing of the brook before scrambling up the far bank and continuing along the E side of this extensive open swamp. At 3.4 mi. the trail crosses the outlet to Round Pond in a thick clump of alders, turns sharp R, and heads up a gentle grade. At 3.5 mi., just before coming within sight of Round Pond, the trail turns sharp R off the old road and proceeds to the outlet of Round Pond at 3.9 mi. (The old road leads straight ahead to the NW shore of Round Pond with a good campsite located across the pond on some low rocks.)

From the outlet, the trail climbs S away from the pond and skirts numerous small swampy areas as it crosses a low divide and proceeds down to a jct. with an unmarked trail leading L at 4.5 mi. (Trail L leads along E shore of Trout Pond to a rough access road.) Continuing R, the trail makes its way along the W shore of Trout Pond and comes to the North Hudson–Moriah Rd. at 5.2 mi. This trailhead is approximately 5.3 mi. from US 9, N of North Hudson, and is not marked by any sign.

Distances: *Sharp Bridge Campground to East Mill Flow, 2.7 mi.; to outlet to Round Pond, 3.9 mi.; to North Hudson–Moriah Rd., 5.2 mi. (8.4 km).*

(24) Howard and Munson Ponds   Page Map

These are two more jewel-like ponds along the Moriah Rd. in the town of North Hudson.

Trailhead: *Drive 5.7 mi. E of NY 9 on County Route 4, the Moriah Rd. Park at a turn-out on the R. Walk back W along the road 250 ft., passing a huge double white pine until you come to the marshy opening of the trail on the N side of the road. There are no signs or markers, and the beginning of the trail may be a little tricky to spot.*

Despite a wet beginning, the trail is mostly dry, first going W parallel to the county road and then at 0.1 mi. turning N and uphill within earshot of a stream. The trail levels out at 0.2 mi. along a stream with a steep hillside to the R. The trail goes up again and at 0.3 mi. Howard Pond can be seen. A sign says these are Special Brook Trout Waters.

At 0.4 mi. the trail reaches the edge of Howard Pond. Retracing your steps 100 ft., follow a path to the L at the height of land just before the pond edge. This faint trail goes through a beautiful cedar and hemlock forest along the E side of the pond. At 0.6 mi. the trail passes a large white pine with a fire circle by the edge of the pond. At 0.7 mi. it leaves the NE edge of the pond and starts uphill, soon going through a large stand of maidenhair fern. It ascends steeply, at 0.9 mi reaching the top of a ridge. On the short descent the trail is faint. After a slight rise, it goes downhill to a tiny, swampy pond.

At 1.0 mi. the trail starts heading more steeply downhill. At 1.1 mi. Munson Pond can be seen through the trees, and in a few hundred yds. it is attained. The beavers have been doing heavy-duty logging here, felling large birches around the perimeter of the pond. The pond level has been raised considerably. Although there is no formal path around this pond, it is not difficult to thread your way among the hemlocks, white pines and birches, since their canopy is quite high.

Distances: *Moriah Rd. to Howard Pond, 0.4 mi. (0.7 km), to Munson Pond, 1.2 mi. (2 km). Elevation of Howard Pond, 1227 ft. (374.1 m). Elevation of Munson Pond, 1260 ft. (384.1 m).*

(25) Bass Lake Trail   Map: p. 76

This is the first body of water among the family of ponds along the Moriah Rd. These ponds all feed the Schroon River to the S.

Trailhead: *Drive 2.4 mi. N of North Hudson on US 9 to a R (NE) on Essex Co. Rt. 4, known locally as the Moriah Rd. There is a sign that says "Port Henry." After this turn go only 0.2 mi. to an old paved road to the R (E). At the end of this is the trailhead with yellow markers.*

The old paved road turns to dirt in several hundred yds. at an old bridge abutment on both sides of the stream on the L. A fisherman's path goes down the steep bank to the stream. The trail passes a wide place in the stream below at 0.2 mi. Now the trail cuts along the bank and at 0.3 mi. passes shelving falls through the trees on the L. The trail now bends R uphill and away from the stream.

At 0.4 mi. the trail levels off. Crossing a stream, the road heads up steeply through a birch and hemlock woods. At .8 mi. it crosses a small brook. At 1.0 mi. the trail, still climbing, becomes muddy, eroded and rocky. It soon levels off in a beech woods and then descends along a ridge.

At 1.4 mi. the trail turns L to avoid a blowdown, goes through a sunny area and then enters some tall hemlocks. At 1.6 mi. Bass Lake is visible through the trees, and there is a side trail on the L that leads 0.2 mi. to the W end of the lake by a huge boulder.

The trail continues on to the R parallel to the S shore of Bass Lake. It soon crosses a stream and then at 1.8 mi. comes to another side trail that leads a short distance to an informal campsite on Bass Lake. The trail continues on along the shoreline, reaching the outlet at 2.2 mi. where there are signs of beaver activity. At 2.3 mi. the E end of the lake is reached with nice views back across the water. After passing through a wet area, the trail levels off in open hemlocks at 2.5 mi.

The trail soon descends gradually, with Berrymill Flow visible through the trees at 2.9 mi. The trail now roughly parallels the shoreline of the flow, and reaches the junction with the Moose Mt. Pond Trail (27) at 3.15 mi. From this point it is 1.35 mi. to the Hammond Pond trailhead on the Moriah Rd. following the Berrymill Flow and Moose Mt. Pond Trail (27).

Distances: *From trailhead off US 9 to first side trail to Bass Lake, 1.6 mi. (2.6 km); to E end of lake, 2.3 mi. (3.7 km); to jct. with Berrymill Flow and Moose Mt. Pond Trail (27), 3.15 mi. (5 km). Elevation of Bass Lake, 1231 ft. (375 m).*

(26) Challis Pond Page Map

This is another of the lovely ponds near the Moriah Rd. These are lightly travelled trails which are used mostly by trout fishermen. It would be pleasant to hike in with an inflatable raft or ultralight canoe for further exploring.

Trailhead: From Northway exit 29 (Newcomb–North Hudson), turn E to the jct. with US 9 at 0.4 mi. Turn L, drive 2.4 mi. N and turn R at a sign for Port Henry. At 2.6 mi. pass the old road on the R which is the trailhead for Bass Lake (25). At 2.7 mi. turn R again at signs for Moriah and Champlain Bridge. This is a beautiful, winding road. At 4.3 mi. cross a small bridge over a brook and at 5.3 mi. park at a small turn-out at the trailhead for Challis Pond (0 mi.). There might not be a sign, but someone has built a cedar railing on both sides of the trail about 50 ft. up from the road.

The clearly defined trail leads up through hemlock and cedar woods. At 0.3 mi. a stream can be heard on the R but is unseen. There are orange paint blazes on trees.

At 0.4 mi. the outlet stream is on the R. The trail crosses dry ground above a small seep. At 0.5 mi. it enters deciduous woods; at 0.6 mi. the pond comes into view through the trees.

A campsite with a blackened boulder is near the edge of the pond. The pond seems to be almost a perfect circle. Bullfrogs call a welcome, as well as chickadees, warblers, thrushes and nuthatches. Bog laurel, pickerel weed and pond lilies bloom along the shoreline. There are no beavers here.

To the R, an informal path crosses the outlet stream and then continues through hemlocks around the shoreline but peters out after 0.2 mi. This is probably used by hunters and anglers.

Distance: Moriah Rd. to Challis Pond, 0.6 mi. (1 km). Pond elevation, 1150 ft. (350.6 m).

Hammond Pond Wild Forest, Crown Point, Moriah Section **75**

USGS 15 Min.
Elizabethtown
Paradox Lake

N ← | 1 MILE

Howard and Munson ponds (24), Bass Lake Trail (25), Challis Pond (26),
Berrymill Flow and Moose Mt. Pond (27), Hammond and Bloody ponds (28)
Based on Elizabethtown and Paradox Lake quadrangles, both 15-min. series,
1973.

(27) Berrymill Flow and Moose Mt. Pond

Map: p. 76

This is an easy trail into some nice wild lands. There's a good opportunity to see some wildlife on the way past the flow. There's a lot of beaver activity near Moose Mt. Pond, so you get a close-up opportunity to see what they can do with some fairly level drainages.

Trailhead: This trailhead is a recently constructed parking area on the R (S) side of the Moriah Rd. just 0.1 mi. past the Challis Pond trailhead (26). It is 3.0 mi. from Rt. 9 and 5.4 mi. from North Hudson.

The trail begins at a rustic set of steps at the S end of the parking lot (0.0 mi.) and follows blue markers. It soon joins an old tote road and parallels a stream on a very gradual incline. At 0.4 mi., just before entering an open area with some substantial beaver activity, the trail cuts off to the R (W) and begins climbing a hill. It continues up and down along the hillside until descending to the old tote road again at 0.7 mi.

The trail continues S along the stream through a pretty woods, reaching a 5-ft. waterfall on the L (E) at 0.9 mi. It continues on at a gradual grade, reaching the jct. with the Bass Lake Trail (25) at 1.35 mi. This jct. is marked with a DEC signpost.

Just beyond this jct. there is an informal campsite on a small knoll. From here is a nice view S across Berrymill Flow. After passing through the campsite, the trail crosses the recently constructed bridge across the outlet of the flow, climbs a few stairs, and then begins to follow S along the shoreline of the flow. At 1.7 mi., about half way down the flow, the trail swings L away from the flow and gradually ascends a couple of small sets of stairs. It soon meets and follows the L bank of a small stream.

At 2.1 mi., still heading E, the trail begins following an old tote road above the stream. The forest is relaxing here, with a lot of tall pines, hemlocks, poplars and cedars. The trail soon rejoins the stream, but at 2.3 mi. veers L away from the stream again. At 2.4 mi. an opening in the trees far to the L gives hope that the pond isn't too far away, but this is just an isolated wet area.

The trail soon ascends a short steep section and at 2.75 mi. reaches the first of a couple of recent beaver ponds that flood the trail. This first flow is skirted through the woods on the L side, and rejoins the trail in a short distance. Following along the beaver ponds, the trail is again flooded at 3.1 mi. Moose Mt. Pond isn't far away, and at 3.2 mi. a side trail to the R leads to an informal campsite on the W shore of the pond. It's a nice view from here across the pond to the rugged hills beyond.

The trail continues E within sight of the shoreline of the pond through a nice woods, reaching the recently constructed lean-to at 3.5 mi. This is a great site with views from the shoreline looking across the pond to Moose Mt. and Owl Pate.

Distances: Parking lot to Bass Lake Trail (25), 1.35 mi. (2.2 km); to where trail leaves Berrymill Flow, 1.7 mi. (2.7 km); to Moose Mt. Pond, 3.2 mi. (5.1 km); to lean-to, 3.5 mi. (5.6 km). Berrymill Flow elevation, 1090 ft. (332 m); Moose Mt. Pond, 1265 ft. (386 m).

(28) Hammond and Bloody Ponds Map: p. 76

Trailhead: This uses the same trailhead as for the Berrymill/Moose Mt. Pond Trail (27). The Hammond Pond Trail, however, heads L (SE) from the parking lot.

You will have a choice in 0.1 mi. of taking off your boots and crossing a wide ford in a stream or walking across an ingenious "double-decker bridge" upstream. (A trail forks R to the bridge.) Walk on the middle log, which is four ft. below the upper two logs, which act as railings.

Now the trail is level along the bank above the stream on the R. At 0.2 mi. the trail leaves the stream. At 0.4 mi. a swamp is visible through trees on the L. The trail, strewn with pine needles through woods of white pine, hemlock, birch and maple, dips gently. After a stand of red pines, it continues on the level through a stand of hemlocks.

At 0.6 mi. there is a stream on the L. There is a culvert for a small feeder stream at 0.7 mi., after which the trail divides. Uphill to the L on a spur trail to a wide plank spillway at a dam at 1.0 mi., there is a good view of Blood Mt. across Hammond Pond. In July the deerflies are pesky, but in winter this would be a good cross-country ski destination.

Returning to the trail, continue uphill. At 0.8 mi. Hammond Pond comes into view again, and at 0.9 mi. another opening gives a view of a weedy edge of the pond. Wildlife is prolific here. Great blue heron fish in the shallows. Some huge hemlocks have been cut and left along the trail here near an orange snowmobile trail marker. Perhaps they blew down across the road.

At 1.2 mi. there is a cement culvert over a dry brook. The trail goes along a small weed-filled pond, at 1.4 mi., descending to a broken bridge at 1.5 mi. The trail is growing in considerably. There is a stream on the R.

At 1.7 mi. another rotting bridge crosses the outlet from Bloody Pond. To hike the 0.2 mi. to Bloody Pond, turn L at a yellow paint blaze on a tree after crossing the bridge. Follow the old yellow paint blazes carefully since the trail is faint and there are some blowdowns. This is a steep, rocky trail with a wonderful chimney to climb through. The pond is a tiny jewel surrounded by thick woods.

Rejoining the trail after the detour to Bloody Pond, it is only another 0.2 mi. before the road is interrupted at 1.9 mi. by beavers at work. Since the road goes onto private land soon, it is time to turn back.

Distances: *Moriah Rd. to jct. for Hammond Pond, 0.7 mi.; to Hammond Pond, 1.0 mi.; to Bloody Pond jct, 1.7 mi. (to Bloody Pond, 1.9 mi.); to beaver swamp, 1.9 mi. Cumulative distance to Hammond Pond, Bloody Pond and the beaver swamp, 3.0 mi. (5 km). Elevation of Hammond Pond, 980 ft. (298.8 m). Elevation of Bloody Pond, 1200 ft. (365.9 m).*

(29) Peaked Hill and Peaked Hill Pond

Page Map

One of the charms of this trail is being able to combine some canoeing and hiking and then finish up with a swim at the end of a hike on a hot summer day. The trail is not heavily used, so once away from the lake you'll probably have it to yourself.

Trailhead: *The only public access to the lake and the trail is from the Paradox Lake state campground boat launch. From the intersection of NY 74 and US 9, N of the hamlet of Schroon Lake, head E on NY 74. At 0.6 mi. a canoe and fishing access site on the Schroon River is passed on the S side of the road. A trailhead for the Pharaoh region is on the R at 4.1 mi., with the Paradox Lake state campground on the L (N) side at 4.3 mi. The boat access site is 0.3 mi. on the R along the campground road, just past the entrance gate. There is no sign for the campground once it's closed for the winter. A day-use fee is charged during the summer when the campground is operating. From the boat launch it's about a 0.5-mi. canoe to the N across the lake, following along the point the campground is on, to the trailhead in a small bay on the N side of the lake.*

On the lakeside there is a DEC trail sign for the pond and the

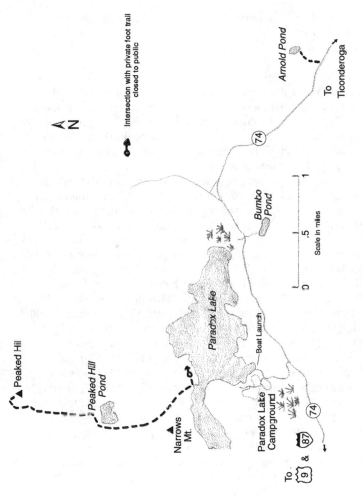

N

Intersection with private foot trail closed to public

Arnold Pond

Peaked Hill

Peaked Hill Pond

Paradox Lake

Boat Launch

Narrows Mt.

Paradox Lake Campground

Bumbo Pond

To Ticonderoga

To 9 & 87

74

74

0   .5   1
Scale in miles

Peaked Hill and Peaked Hill Pond (29), Arnold Pond (30)
Based on Paradox and Eagle Lake quadrangles, both 7.5-min. series, 1973.

mountain and a No Camping sign. Here (0.0 mi.) the well-marked, blue-marked trail heads in a northerly direction away from the lake. Avoid going R on a side trail which leads to a private road in about 0.2 mi.

The trail climbs on a moderate grade, crossing under a major power line at 0.1 mi. It continues climbing and soon swings L up and across some boulders and through the evergreens and hardwoods. At 0.25 mi. the grade levels off as the trail crosses a small mossy stream that cascades down the hillside on the L. The trail soon swings R and gently uphill through the hardwoods, roughly following the brook on the R.

At 0.4 mi. the trail levels off again and meanders through the evergreens. A small rock ledge is traversed at 0.7 mi., then, after crossing a small stream, the trail heads up a small hill and through a beautiful mature evergreen forest. Peaked Hill Pond is visible through the trees at 0.9 mi. as the trail soon drops to near the level of the pond. A small opening on the shoreline is reached at 1.0 mi. with a DEC sign marked "Peaked Hill 1.1 miles." Here there is a view out across the pond that is ringed with cedars, hemlock and birch.

The trail continues around the shoreline of Peaked Hill Pond until at 1.3 mi. it turns L (N) away from the pond on a very gradual climb through the hardwood forest. After descending slightly, the trail winds along the side of a hemlock-covered hill and drops to cross a stream at 1.6 mi. Climbing along the L branch of the stream, the trail crosses a wet area on some rocks. Very shortly the climbing begins through the hardwoods, first gradually, then rather steeply in a few spots. The trail turns R just below a boulder, a large glacial erratic, then turns up along a rocky streambed. It veers slightly L around the W side of a small hill at 2.0 mi. Avoid heading straight ahead toward the boulders and bottom of the cliff.

At the top of the hill the trail levels off for a short distance but soon turns R and climbs fairly steeply again up the mountain top.

After crossing a small level area near the top, the trail leads up over the ridge of rock to the wooded summit ridge. It is a short distance R to a rocky outcrop at 2.2 mi. with views to the S. Peaked Hill Pond and then Paradox Lake are in the foreground, with Pharaoh Mt. on the L horizon, and on a clear day, Crane Mt. in the distance beyond Schroon Lake.

Trail in winter: This route would be an excellent ski-shoe. Start out skiing on the campground road on NY 74, and ski across the lake to the lakeside trailhead. Good skiers might ski some of the first climb, but snowshoes would be easiest for the ascent. Once on top of the first hill it's a great ski in to the start of the climb up Peaked Hill. The climbing there is best on snowshoes as this trail climbs almost 700 feet in the last 0.5 mi.

Distances: *From lakeside trail sign (0.0) to top of first hill, 0.4 mi.; to sign on Peaked Mt. Pond, 1.0 mi. The trail leaves N shore of pond at 1.3 mi. (2.1 km) and begins climb up Peaked Hill at 1.6 mi. (2.6 km). The lookout on top is reached at 2.2 mi. (3.5 km). Ascent from Paradox Lake to Peaked Hill Pond, 342 feet (104 m); from Peaked Hill Pond to top of Peaked Hill, 750 ft. (229 m). Total ascent from Paradox Lake, approx. 1100 ft. (335 m). Elevation of Peaked Hill, approx. 1900 ft. (579 m).*

(30) Arnold Pond

Map: p. 81

Trailhead: *This short, very steep trail on the side of Skiff Mt. starts on the N side of NY 74, just W of Eagle Lake and only 0.1 mi. E of the trailhead to Tubmill Marsh Trail (39) in the Pharaoh Lake area trail. The trailhead for Arnold Pond is 7.9 mi. E of Northway exit 28 (Ticonderoga–Paradox). Park in a lot just E of the trailhead on the S side of the road.*

The trail starts up the hill by a trail sign for Arnold Pond on the N side of the road. This steep hillside has loose rock. The trail goes up through rocky woods where wild sweet peas bloom in July. At 0.1 mi. there is a view to the S of Bear and Ragged mts. At 0.2 mi. the trail reaches a small col after a very steep climb with loose rock, and soon reaches the top of a ridge. At 0.3 mi. it reaches the edge of Arnold Pond.

An unmarked, unmaintained trail continues to the L up toward Skiff Mt. A short trail leads R down a solid rock walkway to the pond. A large beaver house is across the pond on the E side and a dam is on the S side. Many dead trees ring the pond, attesting to the work of ambitious beavers. From the rocky cliffs on the N side of the pond, it is possible to hear or see a raven circling.

Distance: NY 74 to Arnold Pond, 0.3 mi. (0.5 km). Ascent from road, 347 ft. (105.8 m). Elevation of Arnold Pond, 1300 ft. (396.3 m).

(31) Old Ironville Road   Page Map

There is not a more pleasant walk in the woods than this one. Although this road is still passable for 4WD vehicles and is sometimes used by snowmobiles, it is usually empty and quiet, perfect for walking or cross-country skiing. An abandoned town road, it starts in the town of Crown Point and ends in the town of Ticonderoga.

Trailhead: From Chilson on NY 74, drive N 4.5 mi. to the Penfield Museum in Ironville.

From the Penfield Museum (0.0 mi.) the route proceeds E along the road and then turns R downhill on a dirt road. At 0.1 mi. there is a bridge over a series of cascades on Putnam Creek, the outlet of Penfield Pond.

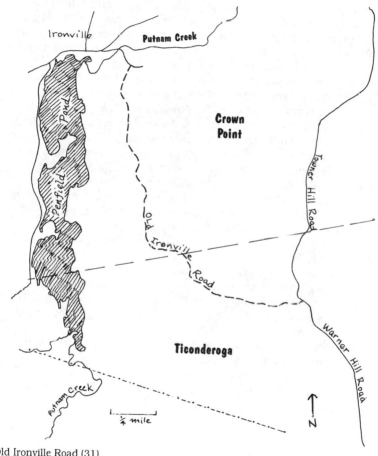

Old Ironville Road (31)
Based on Eagle Lake quadrangle, 7.5-min. series, 1973.

At 0.2 mi. the road splits. Go R past a house, after which the road narrows and goes into deep woods. There are stone walls on both sides. At 0.4 mi. the road splits again; stay straight, not R. The road comes to the top of a hill, then begins to go downhill. It crosses a culvert at 0.6 mi. with a large corner of a stone wall on the L. There is another side road R at 0.7 mi., followed soon by an ascent.

After an old farm clearing, there is a small stream on the R at 0.9 mi., which is crossed shortly afterwards. The going gets steeper, then levels out at 1.0 mi. At 1.1 mi. the road enters a stand of large hemlocks and white pine. It goes uphill again at 1.2 mi., through a clearing at 1.3 mi., and continues uphill past old stone walls. At 1.4 mi. another old road enters on the R. At 1.5 mi. there is a five-ft.-high iron post on the L (probably marking the town line between Crown Point and Ticonderoga). At 1.55 mi. the road passes another old farm clearing at a height of land and another clearing with an old apple tree at 1.6 mi., just before another old road on the R.

Now the road goes uphill again. At 1.9 mi. there is a beautiful rocky cliff L. Past the top of the hill at 2.0 mi., the road passes through another clearing. In summer, milkweed blooms and butterflies gather nectar from the fragrant flowers. The road goes along almost level, then goes uphill slightly to meet the Warner Hill Rd. at 2.3 mi. The Warner Hill Rd. is called Towner Hill Rd. in the town of Crown Point.

On skis, the return trip would be mostly downhill; the elevation changes from 894 ft. in Ironville to 1256 ft. at Warner Hill Rd.

Distances: *Penfield Museum to bridge over Putnam Creek, 0.1 mi.; to clearing, 1.3 mi.; to iron post, 1.5 mi.; to rocky cliff, 1.9 mi.; to clearing, 2.0 mi.; to Warner Hill Rd., 2.3 mi. (3.9 km).*

(32) Sherman Lake and Cubtown Roads

Page Map

These old town roads in the NW corner of the town of Crown Point combine to give a beautiful deep woods walk. A few old farmsites are passed, too. This route would be an excellent cross-country ski route since it is mostly a gentle downhill. A car can be placed at the jct. of Cubtown and Narrowtown rds. to avoid the walk back uphill to your car, but the entire circuit is enjoyable.

Trailhead: From Chilson on NY 74, drive N 4.5 mi. to the Penfield Museum in Ironville. (This museum is worth a stop; it is filled with history of the early days of settlement and mining in the area.) Turn L (N) at the museum onto a dirt road and go 1.2 mi. to a T jct. with North Rd. Turn R here and go 1.3 mi. to the first L onto Hogan Hill Rd. (dirt) and go 2.4 mi. to another T jct. with Breed Hill Rd. Turn L here, then R past Narrowtown Rd. on the L. (If you want to spot a car at the jct. of Cubtown and Narrowtown rds., turn L here and drive 0.4 mi. to the house at the end of Cubtown Rd., which is used only by logging vehicles.) Go uphill (N) 1.2 mi. to a L turn onto Sherman Lake Rd. for 0.3 mi. to the trailhead (unmarked) on the L.

Two old roads start here. A private woods road goes L uphill. The old town road along the S side of Sherman Lake goes R. Park at the beginning of the old town road (space for one car) (0.0 mi.).

The old road descends through some maple saplings and comes along Sherman Lake at 0.1 mi. It then goes gently uphill along Spar Bed Hill. At 0.4 mi. it leaves the S shore of the lake. At 0.5 mi. a faint track to the R leads to an informal campsite on a point (on private property). Now the road goes downhill and along the lake again to a very wet place at 0.6 mi. At 0.7 mi. the road comes to the W end of the lake, curves L (S) and uphill, then follows a long downhill with rocky cliffs to the L. At 0.9 mi. it comes along a swamp.

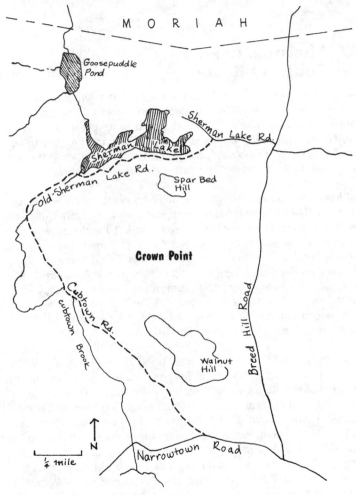

Sherman Lake and Cubtown roads (32)
Based on Eagle Lake quadrangle, 7.5-min. series, 1973.

The road crosses a wet place where deer and bear tracks might be seen, then goes uphill. At 1.1 mi. it enters an open sunny area, then goes downhill.

At 1.2 mi. the road comes to a T jct. Now it meets the Cubtown Rd. Go L here. The road surface improves and goes along the level.

At 1.3 mi. the road enters a sunny, overgrown field. It goes straight through this clearing and down into woods. At 1.5 mi. it crosses a wooden bridge over a lovely brook which is flowing from Sherman Lake.

At 1.6 mi. the road reaches a logging yard and another wooden bridge. A road turns R here just before the bridge; this is private and logging is going on a mile up it.

Crossing the bridge, the road is easy with pleasant walking. At 2.1 mi. there is a piped spring on the L. At 2.2 mi. the road passes through an old farm clearing. Now there is a long downhill, with the roadbed eroded in places. At 2.6 mi. it reaches a house at the jct. of Cubtown and Narrowtown rds. If a car has been spotted here, this is the end of the hike.

On Narrowtown Rd. it is 0.4 mi. to the jct. with Breed Hill Rd. at 3.0 mi. Turn L uphill onto Breed Hill Rd. and walk past several houses to Sherman Lake Rd. at 4.3 mi.; turn L and walk another 0.3 mi. to the start.

Distances: *Old road along Sherman Lake to Cubtown Rd., 1.2 mi.; to first wooden bridge, 1.5 mi.; to second wooden bridge, 1.6 mi.; to Narrowtown Rd., 2.6 mi.; to Breed Hill Rd., 3.0 mi.; to Sherman Lake Rd., 4.3 mi.; to trailhead on Sherman Lake Rd., 4.6 mi. (7.7 km). Elevation of Sherman Lake, 1075 ft. (327.9 m).*

Northway Access Points to the Dix Wilderness Area

(The following is from ADK's *Guide to Adirondack Trails: High Peaks Region,* ed. Tony Goodwin, 2nd edition, 1992; rev. 1994.)

With construction of the Adirondack Northway through this area in the mid-1960s there came a need to provide access across this controlled-access highway, because parking was, of course, prohibited on the highway itself. There are now three points where one can easily cross the Northway along the 10-mi. stretch from North Hudson to Exit 30 near Underwood. These access routes connect with the valleys of Lindsay Brook, West Mill Brook and Walker Brook, and are described briefly below.

(33) Lindsay Brook Access   Page Map

This route, marked with red markers, starts S of the Schroon River opposite Sharp Bridge Campground on US 9. Going up a road for 0.1 mi., the trail turns sharp R and crosses a stream, negotiates a flooded area, and continues on through a pine forest to a culvert under the Northway at 0.9 mi. No marked trail continues beyond this culvert.

(34) West Mill Brook Access   Page Map

This route begins 1.6 mi. S of Sharp Bridge Campground or 5.5 mi. N of the intersection of US 9 and the Blue Ridge Rd. There is a large wooden signpost (but no sign) at the start of a narrow dirt road which leads down to West Mill Brook at 0.2 mi., where there is a good ford. (Park just before on R at times of high water.) From the ford, the road crosses an extensive open sandy area and reaches a

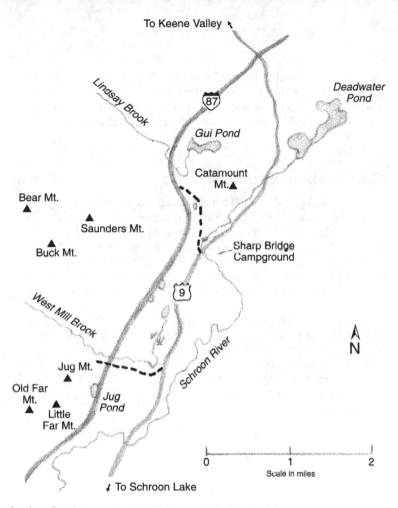

Lindsay Brook Access to Dix Wilderness (33), West Mill Access to Dix Wilderness (34) Based on Mt. Marcy quadrangle, 15-min series, 1953 and ADK's High Peaks Region map.

concrete culvert under the Northway at 0.8 mi. At 1.1 mi. there is a parking area just before a gate controls further access along the old road leading along the R bank of West Mill Brook. This road leads approximately 2 mi. farther W before turning S and becoming obscure.

(35) Walker Brook Access   No Map

This access is 3.7 mi. S of Sharp Bridge Campground or 3.4 mi. N of the intersection of Rt. 9 and the Blue Ridge Rd. Just S of two houses, there is an old green metal signpost at the end of a dirt road. Go down this road for 0.3 mi. and park where a poorer road bears R. Or proceed down the poorer road, which leads to the L bank of the Schroon River, where cars also may be parked. *Bear in mind that this is private land* and that the driveway beyond 0.3 mi. is not a public road.

Cross the stream by wading or find a good log to cross to a good road on the far side, which is followed uphill to a flat area 0.5 mi. from Rt. 9. Bear R just beyond and cross under the Northway through a concrete culvert at 0.7 mi. Walker Brook is approximately 0.2 mi. beyond, with an old road leading up its R (S) bank giving access to Camels Hump, Niagara and Nipple Top mts.

Pharaoh Lake Wilderness, Schroon Lake, Ticonderoga Section

This section contains one of the best known regions in the eastern Adirondacks, the Pharaoh Lake Wilderness. This wilderness area has many lakes and ponds, hills and mountains, and a network of interconnecting trails for trips of varied duration. There are access points to the wilderness from all sides, including the Crane Pond Rd. from the NW corner and the Pharaoh Lake access road on the S central side. These roads are both in a designated wilderness area where vehicles are prohibited. While these roads provide easier access to the interior parts of the region, the special qualities about the wilderness character of the region will be protected by the complete closure of the roads to motorized vehicles. Both of these roads are legally closed by DEC, but access is not yet blocked (August 1994).

All bodies of water within the Pharaoh Lake Wilderness area are trout waters with special regulations. No more than five trout may be taken per day, and the use of fish as bait is prohibited.

This section is bounded on the N by NY 74, on the E by Lake George, on the W by Schroon Lake and on the S by NY 8. The trails on the periphery by Ticonderoga and Schroon Lake are well worth hiking to help give a broader perspective on the whole Adirondack region.

Trails in winter: Snow conditions can vary considerably in the eastern Adirondacks. In years when "nor' easters" come up the Atlantic coast, there can be powder snow on the ground most of the winter. However, when the storms travel down the St. Lawrence valley, this region is on the warm side of them, and rain and ice are the result. When the snow is good, all the trails in the region are great for snowshoeing, and all those except for the mountain climbs are excellent ski routes. Specific suggestions for certain trails are included in the trail descriptions.

Suggested hikes in the region:

Shorter hikes:

Gull Pond—*0.5 mi. An easy hike to a pretty little pond with rock ledges dropping down to the water.*

Rogers Rock—*1.1 mi. A short but quite steep climb to a great outlook over northern Lake George.*

Moderate hike:

Pharaoh Mt. from Crane Pond—*4.3 mi. from the parking lot on the wilderness perimeter. A nice moderate climb with fine views from open areas on top.*

Trail Described	Total Miles (one way)	Page
(36) Crane Pond Road	2.0	96
(37) Goose Pond	0.6	97
(38) Long Swing Trail to Crane Pond Rd.	2.8	97
(39) Tubmill Marsh Trail	6.8	99

(36) Crane Pond Road   Map: B-1

The Crane Pond Rd. is one of the major northern access points for the Pharaoh Lake Wilderness. Within a reasonable distance from the parking lot are trails to Pharaoh Mt., Pharaoh Lake, and many of the interior ponds. At present (August1994) this road is considered closed to motorized vehicles by DEC, but access is not blocked.

Trailhead: From the intersection of US 9 and NY 74 at exit 28, just N of Schroon Lake, head S on US 9. Take the first L (E) on Alder Meadow Rd. (indicated by the sign for the airport). Go 2.2 mi. to a L (E) fork in the road and continue another 2.4 mi. on a narrow road to the Crane Pond parking lot. The road beyond this point is in classified Wilderness and most likely will at some time be blocked to vehicular traffic. The section of the road from the parking lot to Crane Pond isn't plowed in the winter.

This road to Crane Pond changes minimally in elevation. At 0.9 mi. is the trailhead for Goose Pond Trail (37) on the R (S). Some sections of the road from here to Crane Pond are quite rough, with "Wilson Hill" claiming numerous mufflers each year. At 1.6 mi., the NE end of Alder Pond may be flooded. A yellow-marked foot trail heads L just before the hairpin turn before the flooded area of road. At approx. 1.7 mi. the Long Swing Trail (38) from NY 74 comes in from the L. The W end of Crane Pond is reached at 2.0 mi.

Distances: Parking lot to Goose Pond Trail, 0.9 mi.; to Long Swing Trail jct.

*from NY 74, 1.7 mi.; to Crane Pond, 2.0 mi. (3.0 km). Crane Pond elev.,
1081 ft. (329 m).*

(37) Goose Pond

Map: B-2

*Trailhead: The Goose Pond trailhead is on the S side of Crane Pond Rd.
0.9 mi. from the Crane Pond parking lot at the wilderness edge (see trail 36
trailhead description).*

The trail leaves from the S side of the road and has yellow trail
markers. Goose Pond is special trout water. (See regulations in the
introduction to this section, p. 93.)

At 0.1 mi. the trail crosses a high plank bridge over the outlet of
Alder Pond. Upstream a beaver dam can be seen. At 0.2 mi. the trail
crosses a mossy log bridge over a wet place and soon another mossy
log bridge. Now the trail goes gently uphill over rocks and roots,
leveling off at 0.3 mi., then rising again. This section is heavily used
and eroded down to mud and tree roots in places.

The trail goes gently downhill and at 0.5 mi. Goose Pond can be
seen glistening through the hemlocks. At 0.6 mi. the trail reaches a
campsite near the edge of the pond. Across the pond is a view of
Pharaoh Mt. There is a trail to the L that skirts a bay and loops back
to the main trail. Mergansers and loons may be seen here.

*Distance: Trailhead to Goose Pond, 0.6 mi. (1 km). Elevation of Goose
Pond, 1178 ft. (359 m).*

(38) Long Swing Trail to
Crane Pond Road

Map: C-1

Trailhead: From Northway exit 28, cross US 9 heading E on NY 74. Go

4.2 mi. to a small parking area on the R with the DEC sign for Crane Pond. The trailhead is only 0.1 mi. W of the Paradox Lake state campground entrance.

Climb up the bank from the parking area and enter woods. The trail goes back (W) parallel to the road, crosses a cedar log bridge over a stream and soon turns L (S) onto the older trail, marked with blue trail markers. The woods are mature white pine, hemlock, sugar maple and yellow birch.

At 0.2 mi. a smaller hemlock grows so close to a giant white pine that they look like Mutt and Jeff. The trail now heads S away from the road and is quite level. At 0.3 mi. the trail crosses a bridge over the stream, under tall trees including some enormous yellow birch.

Now the trail heads uphill along the stream and under tall hemlocks. At 0.4 mi. it crosses the stream on rocks. The trail heads uphill, then levels off again at 0.5 mi. and skirts a beaver flow on the R side of the flooded marked trail for a short distance.

At 0.7 mi. a new beaver pond filled with dead trees opens up the sky. The trail crosses a bridge over the outlet, with Blue Hill in view ahead. After walking around the edge of the beaver pond, follow the trail gently uphill at 0.9 mi. At 1.0 mi. the trail starts to descend; at 1.1 mi. it heads down more steeply. At 1.2 mi. it levels out at two hemlocks with old gashes, possibly the original trailmarkers.

At 1.7 mi. the trail crosses a stream on rocks, then climbs the bank and levels again. It continues to climb until it levels at 1.9 mi. After passing some giant maples at 2.0 mi., the trail continues uphill through dense hemlock, beech and birch. At 2.3 mi., near its northern limit, there is an enormous red oak.

Now the trail goes gently downhill. At 2.8 mi. is a T intersection with the narrow dirt road to Crane Pond (trail 36). Turn L to walk another 0.3 mi. to Crane Pond and the trailhead to Pharaoh Mt.

Distances: NY 74 to beaver pond, 0.7 mi.; to Crane Pond Rd. (trail 36), 2.8 mi.; to Crane Pond, 3.1 mi. (5.1 km). Elevation at NY 74, 888 ft. (273.2 m); at intersection with road to Crane Pond, 1096 ft. (337.2 m); at Crane Pond, 1081 ft. (332.6 m).

(39) Tubmill Marsh Trail
(39A) Crab Pond Spur
to Glidden Marsh Trail

Map: C-1

This trail from the N leads in to the Pharaoh Lake Wilderness and connects to the trails leading to the many ponds in the northern Pharaoh region. It also connects directly with some of the interior trails for easy access to Pharaoh Lake and Pharaoh Mt. for nice hiking and backpacking loops through the region.

Trailhead: A large trailhead sign on the R (S) side of NY 74 8.1 mi. from exit 28 on the Northway marks the start. The trail has blue markers except for the spur from Crab Pond to Glidden Marsh (39A) which is marked in red.

From the parking lot (0.0 mi.), the trail heads E, parallel to the road, above a wetland with beaver activity, then uphill through woods of cedar, oak, birch, hemlock and white pine, reaching the Eagle Lake dam at 0.25 mi. After crossing a bridge the trail turns R (W) and follows the S side of the outlet stream. The fairly level trail soon crosses concrete culverts at 0.6 mi. and then heads gradually uphill at 0.75 mi. After leveling off for a bit, the trail begins a long gradual decline until it reaches an intersection at 1.0 mi. with two private trails from the Pyramid Lake Camp.

Bear L (SW) around the base of Ragged Mt. The trail soon begins ascending through the pass between Ragged Mt. on the L (E), and Bear Mt. on the R (W). At 1.8 mi. the trail reaches the top of a triple col between Ragged Mt., Bear Mt. and Potter Mt. at about 1300 ft. After a descent along a side hill, the side trail for the Tubmill Marsh lean-to is reached at 2.2 mi. The lean-to is 0.1 mi. to the R (W). It's about 500 ft. downhill to the marsh from the lean-to. This is a great place to see wildlife and is pretty when the blue flags are blooming in summer.

From the sign for the lean-to, a sign for Honey Pond is reached at 2.4 mi. After crossing a couple of streams, the trail cuts up along a ridge to a beaver pond at 2.9 mi. Across the beaver pond is a view of Big Clear Pond Mt., elev. 2000 ft., about 500 ft. above the beaver pond. The trail soon crosses a stream and turns away from the pond.

At 3.2 mi. the trail turns R and goes around Honey Pond and along a high ridge into a stand of birches. At 3.4 mi. the trail reaches the jct. with the Lilypad Pond Trail (45) coming in from the L (E). It is 1.8 mi. along this trail to Rock Pond.

Continuing S, the trail climbs for a short distance and then passes an old indistinct side trail for Treadway Mt. at 3.8 mi. The trail soon crosses the outlet of a small pond, and at 4.2 mi. Horse-shoe Pond comes into view. Soon there is an anglers' trail to the R across an old beaver dam. The trail descends along the outlet of the pond and then crosses the inlet to Crab Pond. Crab Pond is soon visible through the hemlocks.

The trail crosses another inlet stream and continues along the S side of the pond, reaching a jct. at 4.9 mi. L is the Crab Pond Spur Trail (trail 39A) that is a direct route 0.4 mi. S from Crab Pond to the Glidden Marsh Trail (41). It is marked with red markers.

Continuing straight (W) around the outlet of Crab Pond, the trail reaches Oxshoe Pond at 5.4 mi. and the Oxshoe Pond lean-to at 5.6 mi. It's a pretty view from the lean-to with rock ledges and pines around the shore of the pond.

At 5.9 mi. the trail reaches the shoreline of Glidden Marsh and intersects with the W end of the Glidden Marsh Trail (41). Turning R, the trail heads NW, away from the shoreline, and enters a nice hemlock forest. After crossing a bridge the trail climbs slightly and intersects the Pharaoh Mt. Trail (40) at 6.4 mi. From here it is 0.7 mi. to the end of the road at Crane Pond (trail 36).

Distances: *Parking lot at NY 74 to Tubmill Marsh lean-to cutoff, 2.2 mi.; to Rock Pond/Lilypad Pond Trail (45) jct., 3.4 mi.; to Crab Pond jct., 4.9 mi.; to Oxshoe Pond lean-to, 5.6 mi.; to Glidden Marsh Trail (41) jct., 5.9 mi.; to jct. with the Pharaoh Mt. Trail, 6.4 mi. (10.2 km). Distance of the Crab Pond Spur Trail (39A), 0.4 mi. (0.6 km). Elevation at NY 74 parking lot, 953 ft. (290 m); at col, 1300 ft. (396 m); at Tubmill Marsh, 1100 ft. (335 m); Lilypad Pond, 1240 ft. (378 m); Crab Pond, 1283 ft. (391 m); Oxshoe Pond, 1180 ft. (360 m); Glidden Marsh, 1081 ft. (330 m).*

(40) Pharaoh Mt. Trail (from Crane Pond to Pharaoh Lake) (40A) Lean-to Spur

Map: C-2

Pharaoh Mt. is a very dominant feature when looking across Schroon Lake from the Northway into the Pharaoh region. It rises sharply from the landscape with its steep rock faces dominating the western side. It's a pleasant mountain to climb, and the views offer an all-round perspective on the eastern Adirondack region.

Trailhead: *The trail starts at the W end of Crane Pond at the end of Crane Pond Rd. (trail 36). The trail is marked with red markers.*

Cross the plank bridge at the outlet of Crane Pond. The trail register is a short distance along the trail from the bridge. The trail follows an old tote road through a pretty woods of tall evergreens. At 0.7 mi., the trail reaches a jct. with the Glidden Marsh Trail to

Pharaoh Lake (trail 41). The trail to Pharaoh Mt. bears R by an old cellar hole. The trail soon passes a beaver pond, Glidden Marsh on the L, and big white pines. There are red markers on the trees.

The trail begins ascending at 1.9 mi., soon bearing R and becoming steeper. At 2.0 mi., the trail crosses a stream (dry in late summer). Now the trail is fairly steep and eroded down to rock. At 2.8 mi., at a good view, the trail is on an open ridge of bare rock. The top isn't far away. The trail soon reaches the site where the observer's cabin once stood and then at 2.9 mi. the open rock summit where the fire tower once stood. The actual summit is just a short distance to the N of the observer's cabin site.

There are great views to the High Peaks and Hoffman Notch Wilderness across Schroon Lake from the rock ledges on the W side of the summit. By exploring the summit to the N and E it is possible to view the High Peaks, the northeastern Adirondacks, Lake Champlain and Vermont, Pharaoh Lake, and the mountains of the Pharaoh Lake Wilderness. Try to pick out Crane Mt. to the SW and the Tongue Mt. Range to the SE.

The route continuing across the summit and down the E side of the mountain is a pleasant, lightly used trail. From the site of the old observer's cabin, the trail heads E across the summit. After a couple of short, steep descents, at 3.2 mi. (mileage from Crane Pond) the route crosses a stream, soon comes to an opening, then crosses the stream again. At 3.5 mi. there is an outlook to the rocky face of Treadway Mt. to the NE. There are blueberries here, in season, along the open rock, as well as trailing arbutus which is on the NYS list of protected plants.

At 3.7 mi. the clearing ends and soon Pharaoh Lake can be seen below. After crossing and then recrossing a stream, the trail crosses a couple of bridges and wooden walkways, coming close to the shoreline of Pharaoh Lake at 4.5 mi.

Turning R (S) along the shore of the lake, the trail parallels the shoreline, passing over a couple of streams, then a wetland on the L, and reaches a jct. with a side trail at 5.3 mi. This Lean-to Spur Trail (40A) leads to Pharaoh lean-to #5 and the point that protrudes into the lake. There are great views from the tip of the point, 0.2 mi. from the main trail.

Continuing along the main trail, there is another lean-to (#6) visible through the trees at 5.7 mi. The outlet of the lake and the jct. with the Mill Brook Trail (50) are reached at 6.2 mi. It is another 2.5 mi. to the parking lot at Mill Brook and 3.6 mi. to the parking lot by the wilderness boundary via trail 50.

Trail in winter: This would be an excellent ski-shoeing route in the winter, skiing in on the road and part way up the trail, then snowshoeing to the summit. A group could return the same way, or continue down the other side, skiing out the Pharaoh/Mill Brook Trail (50) to another car parked at the end of the access road.

Distances: *Crane Pond end of the Crane Pond Rd. (trail 36) to jct. with Glidden Marsh Trail (41), 0.7 mi.; to summit, 2.9 mi.; to shore of Pharaoh Lake, 4.5 mi.; to side trail to lean-tos, 5.3 mi.; to jct. with Pharaoh/Mill Brook Trail (50), 6.2 mi. (9.9 km). Ascent from Crane Pond, 1470 ft. (448 m); ascent from Pharaoh Lake, 1390 ft. (424 m). Elevation of Pharaoh Mt., 2551 ft. (778 m).*

(41) Glidden Marsh to Pharaoh Lake

Map: C-2

This trail connects the Crane Pond area with the Pharaoh Lake area and the Grizzle Ocean Trail (47). This way it's possible to hike from the Crane Pond area to the Pharaoh Lake area, then up to the Putnam Pond area (trail 43) and back to Crane Pond via Crab Pond and Oxshoe Pond (trails 45 and 39) without having to retrace many of your steps. It's a long route, but it would make a nice 2- to 4-day backpacking trip (depending on how much time you have to relax and enjoy or explore).

Trailhead: *The Glidden Marsh Trail begins along Glidden Marsh at a jct. with the Tubmill Marsh Trail (39), 0.4 mi. E of the Pharaoh Mt. Trail (40), and 1.1 mi. from the end of Crane Pond Rd. (trail 36). The trail is marked with yellow markers.*

Glidden Marsh is a great place to see wildlife. Herons and other waterfowl frequent this area and there are lots of signs of beavers. At the jct. with the Tubmill Marsh Trail (39) 0.0 mi., the trail heads SE along the shoreline of Glidden Marsh. The trail soon begins a gradual ascent and at 0.6 mi. reaches a jct. on the L with the Crab Pond Spur Trail (39A). There is a sign here for Crab Pond 0.4 mi to the L. The trail now climbs very gradually through the rolling woods on the E side of Pharaoh Mt., crosses a couple of streams and passes a small pond.

At 2.1 mi. the trail begins a fairly steep descent toward Pharaoh Lake, coming near the shoreline at 3.1 mi. where there's a sign marking the trail to the L. The trail now follows to the E around Split Rock Bay on Pharaoh Lake, and then swings S along the bay toward the lean-to. At 3.7 mi. the trail reaches Pharo Lean-to (#4) situated on a fine broad point with views of the lake. Heading E, the trail soon crosses a stream and then heads more S and away from the lake.

At 4.4 mi. there is a side trail for Wintergreen Point (0.3 mi., with some great views). Continuing on, the trail almost immediately comes to the jct. with the Grizzle Ocean Trail (47) and the East Shore Pharaoh Lake Trail (51) at 4.4 mi.

Distances: *From Tubmill Marsh Trail along Glidden Marsh Trail (39) to jct.*

with Crab Pond Spur Trail, 0.6 mi.; to Pharaoh Lake shoreline, 3.1 mi.; to Pharo Lean-to, 3.7 mi.; to jct. with Grizzle Ocean Trail (47) and East Shore Pharaoh Lake Trail (51), 4.4 mi. (7.0 km).

(42) Otter Pond

Map: D-1

This is one of two ponds with trails in this area, and the only one that is open for public access. The only legal public access is from the boat launch on Eagle Lake, since the shoreline on the S side of the road is privately owned. (There is access for the town of Ticonderoga to get to Gooseneck Pond, but this is not a public easement. While Gooseneck Pond is entirely on state land, the easement crosses private land to reach the pond.)

Trailhead: On NY 74, approximately 9.5 mi. E of Northway exit 28 (approx. 8 mi. W of Ticonderoga), is a boat access site for Eagle Lake, just W of the causeway. It is a short canoe almost due S across the lake to the trailhead and sign for Otter Pond in a small cove on the SE shore of Eagle Lake.

From the canoe landing, walk L on the road along the shore for 0.1 mi. to a low place on the R where two dark blue DEC trail markers lead into the woods. The trail is well marked, but the start is easy to miss.

Continuing on the level for a short time, the trail quickly goes uphill. It climbs steeply through a draw on a north-facing slope of hemlocks and boulders. The trail is so little used that you must depend on the trail markers. At 0.2 mi. the trail levels, curves L and goes gently uphill to Otter Pond at 0.3 mi. Trail markers on the trees here show that the beavers are busy at work. To the R at about 100 ft. is a beaver dam at the outlet.

Distance: *Canoe landing to Otter Pond, 0.3 mi. (.5 km). Elevation of Otter Pond, 1300 ft. (396 m).*

(43) Clear Pond Trail
(43A) Rock Pond Spur
(43B) West Clear Pond Trail
(43C) Putnam Pond to Clear Pond Trail

Map: D, E-1

This trail circles around the Putnam Pond area and provides access to the several small ponds W of Putnam Pond. When the Clear Pond trail is combined with a portion of the Grizzle Ocean Trail (trail 47), it's possible to make a complete circuit of Putnam Pond.

Trailhead: *Drive 13.3 mi. E on NY 74 from Northway exit 28 (Ticonderoga–Paradox) to a large sign on the R for Putnam Pond State Campground. Drive S 3.8 mi. to the entrance. Day-use fees are charged in season. A boat launch is just beyond on the R and the parking lot is reached at 0.4 mi. From the parking lot walk along the entrance road 0.4 mi. to the entrance booth, then another 0.4 mi. into the campground to the trailhead at campsites 38 and 39. The trail is marked with yellow markers up to the end of Clear Pond, and then blue markers from Clear Pond to its jct. with the Grizzle Ocean Trail (47).*

Starting at the campsites 38 and 39, 0.0 mi., the trail heads N toward Heart Pond. The trail crosses and recrosses a stream, reaching the jct. with the Bear Pond Trail (44) at 0.4 mi. Continuing L to the S of Heart Pond, at 0.5 mi. there is a side trail to the N that goes to a point that overlooks this pretty little pond. The trail continues W over rolling terrain, soon follows the N shoreline of North Pond, and crosses a bridge at 1.1 mi. At 1.5 mi. the trail reaches the shore of North Pond. (North Pond is actually a long extended bay to the N of Putnam Pond.) The trail heads W, climbs up and then descends over a hill and reaches a jct. with the Rock Pond Spur Trail at 1.7 mi.

Turn L (S) at this jct. for the main trail and the shortest route to Clear Pond, and also the Little Rock Pond lean-to. The trail crosses a stream and comes to the lean-to at 1.9 mi., meeting up with the Rock Pond Spur Trail (43A) at 2.0 mi.

The Rock Pond Spur Trail (43A) heads straight (W) at the jct. at 1.7 mi. to a jct. at Rock Pond in 0.2 mi. This is the jct. with the Rock Pond to Lilypad Pond Trail (45). Turn L (S) at the trail 45 intersection to follow S along the E shore of Rock Pond, meeting up with the Clear Pond Trail at 0.5 mi. This spur is a half mile long or 0.1 mi. longer than the parallel section of the main trail.

After rejoining with trail 43, the trail continues S, with Rock Pond to the W and Little Rock Pond to the E. It crosses an isthmus that separates the two ponds, and then comes to another jct. at 2.1 mi. The trail to the R (W) is the S route of the Rock Pond to Lilypad Pond Trail (45B). Trail 43 continues on to the S, ascending and then descending to the trail jct. at the head of Clear Pond at 2.7 mi. Here again there's a choice: you can go around the E or the W side of Clear Pond. The W Clear Pond Trail (43B) is the shorter by about 0.1 mi. at 0.6 mi. It heads R at this intersection, following the W side of Clear Pond and reaching a jct. with the main trail in 0.6 mi.

The main trail heads L around the E shoreline of Clear Pond, reaching the Clear Pond lean-to at 3.1 mi. Behind the lean to is the Putnam Pond to Clear Pond Trail (43C) that is 0.6 mi. to Putnam Pond. Continuing on the main trail at the outlet of Clear Pond, the jct. with the trail from the W side of the pond is reached at 3.4 mi.

Trail 43 continues S and E past Mud Pond to an intersection with the Treadway Mt. Trail (46) at 3.6 mi. Continuing S across the intersection, the trail soon meets the Grizzle Ocean Trail (47) at 4.0 mi.

The trail L (E) leads to the Putnam Pond parking lot in 1.4 mi.

Distances: *From Putnam Pond campsites 38 and 39 to Bear Pond Trail (44) jct., 0.4 mi.; to jct. with trail to Little Rock Pond and Rock Pond, 1.7 mi.; to Little Rock Pond lean-to, 1.9 mi.; to Clear Pond lean-to and side trail to Putnam Pond, 3.1 mi.; to Treadway Trail (46), 3.6 mi.; to Grizzle Ocean Trail (47), 4.0 mi.; from the parking lot, 4.8 mi. Length of trail 43A spur, 0.5 mi. (0.8 km); length of trail 43B, 0.6 mi. (1.0 km); length of trail 43C spur, 0.6 mi. (1.0 km). Complete circuit of Putnam Pond with return via Grizzle Ocean Trail (47) to parking lot, 6.2 mi. (9.9 km).*

(44) Bear Pond Trail   Map: E-1

This is a trail to one of the special trout waters in the Pharaoh Lake Wilderness area. (See the regulations in the introduction to this section, p. 93.) The trail links with the Clear Pond Trail (43) at Heart Pond at the E end and Rock Pond Trail (45A) on the W end. There is no public access other than the Clear Pond Trail.

Trailhead: *The easiest access to this trail is via the Clear Pond Trail (43) from Putnam Pond Campsites 38 and 39. (See trail 43.) It is 0.4 mi. N on the Clear Pond Trail (43) from the campsites to the beginning of the Bear Pond Trail. The trail is marked with blue markers.*

This is a pleasant, little-used trail to the NE end of Bear Pond. Leaving the Heart Pond jct. with the Clear Pond Trail (43) (0 mi.), the trail heads N along the E shore of Heart Pond. At 1.0 mi. the trail crosses open rocky places with blueberry bushes before descending a small hill to a L (S) turn near Bear Pond at 1.2 mi. Here an unmaintained trail leads to private land. The trail soon leads over a small knoll to a campsite on the E shore of Bear Pond. There are lots of signs of beaver activity around the pond. Following S, the trail soon reaches the edge of Bear Pond and then follows along a narrow, rocky path. The trail passes along the marshy SE corner of the pond with rocky cliffs on the L. The trail crosses an inlet stream and soon leaves the pond at 1.5 mi.

The trail gradually heads uphill, up and over Bear Pond Mt., reaching the height of land at 2.2 mi. The trail is rather washed out for awhile, then levels off on a hemlock-studded hillside before descending gradually along some nice rock cliffs. At 2.7 mi. it drops more steeply to Rock Pond, now visible through the trees. At 2.8 mi. the trail reaches the intersection with the Rock Pond to Lilypad Pond Trail (45A). Head L to reach the Rock Pond Spur Trail (43A) in 0.2 mi. Across the pond are Peaked Hill and Little Clear Pond.

Distances: Heart Pond jct. with Clear Pond trail, 0.0 mi.; to Bear Pond, 1.2 mi (1.9 km); to height of land, 2.2 mi. (3.5 km); to Rock Pond intersection, 2.8 mi. (4.5 km). Elevation of Bear Pond, approx. 1400 ft. (427 m). Height of land elevation on Bear Pond Mt., approx. 1750 ft. (533 m).

(45) Rock Pond to Lilypad Pond
(45A) North Rock Pond Trail
(45B) South Rock Pond Trail   Map: D-1

This trail, besides being the connector trail between the Putnam Pond area on the E and the Crab Pond and Crane Pond area on the W, is a pleasant trail to hike. There are fine views from the shoreline of Rock Pond, and it's a nice walk along Rock Pond Brook to Lilypad Pond lean-to. It's also possible to make a loop around Rock Pond using part of the Clear Pond Trail (43).

Trailhead: This trail utilizes two routes along the shores of Rock Pond: one *at the N and one at the S of the pond. Trail 45A starts from the NE corner of Rock Pond at the intersection with the Rock Pond Spur Trail (43A) at a point 1.9 mi. from the Putnam Pond State Campground. Trail 45B begins at the SE corner of Rock Pond near Little Rock Pond, also at a jct. with the Clear Pond Trail. Trail markers are red.*

Starting at the intersection (0.0 mi.) with the Rock Pond Spur Trail (43A), the trail heads W along the alluring N side of Rock Pond. At 0.2 mi. the Bear Pond Trail (44) intersects on the R. Shortly after a turn R there is a cave-like entrance of an old graphite mine with some brownish water seeping from it. The trail climbs steeply uphill and at 0.25 mi. reaches a bluff on the L that overlooks the pond. A side trail leads to a rock point with some blueberry bushes and several large white pines on the end.

The trail soon passes a campsite with a fireplace, then follows the shoreline, climbs steeply to some more open rock at 0.4 mi., and drops steeply once again to the shoreline. At 0.7 mi. there is another campsite on a huge open rock. It may be easy to lose the trail here because of the rock. Continue straight through the clearing to the trail, which crosses the outlet of Rock Pond and meets up with the S trail extension (trail 45B) at 0.8 mi.

At the SE corner of Rock Pond at a jct. with the Clear Pond Trail (43), near Little Rock Pond (0.0 mi.), the trail heads W around the S shore of Rock Pond. The trail soon follows the shoreline and heads N along the W shore, passing a campsite on a nice promontory on the W side of the pond. At 0.7 mi. the jct. with the trail spur (45A) is reached on the S side of Rock Pond outlet.

Heading W from the jct. of (45A) and (45B), the trail parallels the outlet stream for some distance. At 0.5 mi. from the jct. a waterfall is heard off to the R. In a short distance the trail descends to the waterfall where there is a short side trail leading to the falls. The trail now begins following along a wetland until at 1.1 mi. from the jct. it climbs and reaches Lilypad Pond lean-to at Lilypad Pond. From the lean-to it's a short distance to the jct. with the Tubmill Marsh Trail (39) (1.2 mi. from the jct. of 45A and 45B).

Distances: 45A: *From NE corner of Rock Pond trail jct. to jct. with 45B at Rock Pond outlet, 0.8 mi. (1.3 km).* **45B:** *From SE corner of Rock Pond trail jct. to jct. with 45A at Rock Pond outlet, 0.7 mi. (1.1 km). From Rock Pond outlet jct. of 45A and 45B (0.0 mi.) to Lilypad Pond lean-to, 1.1 mi.; to jct. with Tubmill Marsh Trail (39), 1.2 mi. (2.0 mi. [3.2 km] via 45A, 1.9 mi. [3.0 km] via 45B).*

(46) Treadway Mt. Trail   Map: D-2

This is a unique mountain with large open rocky spaces on top and an interior trail that winds along a U-shaped summit. Trailing arbutus and blueberries grow profusely along the upper parts of the trail. There are good views of Treadway's more popular neighbor, Pharaoh Mt., and surrounding points, as well as Schroon Lake and mountains to the W, S and E. It is possible to cross Putnam Pond by canoe to the Treadway Mt. trailhead, which removes 3.6 mi. from a round trip.

Trailhead: *The trailhead is 1.4 mi. S on the Grizzle Ocean Trail (47) from Putnam Pond State Campground, then 0.4 mi. N on the Clear Pond Trail (43). At a jct. at this point (0.0 mi.), the Treadway Mt. Trail goes L; R leads 0.2 mi. to the landing for the canoe short-cut. To reach the Treadway Mt. trailhead on Putnam Pond by canoe, put in at the boat launch on the E shore near the Putnam Pond parking lot (see trail 43). Then canoe W and S to a small point on the W shore of Putnam Pond. The trail starts by a small stream in the cove behind the point. The trail is marked with red markers.*

From the intersection of the Clear Pond Trail (43) and the

Treadway Mt. Trail (46), the red-marked trail proceeds 0.1 mi. to a deadwood swamp called Mud Pond. Wintergreen grows along the edge of the trail, which follows the S side of Mud Pond. At 0.2 mi. the trail crosses a stream on a log with a beaver dam downstream, turning L along the stream. At 0.3 mi. the trail crosses the stream and soon recrosses it. Now it climbs moderately and can be wet. It is a wide old tote road through hemlocks, with a stream on the R, and then mixed hardwoods.

At 0.9 mi. the trail comes to a swamp with bright green grass and moss. It becomes steeper at 1.1 mi. above a swampy stream. At 1.2 mi. it becomes rocky, winding above a ravine to the L. Then it arrives at the first bare rock with trailing arbutus and a cairn at 1.3 mi. It is important to follow the red paint blazes on the rock. In early July bright pink sheep laurel blooms here.

At 1.5 mi. the trail climbs through a chimney and arrives in a thick growth of blueberry bushes. At 1.6 mi. it goes into woods again; at 1.7 mi. is the first view to the E. At 1.8 mi. the trail comes to the bottom of a dip. Then at 2.0 mi. it comes to a false summit and after another dip arrives at the true summit at 2.1 mi. This mountain deserves more attention; it has a varied and satisfying climb and fascinating summit trail over its open rocky top. Views are excellent.

Distances: *Putnam Pond State Campground parking lot to trailhead for Treadway Mt., 1.8 mi.; trailhead to summit, 2.1 mi. (3.5 km). Parking lot to summit, 3.9 mi. (6.5 km). Ascent, approx. 900 ft. (275 m). Summit elevation, 2240 ft. (683.2 m). Or by canoe: paddle approx. 1.0 mi. across Putnam Pond from boat launch SW to a small point. Walk on trail with red markers 0.2 mi. to a jct., then straight to summit at approx. 2.3 mi. (3.8 km).*

(47) Grizzle Ocean Trail
(47A) Grizzle Ocean Circuit Trail   Map: D-2

This fairly easy trail connects the Putnam Pond and Pharaoh Lake areas.

Trailhead: *The trail begins on the W side of the parking lot at Putnam Pond State Campground. (For directions to the parking lot, see the Clear Pond Trail [43].) The trail has yellow markers.*

The trail crosses a pair of bridges immediately. A side trail goes R to Putnam Pond. At 0.3 mi. the trail crosses a muddy place, and then crosses a brook. At 0.7 mi. the trail goes downhill through hemlocks with a mossy cliff on the L and soon crosses an inlet to the pond on a plank bridge. At 1.2 mi. it reaches a jct. (An unmarked side trail R goes to the S edge of Putnam Pond.) The trail crosses a brook on a plank bridge. At 1.4 mi. it reaches a stream with a bridge. On the other side a trail R goes via Clear Pond Trail (43) back to Putnam Pond State Campground, circling Putnam Pond. The main trail heads L (S) to Grizzle Ocean. At 1.6 mi. the trail crosses the stream on rocks, and at 1.8 mi. reaches a height of land. (The Grizzle Ocean Lean-to side trail goes L 0.2 mi., following blue trail markers. The lean-to is set back under pines from the edge of Grizzle Ocean, a pretty, shallow pond.)

From the jct. for Grizzle Ocean Lean-to, the trail continues to a long wooden walkway which crosses the outlet of Grizzle Ocean at 2.0 mi. The trail turns L at the end of the walkway. At 2.1 mi. it reaches a jct. for the red-marked Grizzle Ocean Circuit Trail (47A) around Grizzle Ocean on the L. This trail circles the pond and reaches the lean-to in 0.9 mi. It is 0.2 mi. from the lean-to following yellow markers back to the Grizzle Ocean Trail for a total of 1.1 mi. around the E side of Grizzle Ocean. Turn R to continue to Pharaoh Lake.

At 2.2 mi. the trail reaches a miniature pond on the R. At 2.5 mi. it crosses a small stream on rocks and soon crosses the stream again. At 2.8 mi. it reaches a wet place which is the start of a stream under high maples, and begins to follow the stream downhill. This is the divide between Putnam Pond and Pharaoh Lake. It is also a pass between Grizzle Ocean Mt. to the N and Thunderbolt Mt. to the S.

At 3.3 mi. the trail comes to a very muddy spot, then a couple of streams.

At 3.7 mi. the trail goes along a hillside with hemlocks and maples, then crosses a bridge. At 3.8 mi. it reaches a small stream tumbling down through rocks, from Devil's Washdish. At 3.9 mi. the trail passes Wolf Pond on the L, seen through the trees. At 4.0 mi. it reaches an inlet to Wolf Pond, and at 4.1 mi. another inlet.

Now the trail goes along a fern-filled hillside above a swampy area. It goes along a ridge, and then through a grove of hemlocks. Then it comes downhill and at 4.4 mi. travels over some rolling terrain.

At 4.6 mi. the trail reaches the top of another small hill and at 4.8 mi. it reaches an algae-filled bay. At 5.1 mi. it crosses a stream that feeds into Pharaoh Lake and then passes under a tall stand of red pines; a waterfall is audible down to the L.

At 5.2 mi. the trail reaches an intersection at Pharaoh Lake. The Glidden Marsh Trail (41) R goes to Wintergreen Point and to Pharaoh Lean-to at Split Rock Bay (see trail 41). The East Pharaoh Lake Trail (51) L goes along the E shore of Pharaoh Lake. Just before the trail jct. it is about 100 ft. downhill through the woods to a view of the waterfall. From the jct. it is 0.1 mi. L to a good plank bridge directly below the waterfall. This is good place for a rest stop and picnic, with a good view of Wintergreen Point and its shallow bay filled with pond lilies.

Distances: *Putnam Pond State Campground parking lot to Clear Pond trail jct. (43), 1.4 mi.; to Grizzle Ocean Lean-to jct., 1.8 mi.; to divide of watershed,*

2.8 mi.; to Pharaoh Lake, 5.2 mi.; to waterfall and plank bridge, 5.3 mi. (9.1 km). Elevation of Putnam Pond, 1308 ft. (399 m); elevation of Grizzle Ocean, 1475 ft. (449.7 m); elevation of Pharaoh Lake, 1146 ft. (349.4 m).

(48) Berrymill Pond from the North

Map: E-2

Trailhead: The trailhead is near the exit of the parking area in the Putnam Pond State Campground (see trail 43).

The trail starts uphill on an old tote road, crosses a a stream, and soon enters a straight section. At 0.4 mi. the road goes up along the brook on the R. At 0.6 mi. the trail crosses a stream and then travels at a gentle pace through the woods. At 1.5 mi. the trail crosses another stream where there may be some beaver activity. The side trail R (W) to the pond and the lean-to is reached at 2.0 mi.

Distances: Parking lot to pond and lean-to, 2.0 mi. (3.2 km).

(48A) Berrymill Pond from the South

Map: E-2

Trailhead: This trailhead is reached from the town of Hague. Turn R (N) onto Summit Drive from NY 8, 3.0 mi. W of Hague. At 0.8 mi. take the sharp R curve. The road soon joins with West Hague Rd. and at 1.4 mi. passes May Memorial Cemetery on the R (E). At 2.0 mi. there is a small trailhead and sign for Berrymill Pond on the L (W) side of the road. The trail has blue markers.

From the Hague side the trail starts on private land at the trailhead (0.0 mi.), crossing onto state land in about 300 ft. At 0.3

mi. there is a jct. with an old logging road on the L. Bear R and continue the gradual climb. The trail becomes steeper at 1.2 mi., and then levels off at 1.3 mi. A wetland is passed at 1.5 mi. The trail crosses a couple of bridges, and then crosses a stream at 2.2 mi. A spring is passed at 2.6 mi. just before a bridge. The jct. on the L for Berrymill Pond is reached at 3.0 mi. The shore of the pond is reached at 3.1 mi. Turning R, there is an old lean-to site at 3.2 mi. After a knoll of white pine and red pine, the trail reaches the end of this point at 3.4 mi. Blueberries grow in abundance here, as do trailing arbutus and ladyslippers. There are signs of beaver activity in the cove to the R, where there is also a lean-to.

To reach the lean-to, go back to the jct. at 3.0 mi. Head L (N) about 100 yds. to another jct. with a sign for Putnam Pond 1.9 mi. to the R and Berrymill lean-to to the L. Another 100 yds. to the L (W) is the lean-to on the cove.

Distances: *W. Hague Rd. parking to first Berrymill Pond jct., 3.0 mi. (4.8 km); to the lean-to, 3.2 mi. (5.1 km). Elevation of Berrymill Pond, 1675 ft. (511 m).*

(49) Lost Pond

Map: E-1

Trailhead: *From NY 74 at Chilson turn S onto the road with a large sign for Putnam Pond State Campground and drive 3.3 mi. to the trailhead sign for Lost Pond on the L (0.0 mi.). The trail is an old tote road with yellow markers. This is a well-used trail popular with campers and anglers.*

At 0.3 mi. the old road enters a stand of hemlocks. There are lots of Indian pipes growing here in July. At 0.4 mi. the trail forks L from the old road. There are exposed roots of beech and maple trees. At 0.5 mi. the trail goes over a knoll, into a dip and then up another knoll. Now it levels off. At 0.7 mi. it crosses a muddy seep.

At 0.9 mi. the trail descends gently, before going through woods of maple, beech and huge birches. At 1.0 mi. it reaches a plank bridge over a stream with huge boulders. A beaver swamp is down to the L. White orchids may be seen growing here on the R in July. The trail passes the outlet of the pond at 1.1 mi., then a private trail on the L over a stream. At 1.2 mi. the trail crosses the stream, continuing uphill.

At 1.3 mi. the trail levels out among mature maples. At 1.4 mi. Lost Pond is in sight, and soon the trail reaches a jct. for a trail around the pond.

Continuing around the pond, yellow markers are very helpful since the path is sometimes faint. There is a fair amount of beaver activity at this pond. At 1.7 mi. the trail comes along a mossy cliff on the R, then crosses a rocky stream at 1.8 mi. At 1.9 mi. the trail comes around one of the end lobes of the pond. At 2.0 mi. it reaches an outcropping of boulders. This is a good picnic spot. Huge bullfrog tadpoles loll in July in shallow water above submerged boulders. Fish glide by in deeper water. Trout fishing here is quite good. Chickadees, warblers, thrushes and veeries sing their various songs along the edge of the deep forest.

In a few hundred yds. there is a campsite with a fire circle. Another campsite is at 2.2 mi. and below, at water's edge, is a huge beaver house. Blueberries are thick along the trail here in summer.

Now the trail climbs steeply up through boulders along Abe's Hill. At 2.5 mi. the trail reaches another campsite, and at 2.6 mi. it ends at the trail jct. where the loop around the pond began.

Distances: *Putnam Pond State Campground road to Lost Pond, 1.4 mi.; to complete walk around pond, 2.6 mi. (4.3 km). Elevation of Lost Pond, 1553 ft. (473.7 m).*

(50) Pharaoh Lake via Mill Brook   Map: B-3

This is the easiest and most popular trail into the Pharaoh Lake Wilderness from the S. The trail is a nice walk directly into the S end of Pharaoh Lake, from where there is access to the rest of the Pharaoh region via the Pharaoh Mt. Trail (40) and the East Shore Trail (51).

Trailhead: From exit 25 on the Northway, head E on NY 8 to the NE end of Brant Lake. After following the main part of the lake, take the first L (N) onto Palisades Rd. (around the N end of the lake), 0.0 mi. After passing a nice old stone barn on the L at a L bend in the road, and then the Point O' Pines Farm Rd. soon after on the R, take the next R at 1.5 mi. onto Beaver Pond Rd. At 2.6 mi. on a bend, the dirt Pharaoh Lake Rd. cuts off to the R. At 3.1 mi. the road reaches the wilderness boundary and a parking lot. From this point the DEC considers this road closed to vehicular traffic, but access is not denied. At some time in the future, this point may be the trailhead. It is another 1.1 mi. over a very rough road to the trailhead at Mill Brook. This last section of the road is not plowed in the winter.

From the Mill Brook parking lot (0.0 mi.), the trail heads N across Mill Brook on a nice plank bridge; however, the open area on the other side of Mill Brook may often be flooded with knee-deep water for about 300 ft. Trail work is planned (July 1994) to improve this situation in the near future. The trail register (which sometimes is missing) is in the woods along the trail just after the wet area ends. The trail soon follows an old tote road on a gradual grade NE through a nice woods.

At 1.2 mi. the trail bears R and crosses a bridge over a stream. A side trail before the bridge to the L leads to an evergreen knoll with an informal campsite that overlooks the beaver pond and large wetland. After crossing the bridge the trail swings L and uphill on the tote road again. At 2.0 mi. the road begins descending, soon joining a stream on the L.

An unmaintained footpath enters on the R at 2.4 mi. To the L but poorly marked at this point is the end of the Sucker Brook Horse Trail (54) from Adirondack. The footbridge at the outlet of Pharaoh Lake is reached at 2.5 mi. The Sucker Brook Trail spur foot trail intersects just beyond the bridge. This is also the intersection with the Pharaoh Mt. Trail (40), and the East Shore Trail (51).

Distance: Mill Brook to Pharaoh Lake outlet trail, 2.5 mi. (4 km). Elevation of Pharaoh Lake, 1146 ft. (349 m).

(51) East Shore of Pharaoh Lake   Map: C-2

This is a fine trail along the E shore of Pharaoh Lake with some great views along the way of the lake and the surrounding mountains. It passes by three lean-tos and the trails to Whortleberry Pond (53) and Springhill Ponds (52). It's also the connector trail between Mill Brook and the Putnam Pond and Crane Pond area via the Grizzle Ocean Trail (47) and the Glidden Marsh Trail (41).

Trailhead: The trail starts at the jct. with the Mill Brook Trail (50) and the Pharaoh Mt. Trail (40) by the outlet bridge at the S end of Pharaoh Lake. The trail is marked with yellow markers.

The trail goes uphill to the R, crossing the clearing and into the woods on the E side of the lake. At 0.4 mi. lean-to #1 is reached on the lakeside. From the lean-to are nice views across the lake to Treadway Mt. At the top of the hill beyond the lean-to on the main trail on the R side is the unmaintained side trail for Whortleberry Pond (trail 53). The trail soon crosses open bedrock with bracken, blueberry bushes, reindeer moss and trailing arbutus. At 0.7 mi., lean-to #2 is set back in the woods on the L.

The trail is now narrow and alluring with views of the lake and Pharaoh Mt. In a short distance, at 0.8 mi. the cutoff for Springhill Ponds (trail 52) is on the R. Bear L to continue around the shore of the lake. In about 500 ft. the trail reaches the jct. for lean-to #3, beautifully located about 100 ft. to the L on a small point on the lake. There's good swimming and great views of the lake and surrounding mountains from the ledge beyond the lean-to.

The main trail heads R and soon crosses a couple of rocky bluffs with nice views across the lake. After climbing over a huge rock, the trail drops and crosses a bridge. Soon after going along another high bluff that faces a cove and some islands, the trail reaches another promontory at 1.3 mi. From this point there is a beautiful panorama of the lake, the islands and the surrounding mountains. The trail then enters a woods of cedars, hemlocks and pines. After passing along a steep hillside with red pines, the trail reaches an informal campsite with a fire circle at 1.9 mi.

Turning R, the trail follows around a large bay, crosses an inlet and then wanders through some boulders. After crossing a rocky stream near the shoreline, it crosses the bridge over the outlet from Wolf Pond at 2.3 mi. From here there's a fine view of Wintergreen Point across the water lily-filled bay. At 2.4 mi. the trail reaches its N end at the jct. with the Glidden Marsh Trail (41) straight ahead, and the Grizzle Ocean Trail (47) on the R.

Distances: *From the outlet at the S end of Pharaoh Lake to lean-to #1, 0.4 mi.; to Springhill Ponds Trail (52), 0.8 mi.; to jct. with the Glidden Marsh Trail (41) and the Grizzle Ocean Trail (47) at the NE end of Pharaoh Lake, 2.4 mi. (3.8 km).*

(52) Springhill Ponds

Springhill Ponds is an interesting destination and a desirable one for those who wish a bit more solitude than the usually popular Pharaoh Lake area affords. The round trip from the Pharaoh Rd. parking lot at Mill Brook is 15.4 mi., so it is not a casual or late-start trip. It would be more feasible for a party camped at one of the Pharaoh Lake lean-tos or as a camping destination itself. Hikers should be prepared for wet going in many places and occasional overgrown sections. With less human presence, opportunities for observing wildlife are much improved and signs of their activity are more evident than in the Pharaoh Lake vicinity.

Trailhead: *The Springhill Ponds trail departs R from the yellow-marked trail around the E shore of Pharaoh Lake 0.8 mi. from the outlet bridge (and 3.3 mi. from the trail register at Mill Brook) near lean-to #2 near the lake.*

The trail leaving the E side trail is initially well marked with yellow trail markers. It zigzags around in an E direction to find the driest ground. After 0.2 mi. the trail crosses a small stream and starts to ascend. At this point it is a wide path through an attractive hemlock forest and shows few signs of heavy use by man or beast.

Continuing to ascend, the trail now enters a shallow divide with a rock outcropping on the R. After 0.5 mi. it reaches a height of land and a wet area. The trail is now harder to follow. Bear along the L shore among the rocks. Soon afterwards it begins a gradual descent through deciduous growth, still travelling E. When leaf cover is light the rocky bulk of Thunderbolt Mt. is visible through the trees, slightly to the L.

After 1.0 mi. the trail enters a glen of conifers where new growth narrows the path, giving it a more intimate feel. Soon afterwards, it crosses a stream and turns to the SE. It now climbs steeply but briefly above the stream and resumes an E direction.

In a now familiar pattern, the trail once again descends to a wet area. It has edged around to the S and at 1.5 mi. crosses the largest stream since leaving Pharaoh Lake. In spring or other wet periods the crossing may result in wet feet. Easier crossing is to be found downstream rather than upstream.

Leaving the stream, the trail ascends gently, going from evergreens into a mature deciduous growth. Occasionally the open rocks along the length of Thunderbolt Mt. can be seen more closely to the NE. The trail has been showing progressively less and less usage and by now the secondary growth is often waist-high and footsteps less secure.

After climbing gradually for 0.3 mi., the trail enters a cozy glen of hemlocks and a shallow depression. It emerges at a large bog and follows its R bank. The going is level now and offers easy and soft travel over pine needles.

Leaving the bog, the trail parallels a nice feeder stream on the L. There are several rocks that offer good resting spots with the murmur of the stream for background music. Continuing S, the path again becomes quite overgrown. At 2.7 mi. it passes through a cut made in a fallen tree. The walking becomes more level now and, unfortunately, wetter. As the trail climbs slightly, a stream enters from the L and crosses the trail.

Not long afterwards the sound of a larger stream is heard. Follow it upstream to the E. The route is now on an old road, which becomes gullied ascending to a crossing with a small set of falls on Spuytenduivel Brook. At 3.5 mi. the path is narrow again and ascends quite steeply from the brook. You must push your way through thick undergrowth again. At the top the trail is quite indistinct. Turn R and cross a feeder stream. The path bears L shortly and passes through another wet area where trail markers are few and far between amidst much low growth.

Turning R and due E, the trail follows a washed-out roadbed

steadily uphill and reaches the turn-off for Springhill Ponds on the L and to the N at 4.0 mi. (The road continues S to the West Hague Rd. and is now closed to the public from that direction because of private property and lack of an easement. As of this writing [1994] the Unit Management Plan for the Pharaoh Lake Wilderness Area calls for the relocation of the trail over public lands to link up the trail to Berrymill Pond [see below] and share that trailhead location. No firm schedule for this relocation has been established so hikers are urged to call the DEC in Warrensburg to check on the status of the trail from the West Hague Rd.)

The remaining 0.4 mi. to Springhill Ponds involves three more stream crossings, the last being the hardest. Looking upstream from the last one, a very large beaver dam can be seen. A last rise is ascended, then the trail descends to the SE shore of the larger Springhill Pond. A smaller pond is to the E. An informal fishermen's trail continues around the E shore. On the W end of the pond an attractive rocky promontory with pines overlooks the pond.

Distances: *From lean-to #2 at Pharaoh Lake to small stream, 0.2 mi.; to large stream, 1.5 mi.; to falls on Spuytenduivel Brook, 3.5 mi.; to turn-off to ponds, 4.0 mi.; to larger Springhill Pond, 4.4 mi. (7 km). Distance from Pharaoh Rd. parking lot at Mill Brook to Springhill Pond, 7.7 mi. (12.9 km). Ascent, approx. 700 ft. (213 m). Elevation of Springhill Ponds, 1818 ft. (554.3 m).*

(53) Whortleberry Pond   Map: C-2

Trailhead: *The trail begins on the East Shore Pharaoh Lake Trail (51) 120 ft. E of a lean-to on the L and privy on the R at the loop trail's 0.4 mi. mark. The Whortleberry Pond Trail turns R (S) off the loop trail; coming from the E, one can see a yellow painted arrow on a hemlock at the start of the trail.*

The large hemlocks have carpeted the forest floor with their needles, so there is no underbrush. This trail is unmaintained by DEC, but is easy to follow and occasionally marked with yellow paint blazes.

At 0.2 mi. the trail turns R above the pond, reaching an inlet brook. Turn L here and follow the trail along the inlet and through the woods to the water's edge at 0.3 mi. Hemlocks and white pines line the shore. A lovely point across the pond on the E side has a bog on its N side. A great blue heron, crows, bluejays, ravens, chickadees and woodpeckers are among the resident species. Stevens Mt. (elev. 2103 ft.) and Little Stevens Mt. are directly S. Bushwhacking is not difficult in these open woods. This secluded pond is a birdwatcher's paradise.

Distance: East Shore Pharaoh Lake Trail to Whortleberry Pond, 0.3 mi. (0.5 km).

(54) Sucker Brook and Desolate Brook Trail to Pharaoh Lake   Map: A-3

Trailhead: From the Adirondack General Store in the town of Adirondack on the E shore of Schroon Lake, drive E 0.5 mi. on Beaver Pond Rd. to a large sign for the Pharaoh Lake Horse Trail. Turn L at the sign, drive 0.2 mi. to a T, then L again for 0.6 mi. to a parking lot at a dead-end. This is a horse trail marked with yellow markers.

An old road leaves the Pharaoh Lake Horse Trail parking lot and rises gently, heading N through beautiful woods. At 0.9 mi. the road crosses a stream. Then it goes through a cedar grove. Another small stream intersects the road at 1.0 mi. and another at 1.3 mi. At 1.4 mi. another old road enters on the L. Continuing straight ahead, the road steadily climbs at a gently grade.

At 1.6 mi. an old driveway goes up to the R with a stone wall opposite. On the R is the foundation of a farmhouse with a deep cellar. Now the road goes down again. At 1.7 mi. and 2.1 mi. it crosses streams.

A beaver pond is visible down to the L at 2.5 mi. It is interesting to walk downhill through the woods over an old dump of bottles, cans and an old cast iron stove to get a better look at the pond. A huge beaver house is along the close shore to the L. This pond is a wide place in Sucker Brook.

Now the old road ends and walking becomes more difficult after a R turn (E) to follow the pass that Sucker Brook flows through. It is necessary to thread your way through the woods on a narrow trail that crosses Sucker Brook at 2.6 mi. and again at 2.7 mi., then winds up and over the N side of Orange Hill. At 2.9 mi. the trail starts down again, then up and downhill some more. At 3.3 mi. it crosses Sucker Brook again, generally following the valley of the brook.

At 4.7 mi. the trail makes the first of several turns down the N side of No. 8 Hill, first R, then L until crossing Desolate Brook at 5.0 mi.

At 5.1 mi. the trail crosses another branch of Desolate Brook, aptly named, for these are dark, dank woods. Huge hemlocks and maples tower above. A carpet of bunchberry covers the barely discernible trail. At 5.4 mi. it climbs a short hill, with the brook occasionally visible winding a sinuous course down to the L.

At 5.6 mi. the trail turns R and at 5.8 mi. climbs around a low shoulder on the SW side of Pharaoh Mt. At 6.1 mi. it starts downhill, crossing a muck hole and climbing briefly before beginning a steep descent through beech woods. The trail crosses a small brook at 6.4 mi. in a level stretch among incredibly tall, straight trees.

In the next half mile the trail crosses several small streams. At 7.1 mi. it goes more steeply uphill, soon leveling out. At 7.4 mi. the trail becomes an old road going downhill to a clearing. The horse trail goes R and then L to a wet crossing of Pharaoh Lake Brook. It meets the Mill Brook Trail (50) at 7.5 mi. On trail 50 it is a few hundred ft. L to the picturesque outlet of Pharaoh Lake, the first long-distance view of the trip, and an intersection with the Pharaoh Mt. Trail (40) and the East Shore Trail (51).

A drier crossing of Pharaoh Lake Brook is possible via the foot-trail spur at a L turn in the clearing at 7.4 mi. It is a short distance to the bridge on the spillway at the Pharaoh Lake outlet.

A good cross-country ski run would be a trip on the old road from Adirondack to the beaver pond, a round trip of 5.1 mi.

Distances: *Adirondack on old road to beaver pond, 2.5 mi.; to Pharaoh Lake, 7.5 mi.; to parking lot at Mill Brook, 10.1 mi. (16.9 km). Ascent from Adirondack trailhead (880 ft.) to Pharaoh Lake (1146 ft.), 266 ft. (81 m).*

(55) Spectacle Pond   Map: A-2

Trailhead: *This is a beautiful and relaxing walk in deep woods. From Northway exit 25 (Chestertown–Hague) turn E onto NY 8, then L (N) immediately after the northbound entrance ramp at a brown and yellow sign for Adirondack. After 8.0 mi. turn L at a T then take the first R at Adirondack General Store. After the store, the road turns to dirt. Go straight onto this. After 5.0 mi. there are State Forest Preserve signs on trees. After another mile there is a wide turn-out on the R for the trailhead. A sign says Spectacle Pond, 2.0 mi. Actually, the walk is a little shorter, at 1.7 mi.*

There is a yellow DEC trail sign here at the start of this old logging road, which bends L. At 0.1 mi. the trail crosses Spectacle Brook on a bridge. At the end of May there is a profusion of wildflowers in these rich woods: ladyslippers, foamflower, clintonia borealis, jack-in-the-pulpit and violets. At 0.2 mi. the trail crosses a second bridge over the stream and at 0.5 mi. a third bridge.

At 0.6 mi. the trail begins to climb. The stream provides a pleasant companion with its many small cascades, twists and turns around moss-covered rocks. At 0.9 mi. the trail crosses a small stream. At 1.0 mi. it passes a wetland, then turns L at 1.2 mi. and reaches the foot of Spectacle Pond at 1.3 mi.

At 1.4 mi. the trail comes to beaver dams above and below a bridge over the outlet of the pond.

After crossing the bridge, the trail turns L and follows a ridge that ends as a rocky promontory in the pond at 1.7 mi., giving an excellent view of Pharaoh Mt.

Distances: Trailhead to third bridge, 0.5 mi.; to foot of Spectacle Pond, 1.3 mi.; to end of trail on point, 1.7 mi (2.9 km). Elevation of Spectacle Pond, 1165 ft. (355.2 m).

(56) Gull Pond   Map: A-1

Trailhead: Drive N from the Adirondack General Store (see trail 55) 7.1 mi. This is 1.1 mi. N of the trailhead for Spectacle Pond (trail 55). The trailhead parking area for Gull Pond is off the road on the R.

From the parking area the trail goes through deep woods, wet in places, until it climbs a rocky outcrop overlooking Gull Pond at 0.5 mi. This is a jewel of a pond with sheer rock cliffs across on the E side. There are blueberry bushes on the rocks. No camping is permitted at the lookout.

Distance: Trailhead parking lot to Gull Pond, 0.5 mi. (0.8 km). Elevation of Gull Pond, 1193 ft. (363.7 m).

(57) Wilcox Pond

Trailhead: *The Wilcox Pond trailhead is 7.7 mi. N of the Adirondack General Store (trail 55). This is 0.6 mi. N of the trailhead for Gull Pond (trail 56). There is a small pull-in place on the E side of the road just large enough for a car. There are three huge maples on this side of the road just N of the trailhead. There is a Forest Preserve sign on a tree on the W side of the road. The trailhead and the trail are not marked and are not maintained by DEC.*

    This unmaintained and possibly overgrown trail starts beyond an iron cable strung between two large white pines 50 ft. E into the woods. It leads generally L 0.1 mi. to a pile of rocks, then gently downhill, requiring a bushwhack to the brushy pond edge at 0.2 mi. The pond is filling in around the edges, which frustrates getting a good view. From the wet ground there is a nice view of the pond and Carey Hill. It might be a good idea to bring an inflatable boat or ultra light canoe for fishing or exploring.

    For fishing, it is possible to investigate Wilcox Pond, Gull Pond (trail 56) and Spectacle Pond (trail 55) all in one day, as well as Goose Pond (trail 37).

Distance: *Adirondack Rd. to Wilcox Pond, 0.2 mi. (0.33 km).*

(58) Severance Mt.

Trailhead: *Drive 0.6 mi. S of Northway exit 28 on NY 9. Turn R into a large parking lot on two levels—with a hitching post for each car. The lot is clearly marked with a large sign for Severance Mt. by the road (0 mi.).*

    Two long culverts carry the trail under the N and S lanes of the Northway. The trail ducks into the woods at 0.1 mi., following yellow

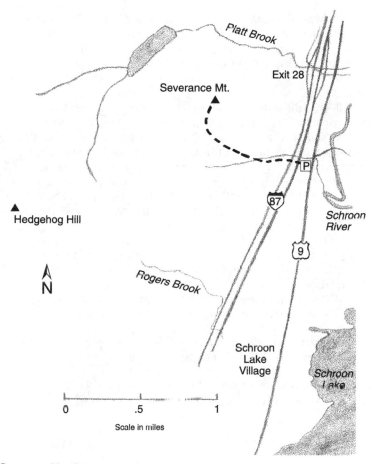

Severance Mt. (58)
Based on Schroon Lake quadrangle, 15-min. series, 1989.

trail markers. The path is wide and starts to go up at 0.2 mi. The grade becomes steeper at 0.3 mi. The trail climbs steadily through mixed woods of maple, white pine, birch, hemlock and white cedar. Unfortunately, the noise of traffic on the Northway is quite loud. Soon take the sharp turn R, avoiding the old log road to the S side of the trail.

At 0.5 mi. the trail levels off. At 0.6 mi. it crosses two plank bridges and then at 0.7 mi. another plank bridge over the same small stream. Now the sound of traffic is faint. The trail begins to climb again, at 0.8 mi. winding on the level through a lovely hemlock grove. Then after a large boulder on the L at 0.9 mi., the trail climbs again. At 1.0 mi. it winds uphill through beech and hemlock woods. At 1.2 mi. the trail reaches an overlook with a view of Schroon Lake and Pharaoh Mt. to the E. A second overlook about 100 ft. farther overlooks Paradox Lake. The rest of the summit is covered with trees.

Curious ravens with beady eyes often swoop over the treetops, then perform their feats of skydiving skill in front of the cliff directly below. Ravens are becoming common in many sections of the Adirondacks.

A DEC sign says the ascent is 813 ft., but the USGS map shows about 700 ft. ascent from the parking lot to the summit.

Trail in winter: *This is a pleasant snowshoe in winter and a nice ski trip for good skiers (intermediate and better).*

Distance: *Trailhead to summit, 1.2 mi. (2 km). Ascent, 700 ft. (213.4 m). Summit elevation, 1638 ft.*

(59) Cooks Mt. Map: p. 133

This is the northernmost climb in the Lake George Basin region. From the top are views south to Anthony's Nose, Lake George and

Roger's Rock, with Black Mt. and the Tongue Mt. Range off in the distance. To the E is Mt. Defiance, with Lake Champlain and the Green Mountains beyond. The Cooks Mt. Preserve is owned and maintained by the Lake George Basin Land Conservancy and is open to the public for recreational, educational and scientific purposes. For more information, please contact them at PO Box 386, Lake George, NY 12845, phone (518) 668-4786.

Trailhead: *Approximately 1.0 mi. south of the monument and traffic circle in Ticonderoga on Rte. 9N, turn E onto Essex Co. Rte. 5. The Ticonderoga Elementary and Middle School is soon passed on the R, and a pair of intersections is reached in about 1.2 mi. Lord Howe Rd. is on the L (N), and Baldwin Rd. on the R (S). The trailhead is exactly 1.5 mi. S on Baldwin Rd. on the right at a gate on an old logging road with L.G. Basin Land Conservancy signs. Just beyond on the L is a state historical marker referring to this area as "Abercrombie's landing, where 15,000 men landed to attack Ticonderoga which was successfully defended by Montcalm in July 1758."*

From the gate (0.0 mi.), the trail follows the grassy old road W toward Cooks Mt. In just 0.1 mi. a very active beaver flow with several ponds and lodges is passed on the R. The road soon turns L (S) and begins climbing. At 0.25 mi. the trail turns right at the Y and then R again at the next intersection. The forest floor in this area is covered with horsetails with lots of signs of wildlife around.

In a short distance, an unmarked path leads to the L. Stay straight ahead on the old road, until at 0.5 mi. the trail marked with red markers heads sharply L at the sign that says Summit Trail.

From here the trail climbs at a steady pace up terrain that varies from gradual to moderate steepness. The well-marked trail climbs steadily up a series of small ridges up the side of the mountain through a nice open hardwood forest of oak, beech and maple. At 0.75 mi. the trail joins what appears to have been an old logging road and turns R (NW), then soon heads more westerly again. A level plateau is reached at 1.0 mi., but the trail soon swings L with some rock cairns near another posted private land boundary. Climbing moderately again, the trail reaches an open area at 1.2 mi. It's pretty here with a variety of mosses, junipers and pines, and a view to the N above the trees. Before reaching the S end of this open area, the trail takes a sharp L into the woods. From here the hiking is much more gradual. Climbing over a series of small ledges, the trail turns to the R and proceeds in a SE direction up over more small ledges.

The rocky top is reached at 1.3 mi. with the trail marked mostly by rock cairns. Here there are great views to the S and E above the scrub oaks.

The trail continues S across the rock toward the main part of Lake George, descending gently on an almost indistinct path with red markers, then soon turns R in a more SW direction at 1.4 mi. More trail work is in the plans, but as of April 1994 it's an open woods ramble with some flagging along the way from this point to a small open ledge about another 0.3 mi. to the S. For the adventurous, the reward is a great outlook over the entire north Lake George basin, with nice views to the E from the open rocky areas along the way. There should be lots of blueberries in the right season.

Trail in winter: *With adequate snow cover, this would be a great snowshoe, though rather steep in a few spots. Snowshoe crampons are recommended. Views are great without leaves on the trees.*

Distances: *From gate on Baldwin Rd. to two right turns on road, 0.25 mi. (0.4 km); to red-marked trail on the L, 0.5 mi. (0.8 km); to highest point, 1.3 mi. (2.1 km); to open ledge at S end of summit, 1.7 mi. (2.7 km). Ascent from Baldwin Rd., 895 ft. (273 m). Elevation, 1230 ft. (375 m).*

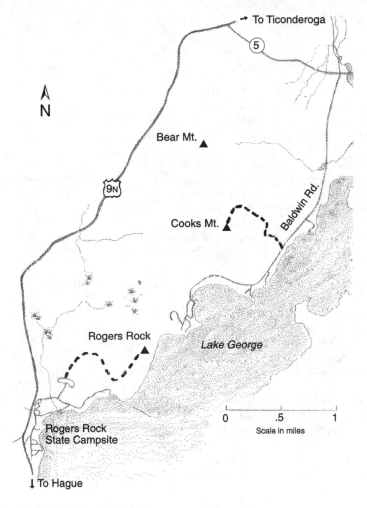

Cooks Mt. (59), Rogers Rock (60)
Based on Ticonderoga quadrangle, 7.5-min series, 1950.

(60) Rogers Rock

Map: p. 133

This is a short hike with a very steep trail to climb so it is not a recommended trip for small children. The view is spectacular. Ravens can be heard "talking" below on the lakeside cliffs and maybe one will glide out over the lake within sight.

Trailhead: *From the village of Hague on Lake George, drive N on NY 9N 4.0 mi. to Rogers Rock State Campground. There is also a beach and boat launch site here. There is a day-use fee in spring, summer and fall. This trail is not marked or maintained by DEC.*

After the entrance booth, take a sharp L and drive 1.2 mi. to a turn-off on the L for campsites 148–214. The trail starts at campsite 184 (0.0 mi.). There is no sign.

A small, well-defined path follows red paint blazes through hemlock woods. At 0.2 mi. it turns L (W) at a rock cliff. Then at red and blue arrows on a boulder it turns R up to the face of the cliff. At 0.3 mi. it climbs up a steep ledge.

The first view opens as the trail continues up steeply, with Cook's Bay below on Lake George. From 0.5 mi. to 0.7 mi. there is a succession of fantastic views along the ridge. There are plenty of blueberries here in summer. Now the trail ducks into oak and white pine woods. Pale corydalis blooms in the shallow soil on top of the rock shelf. At 0.9 mi. the trail reaches another outlook. Wild roses bloom in summer as the trail descends to an open rock face at 1.0 mi. It continues along this rock until reaching the end of the trail at 1.1 mi.

It is possible to walk a little farther but trees obstruct the view and then there is no further passage. It is easy to imagine Robert Rogers struggling to put on his snowshoes backwards near here and then beating a hasty retreat which successfully fooled the Indians pursuing him. They concluded from the snowshoe tracks that

Rogers had fallen to his death over the cliff.

From this perch one can see E to Vermont, S down Lake George and W to the southern Adirondacks. Along the E shore of Lake George are Anthony's Nose jutting into the lake, Record Hill, South Mt., Spruce Mt., Elephant Mt. and Black Mt.

Trail in winter: *This is a steep trail, even for snowshoes. The snow conditions can often be crusted or icy so it's important to have crampons on the snowshoes, or to be able to switch over to just crampons.*

Distances: *Campsite 184 to steep ledge, 0.3 mi.; to level ridge, 0.5 mi.; to Rogers Rock, 1.1 mi. (1.9 km). Elevation of Rogers Rock, 1027 ft. (313 m).*

Rock Pond

Lake George and the Narrows

Rick Stevens

Northwestern Lake George Wild Forest Section

This region is a fairly extensive area with a combination of old roads and some motorized access, and some fine hiking trails. It is bounded by NY 8 on the N, US 9 on the W, and the Warrensburg/ Diamond Point area on the S. The shoreline of Lake George forms the E boundary. Along this section of Lake George is the Tongue Mt. Range and some great hiking, with fine views looking into the wildest parts of the lake. While parts of the Tongue Mt. Range are heavily used, there are more isolated areas, both on Tongue Mt. and in the rest of this region, that see very minimal use through the year. Access to some of the region is over 4WD roads, but that doesn't diminish the experience at the destination.

A number of the roads in this region head toward good fishing ponds and are great for portaging in a small ultralight canoe. While some of the snowmobile trails are suggested as foot trails, these trails are maintained for winter use and may be quite wet at some times in the spring, summer, and fall. Since this is a Wild Forest area, these roads can also be used for mountain biking. Many of them are rather rough and unimproved, so expect a good challenge, not a groomed surface.

The Tongue Mt. area is home to the endangered eastern timber rattlesnake. The snakes are not aggressive and are seldom seen; however, please observe the cautions in the trail descriptions that mention the snakes and remember that this is their home, not ours.

Trails in winter: This region has some nice skiing and snowshoeing possibilities. Most trails, with the exception of the Tongue Mt. region, are great for skiing when there's adequate snow. There is snowmobiling on some of the old roads, and there are snowmobile routes through the region, so you may not have the trail to yourself. These routes, though, are not too heavily used, except sometimes on holiday weekends. Some fresh powder on top of a packed snowmobile trail can make for some fine skiing.

The whole Tongue Mt. area is too rugged for skiing, but there's some good snowshoeing over the mountains. Be sure to carry crampons for poor snow conditions and ice.

Suggested hikes in the region:

Short hike:

Deer Leap—*1.7 mi. From the Tongue Mt. trailhead to an overlook above Lake George. This is a heavily traveled trail because it is near the road, with views of the lake at the end.*

Moderate hike:

Round, Duck, and Buttermilk Ponds circuit from Grassville Rd.—*9.3 mi. (total round-trip distance) A nice rolling hike over dirt roads and trails back to some pretty fishing ponds.*

Harder hike:

Tongue Mt. Traverse—*11.8 mi. From US 9 on the N to Montcalm Point on the S, this is one of the most strenuous and spectacular routes in the eastern Adirondacks. With the Fifth Peak lean-to midway, this can be a fine backpacking trip, or a one-day trip. It's possible to be picked up by boat* from Montcalm Point, or one can return to the Clay Meadows trailhead via the Northwest Bay trail for a total of 16.2 mi.

(61) Lily Pond from Grassville Rd. to NY 8

Map: B-5

This route is a nice walk, and a great ski in the winter, especially when it's linked with further exploration to Round Pond and Buttermilk Pond via the Buttermilk Pond Trail (62). Some sections of this route are old town roads, open to automobiles, while other sections are snowmobile trails closed to all other motorized vehicles. The area is not traveled much, though, except on busy weekends. It's also a great route for an adventurous mountain biker. There are plans to upgrade the road into Lily Pond, so this area may see more traffic. This description proceeds from the highest trailhead to the lowest for the benefit of skiers.

Trailhead: *From the Horicon Fire Dept. (0.0 mi.) in the town of Brant Lake, follow NY 8 E. At 2.3 mi. turn R (S) onto Grassville Rd. At 1.0 mi. follow the road sharp R. At 1.9 mi. the road becomes dirt. A small camp and clearing are reached at 3.0 mi. If parking on the private land just past the camp, be sure to ask permission, or park just along the road. It may be better to park along the wider section of road just before reaching the camp. This is the S access.*

The unmarked N trailhead along NY 8 is 3.7 mi. beyond Grassville Rd. (6.0 mi. from the Horicon Fire Dept.). After an "S" turn on NY 8 with a 25 MPH suggested speed limit, the dirt road to Lily Pond is on the R, just before a fair-sized stream. On the L (N) are cabins on the shore of Brant Lake. The camp named Tak-it-E-Z is just beyond the access road on the L (N), and 0.25 mi. past it is Palisades Rd. on the L (N), which winds around the N shoreline of Brant Lake. A small gray garage is on the R (S) side of NY 8, just to the L of the road to Lily Pond. At some time a small parking lot may be built here, but at present, parking is on the shoulder of NY 8.

Starting at the Grassville Rd. just beyond the camp (0.0 mi.), the road heads gradually downhill. In a short distance a small stream crosses. At 0.25 mi., another stream crosses along a rock water bar. At 0.4 mi. a jct. is reached. A DEC trail marker indicates Grassville Rd. to the L. Avoid the L though, as this travels over private lands back to the sharp R turn on Grassville Rd. Follow to the R for Lily Pond.

The road climbs gradually uphill, then at 0.6 mi. drops back down again on a moderate grade. The keen observer will pick out remnants of the long-abandoned homesteads all through this area. At 0.9 mi. the road begins a long gradual descent, passing a snow-mobile trail (a wet route in the summer) to Island Pond on the R (S) at 1.0 mi., and reaching the S shore of Lily Pond at 1.1 mi. Here there is an informal campsite and fire ring at a nice lookout over the pond. Continuing on the road to the E, there is a bridge over an inlet stream, with a lot of beaver activity visible. A jct. is reached at 1.2 mi. with the road to NY 8 heading L (N). The road straight ahead is the Buttermilk Loop Trail (62A).

Turn L to go along the E shoreline of the lake on the wide path with the two signs reading "No Motorized Vehicles." In a short distance the path splits, then rejoins again soon. The L route more closely follows the shoreline, with some nice views of the pond along the way. After passing over a couple of informal campsites, the trail joins the dirt road from NY 8 at 1.5 mi. Here it is just about 100 ft. to an open area on the L overlooking Lily Pond.

Turning R, the dirt road follows but is out of sight of the E shoreline. At 2.0 mi. it crosses over the outlet of the pond. There has been a lot of beaver activity here in the past, and this section has often been flooded. Work on the road that should take care of the flooding problem is being planned for some time in the future.

The road gradually begins to descend and at 2.25 mi. crosses a bridge over the outlet stream, recrossing it again at 2.5 mi. after passing an old beaver pond. At 2.7 mi. the stream may be heard on the R. From here the road drops steadily at a gradual to moderate rate for the next 0.3 mi., then reaches a jct. with an old road joining on the L (W) at 3.1 mi. At 3.5 mi., the road descends again at a moderate rate almost the whole way to NY 8, which is reached at 3.75 mi.

Trail in winter: While this route is frequented by snowmobilers, it can be a delightful ski trip. Additional routes can be included by going to Buttermilk Pond or taking the cutoff to Island Pond (a snowmobile trail not described because of its wet character in the summer).

Distances: From Grassville Rd. (0.0 mi.) to first jct. on the L to private lands, 0.4 mi. (0.6 km); to first outlook over Lily Pond, 1.1 mi. (1.75 km). At 1.2 mi. (1.9 km) this route goes L at the jct. with Round Pond Rd. and reaches the dirt road from NY 8 at 1.5 mi. (2.4 km). From here it is mostly downhill to NY 8, reached at 3.75 mi. Elevation of Grassville trailhead, approx. 1290 ft. (393 m); elev. of Lily Pond, approx. 1190 feet (363 m); elev. of NY 8, approx. 810 ft. (247 m).

(62) Round, Duck, and Buttermilk Ponds

Map: C-5

This is an enjoyable, though sometimes wet, walk (or bike) to a couple of nice fishing ponds in the Brant Lake area. The terrain is rolling, and the route uses mostly some old roads in the area.

Trailhead: This trail begins at the 1.2 mi. point on the Lily Pond Trail (61) and heads E along the old road.

Continuing straight ahead, the road climbs steadily uphill and at 0.1 mi. reaches another jct. The L fork (trail 62A) is a pleasant route to Buttermilk Pond, which is part of the return loop in this description. To skip Round and Duck ponds for a slightly shorter and drier hike, turn L here to go only to Buttermilk Pond.

Continuing straight ahead, the road is now marked with orange DEC snowmobile trail disks. At 0.3 mi. a small stream which the trail crosses at 0.4 mi. at a wide, shallow place, can be heard on the R.

At 0.7 mi. the trail reaches the top of a rise and then starts downhill. At 0.8 mi. it curves L from E to N and goes slightly uphill. At 0.9 mi it reaches a pile of stones on the L. At 1.0 mi. the road forks L through a very wet intersection. Stay straight. After climbing, the trail goes downhill again towards Round Pond.

At 1.1 mi. the trail makes a sharp curve L. A foot trail that is unmarked and unmaintained by DEC but with painted blazes on trees heads off to the R. The trail heads L and downhill, passing the intersection of the cut-off trail which branched L at the wet intersection.

Still winding downhill, the trail arrives at lovely Round Pond at 1.3 mi. This is an attractive pond with some rocky shoreline. Minnows warm themselves in the shallow and giant dragonflies patrol the air. A pair of ravens may come flying and squawking overhead.

A small foot trail slightly L goes on to Duck Pond at 1.5 mi. after crossing a cedar swamp. There is a large flat rock here for a rest and picnic. A huge beaver house is on the R shore of this pond, which is smaller than Round Pond.

Retracing your steps to the jct., turn L at 1.7 mi. on another narrow trail marked with snowmobile markers. This leads into a swamp with rotten corduroys. There have been cedars cut (for a bridge?) near a flooded corduroy with floating logs. It is important to keep watch for the orange snowmobile trail markers since the trail is faint.

At 1.8 mi. the trail crosses a stream on stones next to a rotten bridge. It soon reaches a wooden snowmobile trail sign pointing S. A turn R leads to the N side of Round Pond. This is a very faint trail, very wet and marked with orange snowmobile trail markers. At 2.0 mi. the trail reaches the N side of Round Pond. A swamp is to the R and a pretty rocky bluff to the L.

At the intersection with the snowmobile sign, the route straight ahead connects to the trail to Buttermilk Pond. (The way L leads back through the swamp to Round and Duck ponds.) The trail goes through cedars following orange snowmobile trail markers. At 2.4 mi. it reaches open rock with moss, bracken and young balsam firs. At 2.6 mi. the trail is in a low, dark and wet cedar swamp with a rocky hill on the R. At 2.7 mi. it curves R and into a birch grove. Now the path is barely discernible. It passes an old fire circle and something that looks like a wooden ladder.

At 2.8 mi. the trail reaches a second jct. with the E end of the Loop Trail (62A). The L route turns N and then S to Lily Pond. R is Buttermilk Pond. The snowmobile signs are orange.

The road quickly narrows to a path as it heads uphill through a pass. At 3.0 mi. the trail reaches a crest. It is growing over with beech and striped maple saplings. Now the trail goes level through huge ferns, birch, beech and maple. At 3.4 mi. it turns abruptly L, after descending from the end of this ridge, and then crosses a stream. Now it turns sharply R downhill along the stream.

The trail leads through a glade of hay-scented ferns. At 3.7 mi. Buttermilk Pond can be seen ahead, and moments later the trail reaches the S end of the pond. To the L is a faint, unmarked path along the shore. At 3.8 mi. there is a huge beaver lodge along the shore. A small point to the L with huge white pines and a large rocky bluff on the opposite shore make this a picturesque and peaceful spot.

Distances: *To jct. with W end of Loop Trail (62A), 0.1 mi.; to Round Pond, 1.3 mi.; to Duck Pond, 1.5 mi.; to N side of Round Pond, 2.0 mi.; to E end of Loop Trail, 2.8 mi.; to Buttermilk Pond, 3.8 mi. Elevation of Round Pond, 1236 ft. (376.8 m); of Duck Pond, 1240 ft. (378 m); of Buttermilk Pond, (approx.) 1460 ft. (445.1 m).*

(62A) Loop Trail

A mile back along the trail is the intersection with the Loop Trail.

An unamed pond glistens on the R just before the intersection. Passing the trail from Round Pond, and from the Loop Trail where there is bare rock for the roadbed, one can walk 300 ft. to the R on a small trail to the edge of this pond. Brush around the edge obscures the view, but it might be a good place to fish.

Returning to the road, it is a pleasure to have easy footing again after several miles of faint and wet trails. The road heads N and then S through lovely woods to lead back to Lily Pond. The road is marked with yellow snowmobile markers and is not marred by the ruts from 4WD vehicles. At 0.8 mi. the road is bare rock.

At 1.0 mi. the road crosses a bridge of stone slabs and goes through an old farm clearing with a rusty shovel jammed into the branches of an apple tree. The walking is level and pleasant. At 1.9 mi. the road passes a large old apple tree and then a pile of rocks on the L. At 2.1 mi. It reaches the intersection with the road to Round Pond. Turn R here to rejoin the Lily Pond Trail (61).

Distance: Length of Loop Trail (62A), 2.1 mi. (3.4 km).

(63) Long and Island Ponds   Map: C-5

Long Pond is a good fishing spot but swimming is not recommended because of leeches. They range in size from $\frac{1}{16}$ inch to 5 inches and are quick to establish a relationship. The pond is used mostly by anglers. Beavers are quite active here. A short connector trail leads from Long Pond to Island Pond, where in winter a snowmobile trail leads from the NW corner of the pond up to Lily Pond.

Trailhead: From Brant Lake Fire Station drive E 1.7 mi. on NY 8 to Duell Hill Rd. on the R. Turn up this steep road and continue on it for 3.1 mi., passing Orin Duell Rd. and Granger Rd. Now turn L and the road turns to *dirt. This is called the Padanarum Spur Rd. After 1.0 mi. the road reaches a green camp called "Cirlew." Here the road turns to a narrow track that is not maintained from December 1 to April 1. Continue another 1.9 mi. down this narrow dirt track to the unmarked trailhead for Long Pond on the L (0.0 mi.). It is an old road going uphill. There is a small space on the R to park.*

The old road on the L (N) goes straight uphill along a washed out section for 0.1 mi. The trail levels out, then there is a series of huge mud holes in the road, made by vehicles. At 0.3 mi. a new wide side trail has been cut on the L around a large wet area, the first of several similar detours.

At 0.5 mi. the road descends gently to another wet spot, then climbs into pines. At 0.8 mi. it goes up, then at 0.9 mi. levels off in birch, white pine, hemlock, balsam and maple woods. At 1.0 mi. the road curves L 90 degrees. At 1.1 mi. there is a trail sign L to Island Pond (see below). At 1.2 mi. the S end of Long Pond is reached after a descent of 250 ft. Beavers have raised the pond level considerably. There is an informal campsite here.

The side trail to Island Pond is pleasant but sometimes wet, first along a ridge and then in and out of ferns. At 0.4 mi. it reaches a flooded edge of pretty Island Pond, which seems to be completely filled in, perhaps the work of beavers. Both ponds are fun to explore in a small ultralight canoe.

Distances: *Padanarum Spur Rd. to Long Pond, 1.2 mi. (2 km); side trail to Island Pond, 0.4 mi. (0.6 km). Total trail distance, 1.6 mi. (2.6 km). Elevation of Long Pond, 1320 ft. (402.4 m); elev. of Island Pond, 1338 ft. (408 m).*

(64) Wardsboro Rd. from N to S
(64A) Wardsboro Rd. Spur

Map: E-4

This trail follows an old road that passes through some nice wild land in the NE part of this region. The N section travels through some private lands, including some timber lands, but there is a public easement to use the road. Approximately the first half mile has been built up to a hard road surface for logging trucks, but the road soon becomes more of a trail after this. This is a great route for skiing (park a car at both the N and S ends of the trail). There no longer is public access to Swede Pond or Swede Mt.

Trailhead: The N trailhead is on NY 8, 1.0 mi. E of the E end of North Pond (approx. 10 mi. E of the firehouse in the town of Brant Lake and about 1.0 mi. W of the town of Graphite). Soon after North Pond, a rock pointed to resemble an elephant is on the R. A posted logging header is passed on the R. In about 0.1 mi. turn a sharp R onto Fly Brook Rd. Park on the R side of Fly Brook Rd.

To reach the S trailhead, drive 5 mi. E from Northway exit 24 to NY 9N, then turn L (N) and drive 6 mi. to Padanarum Rd. (dirt) on the L. At 1.8 mi. cross the bridge, then turn R onto Wardsboro Rd. and drive to a parking turnout across from a red cabin at 3.4 mi. Immediately after parking you'll see the old Wardsboro cemetery.

From the N end, walk along Fly Brook Rd. past the intersection on the R with the gated logging heading. Continue on ahead, walking gently uphill to a L (S) turn onto the side road at 0.4 mi. This is the N end of the Wardsboro road. The logging is soon left behind and the road becomes less rutted. Bear L up the hill, until at 0.9 mi. the road reaches the top of the hill and bears R (S). At 1.1 mi. a fork is reached. The main trail is on the R, while a spur trail (64A) heads to the L. Stay on the main trail.

The road soon heads downhill and comes to a stream on the L at 1.6 mi. At 2.2 mi. there is a large detour around a big beaver pond, and a second jct. with 64A is reached at 2.3 mi.

The Wardsboro Rd. Spur Trail (64A) heads L here from the main trail (0.0 mi.), and descends gradually at first, then more steeply. At 0.4 mi. there is a jct. with an old road on the L. Heading to the R the road becomes eroded and then soon levels off at 0.7 mi. The road descends again to the jct. with the main trail by the beaver pond at 1.5 mi.

From the S jct. of 64 and 64A, below the beaver pond, the road passes over some rolling terrain with some wet sections and reaches a stream at 2.7 mi. The road varies from level to muddy to rolling, and passes occasional beaver handiwork. At 3.8 mi. there is another stream crossing. The road descends on a gradual grade and at 4.3 mi. reaches a cabin on the L. There are some signs of logging, and then the road descends alongside a hill with a pretty glen down to the L at 4.6 mi.

After a stone bridge over the outlet of Spectacle Ponds, a small green house on the R is reached at 5.0 mi. At 5.4 mi. orange markers on the trees on the L announce that the stream is a nursery for Atlantic landlocked salmon. The old Wardsboro cemetery is just ahead at 5.6 mi.

Distances: *From parking along Fly Brook Rd. to L turn onto Wardsboro Rd., 0.4 mi.; to first jct. with 64A, 1.1 mi.; to S jct. with 64A, 2.3 mi.; to Wardsboro cemetery, 5.6 mi. (9 km). Length of 64A, 1.5 mi. (2.4 km). Descent, 908 ft. (277 m). Elevation at large beaver pond by the S jct., approx. 1300 ft. (396 m).*

(65) Tongue Mt. Range from the North to Montcalm Point

Map: E-6

This trail traverses the rugged backbone of the Tongue Mt. Range that extends into the mid-section of Lake George, bounded by the shoreline of Northwest Bay on the W and the narrows of Lake George on the E. Views from open rocky sections along the trail looking to the lake and the mountains beyond are quite inspiring. The streams in the lower sections of this trail are seasonal. The trail can be quite dry for its entire length. Be sure to carry plenty of water.

This region is also home to the eastern timber rattlesnake, a threatened species in New York State. It's a treat to be able to see them in their natural habitat in one of the few places in the state where they may be found. They are not aggressive, and are seldom seen, but it's wise to take a few precautions. Wear high-top boots and use caution when approaching rocky ledges and warm sunny places. Remember, though, that rattlesnakes can be found anywhere on the mountain. It's important never to tease or corner a rattler. If you give them a wide berth and leave them alone, they'll leave you alone. Because their range and population are limited, the timber rattlesnake is protected under New York State law. It is illegal to kill, take, or possess this species without a special DEC permit.

Trailhead: From Northway exit 24, drive 5 mi. E to NY 9N. (Just before NY 9N, there are great views from the road of the Tongue Mt. Range, Lake George, and the surrounding mountains.) Driving N on NY 9N (0.0 mi.), the Clay Meadow trailhead is passed at 4.7 mi. on the R. Continue N on 9N until at 7.7 mi. the N trailhead for the Tongue Mt. Range appears on the R (E). There are blue markers along this trail.

From the parking area along the road (0.0 mi.), the trail at first heads W, somewhat parallel to NY 9N. In about 500 ft., the trail turns L, away from the tote road, and soon begins to climb. Some of this section is eroded and may be wet. At 0.6 mi. there is a jct. with the yellow-marked Deer Leap Trail (66) on the L.

The trail continues climbing steadily, up and over Brown Mt., and reaches an overlook just off the trail at 1.7 mi. The woods varies from hardwoods to hemlocks as the trail reaches a small clearing at 2.0 mi. At 2.4 mi. the trail follows rock cairns across a stretch of open rock, enters the woods, and then begins climbing again across more open rock with cairns. The Tongue Mt. Camp lean-to is reached at 2.6 mi. (no floor). There is a fine view from the lean-to area.

Past the lean-to, a couple of good views look N and W. There's much more open rock underfoot, and there are lots of blueberries in season. Cairns mark the trail. The trail passes through some red pines, descends to a ridge, and at 3.3 mi. reaches a clearing where there may still be an old sign for Tongue Mt. Camp and the highway. The trail soon climbs up and over the ledges near the top of Five Mile Mt., reaching the top at 3.5 mi. Summit elevation 2258 ft.

From the top, the trail descends slightly and then climbs over a couple of rocky outcrops on the trail. There are occasional views to the E, S and W. Be sure to keep in mind the rattlesnakes, and be careful where you put your hands. The trail continues its descent, passing a couple of interesting boulders along the way, reaching a stream (maybe dry) at 4.4 mi. After a couple of small level sections, and some switchbacks, another small stream is crossed just before the intersection at the Saddle at 5.15 mi. The E/W trail is the Five Mile Point Trail (67). From this point it's 1.9 mi. W along the Five Mile Point Trail to the Clay Meadow trailhead, and 1.7 mi. E to the shoreline of Lake George.

Heading straight ahead (SW) toward Fifth Peak, the trail climbs slightly, descends into a glen, and then winds, heading E and then S again. Soon some old stonework along the trail is a reminder of the old CCC days. The trail is cut into the hill and rises steadily along a steep hillside, reaching the yellow-marked spur trail for the Fifth Peak lean-to at 5.6 mi. The fairly new lean-to is reached about a quarter mile off the main trail. It faces away from the fabulous view as protection from the winds. There's a great view to the E, S and W, with a view of French Point Mt. farther down the trail.

The main trail continues S, passes a steep rock face and soon heads uphill more steeply. At 5.8 mi. it passes a small pool at the base of a cliff, and then soon traverses a fairly level enclosed ridge. At 6.0 mi. it passes the site of a fire from the summer of 1985. The undergrowth has pretty well taken over again.

The trail heads downhill at a stone outcrop and soon comes to a good view of the lake and Black Mt. on the E side. French Point Mt. is to the S with First Peak farther S and to the R. After passing a rock cairn, at 6.3 mi. the trail makes a sharp L at a burned-out tree, and soon reaches a lookout with a good view of Northwest Bay.

The trail soon drops sharply W and then follows downhill along a rock wall. At 6.5 mi. there is a sign to turn R. An old unmarked trail traverses this col from E to W at this point. The range trail follows the sign to the R and goes uphill through the hemlocks to another sign pointing to the R. Black Mt. is visible across the lake once again.

The trail climbs steeply again, and at 6.7 mi. reaches the top of Third Peak. After crossing some open rock ledges facing S, the trail reaches a precipitous drop and then another outlook. After heading down and passing a rock cairn, the trail heads into some beeches and then begins to switchback up French Point Mt., reaching the top at 7.5 mi. The summit elevation is 1739 ft. A short distance to the S on the trail there's a great view to The Narrows of Lake George, and the whole southern panorama.

The little-used trail heads S over bare rock with faint, light blue paint blazes and soon reaches another lookout. At 7.8 mi. the trail crosses open rock with ledges on the E, with some fine views. It passes a tiny pond and another S outlook, and continues following the blue-blazed rock, heading directly SW toward Northwest Bay.

At 8.0 mi. the trail descends steeply through a boulder field. After traversing toward the E, it soon turns and heads W and drops steeply to a small stream before climbing again. The trail passes through some huge oaks, comes to another lookout, then undulates up to the top of First Peak at 8.9 mi.

The trail switchbacks down the S side of First Peak through some scrubby oaks and soon comes to a grassy section with a view of the Point of Tongue at 9.6 mi. The route passes another couple of fine views, then turns W through some junipers and at 10.0 mi. goes through a narrow cleft of rock with a slanted side before leveling off for a short distance. After passing a rocky opening with a good view, the trail descends a steep pitch before climbing to a fine view to the E from the top of a flat rock.

The trail descends to another outlook and then enters the deep woods. It begins to level off and soon reaches the jct. with the Northwest Bay Trail (67) at 10.75 mi. Turning L to go to the tip of the point, at 11.0 mi. there's a trail jct. for the state boat dock. Turning R, the trail reaches Montcalm Point at 11.2 mi. From here it's a nice boat ride back to the "mainland," or a 5.0 mi. walk back from the jct. to the Clay Meadows trailhead via the Northwest Bay Trail (67).

Distances: *From N trailhead at 9N to jct. with the Deer Leap Trail, 0.6 mi.; to Tongue Mt. Camp lean-to, 2.6 mi.; to summit of Five Mile Mt., 3.5 mi.; to intersection with Five Mile Point Trail, 5.15 mi.; to cutoff for Fifth Peak lean-to, 5.6 mi.; to French Point Mt., 7.5 mi.; to jct. with Northwest Bay Trail, 10.75 mi. (17.2 km); to Montcalm Point, 11.2 mi. (17.9 km). Elevation at trailhead, 1065 ft. (325 m); Five Mile Mt., 2256 ft. (688 m); Fifth Peak, 1813 ft. (553 m); French Point Mt., 1756 ft. (535 m); Lake George, 320 ft. (97.5 m). Total trail ascent from N to S, approx. 2680 ft. (817 m).*

(66) Deer Leap

Map: E-6

This is a short spur trail that leads from the Tongue Mt. Trail (65) to some nice lookouts over the mid-Lake George area. There are many more spectacular views from along the Tongue Mt. trail, but the advantage of this trail is its short length. This is a fairly heavily used trail. The same cautions about rattlesnakes as described at the beginning of trail 65 pertain here, too.

Trailhead: The trail begins at 0.6 mi. S of the N trailhead for the Tongue Mt. Trail (65). The trail has yellow trail markers.

Starting from the jct. with the Tongue Mt. trail (0.0 mi.), the trail heads E. After reaching an outlook at 0.3 mi., the trail rolls up and down over a couple of hills. After passing a small pond at 0.8 mi., it arrives at a rocky opening overlooking Lake George at 1.1 mi. Here there's a view across the lake to the village of Huletts Landing on the E shore.

Distance: *Trail to Deer Leap 1.1 mi. (1.7 km). Elevation of Deer Leap, approx. 1100 ft. (335 m).*

(67) Northwest Bay Trail from Clay Meadow

Map: D-6

This is an extremely pleasant section of trail that is not used much. It often borders the lake and was originally built as a horse trail by the CCC, but that plan was abandoned once rattlesnakes were discovered. Please read the caution regarding rattlesnakes at the beginning of trail 65.

Trailhead: *From Northway Exit 24 (Bolton Landing–Riverbank) drive 5 mi. E to NY 9N. The steep hill down to NY 9N gives a good view of the undulating ridgeline of Tongue Mt. to the NE. Drive 4.7 mi. N on 9N to a parking area on the R at an old quarry. (When this lot is full, you may find additional parking space a short distance N on the R.) About 100 ft. (S) downhill along the road is the Clay Meadow trailhead for Tongue Mt., with a register (0.0 mi.).*

The trail goes downhill through a grove of white pines planted by the CCC in the 1930s. It crosses a long plank bridge over a stream at 0.2 mi. alongside a beaver dam. At 0.4 mi. it reaches a jct. Straight ahead is the Five Mile Point Trail (68) to the Saddle, Fifth Peak Lean-to, the Ridge Trail and Five Mile Mt. Point on the E side of the mountain. The Bay Trail to Point of Tongue is to the R.

At 0.5 mi. the trail crosses a bridge over a stream with moss-covered rocks. The trail markers are blue. At 0.7 mi. it begins to go up gradually, crossing a stream on stones, then heading uphill and into a hemlock grove alongside another picturesque stream which it crosses. The trail becomes steeper and washed out at 0.9 mi. It reaches the top of the steep pitch at 1.1 mi., then goes downhill and crosses a plank bridge over another beautiful stream. At 1.5 mi. it goes downhill through a deeply shaded hemlock glen.

At 1.7 mi. the trail reaches the marshy head of Northwest Bay. At 1.8 mi. it crosses a stream on another plank bridge. Then it goes up alongside a hill by the shoreline under large hemlocks with a fantastic mossy cliff on the L. At 2.0 mi. a side trail R goes 200 ft. to Bear Point. There is a nice view into Northwest Bay and down Lake George. At 2.1 mi. the trail reaches a high bluff where people have camped. Then it comes downhill and crosses another stream on a bridge at 2.2 mi.

At 2.4 mi. the trail passes a point with a fire circle. At 2.5 mi. it crosses a dry stony brook, then climbs steeply up and then down along a mossy cliff, crossing a bridge. It reaches a small point with a fire circle at 2.6 mi., then goes uphill and under hemlocks, almost level with the lake shore. This is a beautiful stretch of trail.

At 2.7 mi. there is a nice rock to swim from. At 3.1 mi. the trail reaches an opening along the shore with a fire circle. This is also a good place for swimming. At 3.2 mi. it crosses on a log over a stream which cascades 12 ft. down huge mossy blocks of rock. At 3.4 mi. the trail crosses another stream on rocks. At 4.0 mi. it goes uphill, then down steeply to cross a muddy stream and then through a large wet area. At 4.2 mi. it descends a hill and crosses a seasonally dry brook.

The very narrow trail goes along a steep hillside just above the shore. At 4.5 mi. the trail cuts away from the clear lake and goes steeply uphill among jumbled rocks. Then it comes down steeply at 4.7 mi. At 4.8 mi. there is an opening on the shore. At 4.9 mi. the trail crosses a small stream.

At 5.0 mi. the trail reaches a jct. French Point Mt. is 2.9 mi., Fifth Peak Lean-to is 6.2 mi., and the Tongue Mt. trailhead is 11.4 mi., all to the L. Point of Tongue is straight ahead.

At 5.2 mi. the trail divides. A state dock is about 80 yds. to the L on the E side of the point. There is a lovely view of The Narrows from here, as well as islands and Black Mt. (see below) and Shelving Rock Mt. (see below). S is Dome Island (a bird sanctuary owned by the Nature Conservancy), and SW is the elegant Sagamore Hotel on Green Island. Point of Tongue is a good place for a picnic and a swim at 5.4 mi.

Distances: *Clay Meadow trailhead to first jct., 0.4 mi.; to Bear Point, 2.0 mi.; to log bridge, 3.2 mi.; to French Point Mt. jct., 5.0 mi.; to state dock, 5.2 mi.; to Point of Tongue, 5.4 mi. (9 km).*

(68) Five Mile Point

Map: D-6

This is a pretty, little-used route. It's a connecting route with the Tongue Mt. Trail (65) for reasonable-length climbs of Five Mile Mt. and French Point Mt. It then continues down the E side of the Tongue Mt. Range to the shoreline of Lake George. This is a great place to swim on a hot summer day. There are many wildflowers along the trail, and blueberries in season (around open rocky sections). Please read the caution about rattlesnakes at the beginning of the description of trail 65.

Trailhead: *The start is at a jct. with the Northwest Bay Trail (67) 0.4 mi. E of the Clay Meadow trailhead. The trail has red markers.*

The trail starts at the jct. (0.0 mi.), and directly heads uphill. In a short distance, there's a side trail R to a pretty waterfall that drops more than 100 ft. over a series of boulders and ledges.

Continuing up, after crossing a stream at 0.3 mi., the trail becomes steep again. The trail crosses and then recrosses a stream on a couple of plank bridges, and at 0.9 mi. begins a series of switchbacks up a steep and rocky hemlock-covered hill.

The trail reaches a plateau at 1.0 mi., but turns abruptly uphill again at 1.2 mi. At 1.3 mi. the grade moderates along the brook, still on the L. After a level along a moss-covered cliff with overhanging polypody ferns, there's yet another switchback before reaching the Saddle intersection at 1.55 mi. The N/S trail is the Tongue Mt. Trail (65). Five Mile Mt. is 2.7 mi. to the L (N), and French Point Mt. 2.4 mi. to the R (S).

Continuing straight ahead across the intersection, the trail is fairly level, passing a marshy section at 1.7 mi. with the trail hugging the R shoreline. The trail soon turns R and begins descending, leveling off briefly at 2.5 mi. It swings N, passes a small brook and then turns S again.

Descending through a grassy area, there are views to Black Mt., Mother Bunch Islands and Huletts Landing, with another lookout at 2.6 mi., just off the trail. The trail now descends through shrub oaks, junipers and some cedars along an old horse path that was built up with some fine stonework. After a short, steep descent along some ledges and steep rock, the trail levels and enters a stand of maples and oaks. The descent is now much more gradual with lots of wildflowers along the grassy trail. After crossing a small stream, the trail swings L and reaches Five Mile Point at 3.25 mi.

The rock that descends into the lake can be nice for swimming, and makes a good landing place for a boat. Black Mt. seems to rise directly out of the water, Erebus Mt. is to the R of it and Hatchet Island is straight ahead. To the N are the Harbor Islands, Sabbath Day Point, the cliffs of Deer Leap, and Spruce Mt.

Distances: *From jct. with Northwest Bay Trail (67), 0.0 mi.; to intersection with Tongue Mt. Trail (65), 1.6 mi.; to Five Mile Point, 3.3 mi. Total distance from Clay Meadow trailhead, 3.7 mi. Ascent to the Saddle from Northwest Bay, 1180 ft. (360 m). Elevation of Lake George, 320 ft. (97 m).*

(69) Northwest Bay Brook   Map: D-6

This brook has some steep cascades just before it joins Northwest Bay. The short walk through a grove of pines planted by the CCC in the 1930s is pleasant.

After parking at the quarry for the Clay Meadow trailhead (see trail 67), walk across NY 9N and downhill 200 ft. to a gate (0.0 mi.). Going under tall pines on a wide path, the trail continues 0.2 mi. to the edge of a steep hill and then down about 50 ft. to a waterfall of Northwest Bay Brook.

Distance: *NY 9N to Northwest Bay Brook, 0.2 mi. (0.3 km).*

(70) Charles Lathrop Pack Demonstration Forest Nature Trail   No Map

The nature trail at the Charles Lathrop Pack Demonstration Forest is a very appealing walk. While this short trail won't take more than an hour's time, it can be combined with other trips or make a very pleasant diversion on a long road trip. The hiker will see one of the greatest assemblages of truly huge hemlock trees in the Adirondacks as well as one of the largest white pines in the state, known as the "grandmother tree." As of July 1994, this trail is being reconstructed to make it wheelchair accessible. It is an aesthetically attractive trail. Both it and the Warren County Nature Trail (71) are also in ADK's Central Region guidebook by Bruce Wadsworth; they are just west of the border of the Eastern Region.

Trailhead: *Access is off the W side of US 9, 0.7 mi. N of the US 9 and NY 28 intersection N of Warrensburg. A large sign marks the spot. Turn onto the macadam road and drive 0.5 mi. without turns to an intersection with several directional signs. One says "All Parking" and points to the R. Park here in an unpaved open area. Returning to the main road, turn R and walk 150 yds. along the road until you see a small brown sign at L labeled "Nature Trail." This is the trailhead. Nature trail guidebooks are available at the trailhead.*

The trail enters an oak-hemlock forest from the trailhead (0.0 mi.). A gurgling brook is crossed on a bridge at 150 ft. and the valley widens. White pine and yellow birch are now found. The trail gradually circles a glacial hill on the R. Various ferns, mosses and lycopodia keep your interest as the trail swings N among huge hemlocks.

At 0.6 mi., turn L, cross a low bridge, and bear slightly R across a flat area. At 0.8 mi., the nature trail ends, but the pleasant walk continues. Turn R and walk along a woods road to a T-intersection at 1.1 mi. Here is a spring house, where a refreshing drink of water can be obtained. Turn R again and follow the winding dirt road to a pond at 1.2 mi. Then bear L, near lily pads and other water flowers. The paved road is again reached at 1.3 mi. Turn R a third time and walk back to the parking area at 1.4 mi.

Trail in winter: This trail is very short for a winter trip, but several of the roads in this facility can be walked or skied in winter.

Distances: To second bridge, 0.6 mi.; to end of nature trail, 0.8 mi.; to pond, 1.2 mi.; back to parking area, 1.4 mi. (2.3 km).

(71) Warren County Parks and Recreation Nature Trail   No Map

The Warren County Parks and Recreation Department has developed a very informative nature trail beside the Hudson River. An illustrated trail guide is provided to explain the 29 points of interest along the trail. This is a very well designed nature trail.

Trailhead: Access to the trailhead is off the W side of Hudson St., 2.5 mi. NW of the Floyd Bennett Park stoplight in Warrensburg. The other end of Hudson St. intersects NY 28, 1.7 mi. N of the NY 28 and US 9 intersection. The nature trail is 2.2 mi. S from NY 28. A large nature trail–canoe access sign points the way to a parking area. There are a large wooden map and printed trail guides at the trailhead.

The trail leads W toward the Hudson River. Posts with bright red markers and numbers mark each point of interest explained in the guide. The river is reached at 0.3 mi., where a clockwise loop begins. The trail climbs a rather steep hill at 0.7 mi. Avoid numerous ski trails that weave in and out of the route. The hill is descended and the trail ends at 1.4 mi., back at the parking area. Please return the trail guide so others may use it.

Trail in winter: *Many cross-country trails, some requiring considerable skill, weave through this area. While none are very long, when combined they provide a nice circuit.*

Distances: *To Hudson River, 0.3 mi.; to base of hill, 0.7 mi.; to end of trail, 1.4 mi. (2.3 km).*

Shelving Rock Falls

Southeastern Lake George Wild Forest Section

This region to the east of Lake George contains quite a network of trails. Bounded by the Huletts Landing area to the N and West Fort Ann on the S, this area contains a nice mix of mountains, ponds, pleasant forests, and breathtaking shoreline views. Black Mt., to the N in this section, is the highest mountain with a trail in the whole eastern Adirondack section (2646 ft.).

Since this is a Wild Forest area, there is an overlapping mix of hiking trails, horse trails, and snowmobile trails. Many of the trails in this section are part of a large network of carriage paths and trails that was once included in the Knapp Estate on the E side of Lake George. Many of these were logging roads that were improved by the men who worked for Mr. Knapp in the early 1900s. Most were stabilized with some fine stonework and are suitable for a variety of activities. These paths and trails switchback up the mountains and form a maze of paths all through the Shelving Rock area. It's a great area for the hiker, as well as the mountain biker. At present (July 1994) there are no restrictions on mountain biking in the Wild Forest regions except in areas with completed unit management plans. In the near future though, mountain biking will be permitted only on designated mountain biking trails in Wild Forest areas. On the SE side of Lake George, mountain bikers are permitted on all trails except those leading to the summits of Black, Buck and Sleeping Beauty mountains.

To the NE of Shelving Rock are some nice little-used ponds that would be great for portaging in a small ultralight canoe. The trails quite near to Shelving Rock see intensive use, particularly on holiday weekends. You don't have to go too far away, though, to find lesser-used areas and solitude during even some of the busiest times.

Trails in winter: Though this area is marked for snowmobiles in the winter, there's not a lot of use, so there is some great snowshoeing, cross-country skiing, and ski-shoeing potential. Remember though, if parking near the Dacy Clearing area, that most of the trails head downhill to Lake George and have to be climbed on the way back out at the end of the day. With the exception of the mountain trails, all the trails in the region are fine for skiing, and the mountains are great snowshoe tours, especially when combined with a ski in on the more level approach routes. Specific suggestions for certain trails are included in the trail descriptions.

Suggested hikes in this region:

Shorter Hikes:

Inman Pond—*1.3 mi. This is a pleasant walk on an old woods road to a picturesque pond.*

Lapland Pond—*2.1 mi. A walk on an old woods road to a pond with a lean-to and a lot of wildlife.*

Moderate Hikes:

Sleeping Beauty Mt. Loop—*7.6 mi. (total round trip distance). From Dacy Clearing; great mountain views from Sleeping Beauty, and then a descent to Bumps Pond and return.*

Black Mt. from the E—*Some fine views are a good reward for this climb with some steep places up to the fire tower at the summit.*

Harder Hike:

Black Mt. via Shelving Rock Mt.—*6.6 mi. This route climbs first over Shelving Rock Mt., then along the old woods road along the Lake George shoreline, and then ascends steeply up the spectacular W route to the summit of Black Mt.*

Trail Described	Total Miles (one way)	Page
(72) Prospect Mt.	1.7	164
(73) Old Road on the Shoulder of Pilot Knob	1.0	167
(74) Butternut Brook Trail	2.8	168
(75) Inman Pond	0.8	169
(76) Buck Mt. Trail from Pilot Knob	3.3	170
(77) Buck Mt. Trail from Hogtown	2.3	172
(78) Buck Mt. Connector Trail	0.5	173
(79) Shelving Rock Falls Lakeshore Loop	2.0	175
Shelving Rock Falls Trail (unmaintained)		175
(80) W Shelving Rock Falls Connector Trails	0.3	179
(81) E Shelving Rock Falls Connector Trails	0.6	180
(82) Hogtown Trailhead to Fishbrook Pond via Dacy Clearing and Bumps Pond	4.4	181
(82A) W Fishbrook Pond Trail	0.7	183
(83) Sleeping Beauty	2.1	183
(84) Old Farm Road	1.2	185
(84A) E Old Farm Rd. Leg	0.7	185
(84B) W Old Farm Rd. Leg	0.6	185
(85) Shortway Trail	2.4	187

(72) Prospect Mt.   Page Map

This trail would be best rerouted up the mountain with a more gradual rate of ascent and some switchbacks. As it is, it is a steep, rocky trail but a fairly short climb. The present trail will only become more badly eroded as time goes on. There are no vistas along the way.

Trailhead: Turn N off NY 9 in Lake George Village at LaRoma Restaurant

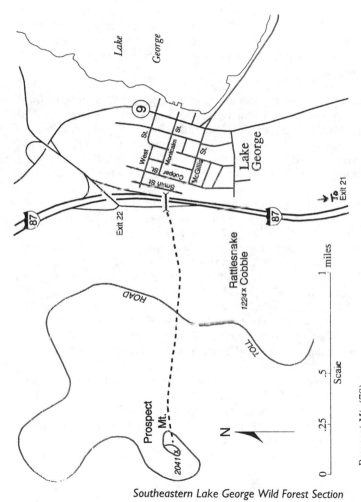

Prospect Mt. (72)
Based on Lake George quadrangle, 15-min. series, 1966.

onto Montcalm St. Pass three churches (the Episcopal church has a youth hostel in summer) and then turn R onto Cooper St. Go one block, turn L onto West St., then L onto Smith St. The trail actually starts at the end of Cooper St. but there is no place to park there. On Smith St. there is space for about five cars at the base of the stairway leading to the trail bridge over the Northway (0 mi.).

The stairway and bridge account for the first 0.1 mi. of this trail. The stairway is the equivalent of about four stories of steps.

The trail markers are red. The trail goes steadily up on a wide rocky path to 0.2 mi. where it makes a gentle L and becomes more moderate. An old foundation on the R has a set of stone steps. More foundations from the inclined railway that once went up the mountain are soon passed.

At 0.3 mi. the trail resumes a fairly steady rate up. At 0.6 mi. it crosses the toll road to the peak. After crossing the road, the trail is badly eroded. It turns R at 0.7 mi. up onto bare rock and then makes a L. At 0.8 mi. it comes to a large sloping rock wall on the R. The trail goes off to the L from this wall, then levels off until at 0.8 mi. it turns R and heads uphill again. At 0.9 mi. a small stream can be heard to the L as the trail climbs steeply over bare slabs of rock.

At 1.0 mi. the trail makes a level L turn, then resumes climbing again. At 1.2 mi. it becomes even more steep, but soon moderates, then goes level through huge hemlocks and white pines. At 1.4 mi. it passes through maples and beeches as it bends S onto a ledge with a partial view E to Lake George.

The trail turns R here and arrives at the toll road at 1.5 mi. near the summit. Turn R up the road, then L into the picnic area at 1.6 mi. Uphill across the road, which has been blasted out of the summit, are the remains of the fire tower at 1.7 mi. In season there are many people at the top, both from the tour buses and those who have driven up. The view from Prospect Mt. includes Lake George village to the E and the mountains of Vermont off in the distance.

Distances: *Smith St. to first jct. with toll road, 0.6 mi.; to second jct. with toll road, 1.5 mi.; to summit, 1.7 mi. (2.9 km). Ascent, approx. 1600 ft. (489 m). Elevation of Prospect Mt., 2041 ft. (622.3 m).*

(73) Old Road on the Shoulder of Pilot Knob

Map: D-9

Many people take the wrong turn onto this road, thinking they are heading for the Buck Mt. Trail. This old road is a lovely deep-woods walk, a connector to Lower Hogtown or the first part of a loop with return past the Buck Mt. trail jct.

Trailhead: *The route begins at 0.2 mi. on the Buck Mt. from Pilot Knob Trail (76). There are no markers, although the road is easy enough to follow.*

The road begins to go uphill beside a stream to the R. At 0.2 mi. it rounds a wide curve to the L as it cuts into the side of a hill. The stream is farther below now. At 0.3 mi. a small trail goes R down to the stream. Now the road is cut into a steep bank and the grade increases.

The road crosses a dry streambed, continuing to climb through beautiful, high, deep woods. The streambed is now down to the L. At 0.4 mi. the road crosses a wet place beneath a huge slanting rock wall on the R partially covered with mosses and ferns. At 0.8 mi. the road crests a hill with a waterfall audible ahead and below on the L. At 0.6 mi. there is an overgrown short spur road to the L down to the stream. It ascends above the stream.

At 0.8 mi. the road crosses a rocky, damp streambed. At 1.0 mi. a trail comes in on the L with blue horse trail markers and orange snowmobile trail markers. The trail downhill to the L meets the Buck Mt. Trail (76) in another 0.4 mi.

The trail uphill to the R continues E to the jct. for the Inman Pond Trail (75) in another 1.9 mi. and at 2.4 mi. reaches the Lower Hogtown trailhead, making a through trip from Pilot Knob of 3.6 mi.

Distances: To dry streambed, 0.3 mi.; to spur road to stream, 0.6 mi.; to jct. with trail to Lower Hogtown, 1.0 mi. (1.6 km).

(74) Butternut Brook Trail   Map: D-9

Trailhead: Drive 6.3 mi. on Buttermilk Falls Rd. (see Buck Mt. from Hogtown [trail 77]) N to the Lower Hogtown trailhead, on the L just past Camp Little Notch, marked with a sign CLN. There is a wide turn-out for parking on the R just N of the trailhead. Perhaps this old road was used by the farmers of Hogtown to drive their hogs and carry vegetables to Lake George for the kitchens of the boarding houses and hotels along the lake.

This is a snowmobile and horse trail. It might be a good route for cross-country skiing with a car at the Pilot Knob trailhead (see trail 73). The road starts gradually uphill past a hillside of jumbled rock on the R at 0.2 mi. At 0.5 mi. the trail reaches a new wooden bridge over a stream. Just before the bridge an old road goes R to Inman Pond (trail 75).

The trail crosses the bridge, follows a rocky, dry streambed, then crosses another stream. Now the road goes more steeply uphill, leveling off at 0.6 mi. Here there is a side road to the R but the trail bends L, following snowmobile and horse trail markers. The road climbs another steep pitch to 0.7 mi., then goes downhill to the level. At 0.9 mi. the road starts uphill again, this time on solid bedrock. At 1.0 mi. an upside down junk car is on the R with a pond visible below through the trees. The road crosses a stream, then another stream at 1.1 mi., before it goes uphill again and then levels out.

At 1.4 mi. an old road goes off to the L at a height-of-land in a pass. Now the road goes gently downhill, coming alongside a stream on the L. It crosses the stream at 1.5 mi., then passes through a fern-filled gully. At 1.8 mi. it crosses another stream, then goes steadily downhill following horse and snowmobile trail markers.

(At 2.4 mi. a side road goes L 1.0 mi. over the shoulder of Pilot Knob [see trail 73], rejoining the trail for Buck Mt. [see trail 76] at 3.4 mi. and reaching the Pilot Knob trailhead parking lot at 3.6 mi.)

The marked trail continues downhill another 0.4 mi. to 2.8 mi. where it meets the trail that turns R up Buck Mt. (see trail 76). From here it is another 1.2 mi. to the Pilot Knob trailhead parking lot, making a through trip from Lower Hogtown to be 4.0 mi.

Distances: Lower Hogtown to turn-off for Inman Pond, 0.5 mi.; to L turn for road over shoulder of Pilot Knob, 2.4 mi.; to Buck Mt. Trail, 2.8 mi.; to Pilot Knob trailhead parking lot, 4.0 mi. (6.8 km).

(75) Inman Pond   No Map

Trailhead: This is a truly delightful walk and pleasing to the eye. From the Lower Hogtown trailhead (see trail 74), walk W 0.5 mi. to a wooden bridge over a stream. Just before the bridge is an old road to the R. Turn onto this road (0 mi.).

Following red horse trail markers, the road goes steeply uphill with a stream down to the L. It levels off at 0.1 mi., then curves up and L around the side of a hill through beech woods.

At 0.3 mi. a path goes off to the R. It is unmarked and overgrown. The road curves L and uphill, passing an orange snowmobile marker and then a red horse trail marker. The road levels out, crosses a tiny stream and splits to fork around Inman Pond at 0.4 mi.

Bearing L, the road crosses an outlet of the pond at 0.5 mi. on giant logs. The pond is visible to the R. The trail passes through a corridor lined thickly with young balsams. It goes into the woods again, crossing a rusty pipe at a wet place.

At 0.7 mi. a wooden sign with "Trail" and an arrow pointing R is nailed to a maple. Snowmobile and horse trail markers are off to the R. This little-used trail leads through hemlocks and then downhill to a small bluff at 0.8 mi. overlooking this lovely pond. There is an informal campsite here as well as an abandoned beaver house in the bog that runs down the middle of the pond to just E of this bluff.

Retracing your steps to the fork (0.4 mi.), walk up the R road which crosses another outlet with a pipe at 0.5 mi. There is an old beaver dam above the outlet. The view down the pond is fascinating since it holds a floating bog. At 0.8 mi. the road continues straight ahead but to the L is a fire circle above the pond edge. This is the end of the official DEC trail.

Distances: *To fork near pond, 0.4 mi.; to S shore bluff, 0.8 mi.; to N shore fire circle, 0.8 mi. (1.3 km). From Lower Hogtown trailhead to both sides of the pond and back is a round trip of 3.1 mi. (5 km). Elevation at Lower Hogtown trailhead, approx. 1000 ft. (304 m); elevation of Inman Pond, approx. 1400 ft. (426 m).*

(76) Buck Mt. Trail from Pilot Knob Map: D-9

Buck Mt. is an enjoyable climb with fine views from the open rock top on the lake side. It can be climbed from both the N and the S. While the N route has less elevation gain, the more heavily used S route has a number of views from the trail on the ascent. The trail is marked with yellow markers.

Trailhead: *To reach the Pilot Knob trailhead, drive 4.9 mi. N on NY 9L from its intersection with NY 149. Turn R (0.0 mi.) at a sign for Kattskill Bay and Pilot Knob and drive 3.5 mi. to the Pilot Knob trailhead for Buck Mt. on the R.*

From the trail register (0.0 mi.) the trail heads E and soon crosses a small brook and then reaches a fork. The unmarked old road to the R (trail 73) goes up a low shoulder of Pilot Knob and then joins the Butternut Brook Trail (74) to Lower Hogtown. Turning L at the fork, the trail passes through a forest of basswood, birch, white pine, oak, maple, sumac, and large grapevines. After Butternut Brook is crossed at 0.4 mi., the trail turns L uphill. After another switchback, the trail climbs steeply, moderates briefly, and resumes the climb by a large boulder.

At 1.0 mi. the trail passes an old stone wall and then levels off. After crossing Butternut Brook again, the trail reaches a fork at 1.2 mi. The trail R is the Butternut Brook Trail (74) to the Lower Hogtown trailhead. The yellow marked trail to Buck Mt. heads L. The route is steep again, with views through the trees of Lake George at 1.3 mi. and the N side of Pilot Knob. The trail soon switchbacks to the L and at 1.6 mi. crosses a stream. It briefly levels off, crosses a small stream at 1.8 mi., and then climbs steadily through a beech woods.

After a large tree whose roots have enveloped a boulder, the steep climbing begins again at 2.2 mi. The grade eases somewhat before another steep ascent at 2.4 mi. At 2.7 mi. the trail passes a small swamp, and then at 2.9 mi. climbs another steep pitch to open rock with a view. At 3.0 mi. the trail ascends steeply up solid rock. Down to the SE is Crossett Pond, site of a Boy Scout camp.

Just before the summit the trail descends into a col where at 3.2 mi. it meets the Buck Mt. Trail from Hogtown (trail 77). The summit is to the L at 3.3 mi. This rocky peak is understandably a favorite with its excellent view of Lake George and the surrounding mountains, although the lesser used trail from the N is shorter, less eroded and easier.

Trail in winter: This is a great snowshoeing trail. It's good to carry instep crampons for the steeper sections and possible ice.

Distances: Pilot Knob trailhead to jct. with Butternut Rock Trail, 1.2 mi.; to summit, 3.3 mi. (5.3 km). Ascent, 2000 ft. (610 m). Summit elevation, 2330 ft. (710 m).

(77) Buck Mt. Trail from Hogtown   Map: E-9

Trailhead: From the intersection of NY 9L and County Rt. 149, drive E 1.6 mi. to the intersection with Buttermilk Falls Rd. Turn L onto Buttermilk Falls Rd. (0 mi.). In 3.2 mi., just after the jct. with Taylor Wood Rd. on the R, the road becomes Sly Pond Rd. and the pavement ends. Continuing straight ahead on Sly Pond Rd., at 8.7 mi. Hogtown Rd. intersects on the R. Continue straight ahead on Shelving Rock Rd., which has a dead-end sign (this road continues on to the Knapp Estate on Lake George at 12.8 mi. from Rt. 149). At 9.4 mi. is the Hogtown trailhead and parking for the Lake George Trails System. Continue on to the L until at 9.9 mi. there is a small parking lot and a sign on the L for Buck Mt.

Starting at the parking lot (0.0 mi.), the trail soon crosses a stream on stones and then starts uphill. At 0.2 mi., the trail crosses another brook in a pleasant hemlock glade. After rolling up and down for a while, the trail passes a miniature pond at 0.5 mi. At 0.9 mi. the trail crosses a stream, and then at 1.0 mi. another, and goes up a steep hill, leveling off at 1.2 mi.

The trail crosses a picturesque stream with shelving rocks,

another stream at 1.4 mi., and then follows along a stream on the L at 1.5 mi. After crossing this stream twice, the trail heads steeply uphill with the stream on the R, passing three huge boulders at 1.7 mi. Now the stream is in a mature stand of hardwoods, and closely follows the stream up a steep pitch at 1.8 mi.

At 2.0 mi. the trail goes through a narrow pass of jumbled boulders and a mossy cliff with a stream cascading through its cleft. After a wet spell, water drips from the moss-covered rock. The trail soon narrows on a gentle grade overlooking the stream. At 2.1 mi. the trail becomes steep again, and crosses and recrosses the stream. Shortly the trail passes between two walls of boulders, levels out, and arrives at 2.2 mi. at the jct. with the Buck Mt. from Pilot Knob Trail (76), which continues on to the Butternut Brook Trail (74) and Pilot Knob. Turn R and climb over bare rock to the summit at 2.3 mi.

The view from the open areas on top is quite fine. It includes a panorama of Lake George and the southern Adirondack mountains, including Tongue Mt., Shelving Rock Mt., Sleeping Beauty and Black Mt. It's a fine place to relax and enjoy the view.

Trail in winter: Buck Mt. is a great snowshoe trip from either side. Skiing would be suitable only on the approach to the climbing. Instep crampons are advised for poor snow conditions.

Distances: *Parking lot (0 mi.) to jct. with Buck Mt. from Pilot Knob Trail, 2.2 mi. (3.5 km); to summit, 2.3 mi. (3.7 km). Ascent, 1130 ft. (345 m). Summit elevation, 2330 ft. (710 m).*

(78) Buck Mt. Connector Trail   Map: E-9

This short trail connects the N trailhead of Buck Mt. with the road to Dacy Clearing. It is not often used since most people park at the Buck Mt. trailhead to climb that mountain or at the Hogtown trailhead or Dacy Clearing. However, it can serve as the start of a very lovely walk or ski trip using other connector roads, providing a loop back to this spot.

Trailhead: *The trail starts directly across from the N trailhead to Buck Mt. on the N side of Shelving Rock Rd., 0.5 mi. W of the Hogtown trailhead parking lot. A sign says, "Sleeping Beauty Mt., 3.4 mi.; Fishbrook Pond, 5.2 mi." Light blue horse trail markers help hikers stay on this little-used trail.*

The trail leads gently downhill N of the road, heading to a small brook, which it crosses. The trees are mostly beech, birch and some hemlock. In October the forest floor is a brown and gold carpet.

At 0.1 mi. the trail descends to a pleasant hollow with the beginnings of a tiny stream. Woodpeckers and chickadees tap and cheep busily.

Now the trail climbs up out of the hollow past maple and ash. A tan DEC marker with "67" on it is on a tree on this slope. The trail winds uphill around a small rock ledge and passes a few yellow DEC markers.

At 0.2 mi. the trail crosses a spring near an uprooted hemlock and passes a moss-covered ledge to the R. The trail continues gently uphill through beautiful woods of beech with some hemlock, oak and ash, crossing another spring at 0.4 mi. At 0.45 mi. the trail meets the road to Dacy Clearing (trail 82), 0.5 mi. from the Hogtown trailhead parking area.

Distance: *Shelving Rock Rd. at Buck Mt. trailhead to road to Dacy Clearing, 0.45 mi. (0.8 km).*

(79) Shelving Rock Falls
Lakeshore Loop
Shelving Rock Falls Trail
(unmaintained)

Map: p. 177

This trail has a lot of variety in it. A nice way to do this trail is to park at one of the lower parking areas (see "Trailhead" below) and end the walk by passing Shelving Rock Falls. This route is the best way to see the falls, from a carriage pull-off near the top of the falls. An unmarked and unmaintained rugged path (trail 79A) leads down to the bottom of the falls and then follows the gorge down to the bridge across Shelving Rock Brook.

This area is a popular place in the summer on weekends, especially holiday weekends, so it might be good to pick off-times to visit. Camping in the Shelving Rock Falls area on the W side of Shelving Rock Rd. is restricted to 21 designated campsites in the level "pines" area along the road just N of the bridge over Shelving Rock Brook. Fires are permitted in existing fire rings. There is no parking after 9 p.m. in the parking areas along Shelving Rock Rd. near the Knapp Estate boundary. Parking is restricted to parking areas only; anyone parking along the road runs the risk of being towed away.

Trailhead: When traveling NW on Shelving Rock Rd. from the Hogtown trailhead (see trail 82), the E access to this trail is 2.5 mi. from the trailhead on the L at the metal barrier gate, just before the bridge over Shelving Rock Brook. The N trailhead is 1.1 mi. farther along (3.6 mi. from the Hogtown trailhead) on the L side of the road, 0.1 mi. before the private Knapp Estate, but the last parking is at the 3.4 mi. point on the L. Five other trails (the first is back in the woods) with metal barrier gates are passed on the L when traveling from the E access to the N access.

The trail begins on the L (0.0 mi.). There are signs for "No Horses

Permitted" and "Motorized Vehicles Prohibited except Snowmobiles."
The trail begins heading downhill to the R, swings L and then
reaches the trail along the shore of Lake George at 0.1 mi. The R leg
ends at a metal gate before a private land boundary in less than 0.1
mi. The public route turns L and passes a pretty rock point with
great 180-degree views from N to S on the lake. The trail closely
follows the shoreline, sometimes right along it and other times a
short distance inland. There are great views most of the way.

At 0.45 mi. the trail takes a sharp L away from the lake, then
soon a sharp R to follow the shore again. It follows around a pretty
little cove, then at 0.6 mi. comes to a jct. The trail L is the main trail.
To the R a trail leads 0.1 mi. to an old camping spot on the shore.
Here's a good view over to Log Bay Island and the shoreline beyond.
There is good swimming off the ledges on a hot summer day.

The main trail contours around Log Bay, soon coming to a nice
view S across a rocky point with the summit of Buck Mt. visible in
the distance. At 0.85 mi., the trail takes a sharp L inland to follow
around a wetland in Shelving Rock Bay. A R turn here leads a short
distance onto the pine-covered point. Herons, beavers and kingfisher
all frequent this wetland.

At 0.9 mi. there's a jct. with the W Connector Trail (80) straight
ahead. Bear R, passing to the W side of an outhouse to continue on the
main trail. In a short distance another leg of trail 80 comes in on the L.

Following along the wetland, the trail comes to Shelving Rock
Brook and crosses it on a plank bridge at 1.1 mi. Just across the
bridge on the L (the S side of the bridge) is the end of an unmaintained foot trail (trail 79A) from Shelving Rock Falls.

This area was used by Native Americans long before it was
claimed by the white settlers. Indian artifacts have been found in
Shelving Rock Bay dating from 2500 B.C., including Vosburg points
(named because this type was first found on the Vosburg farm near
Albany). Pottery shards found here date from the Middle Woodland

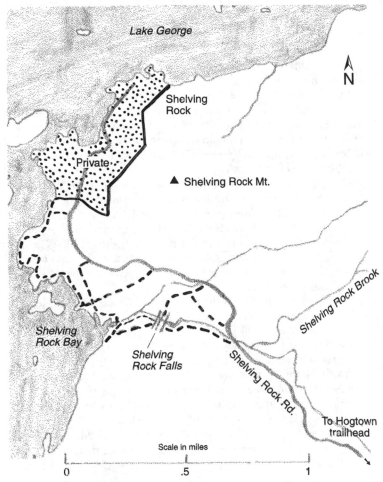

Lake George

Shelving
Rock

▲ Shelving Rock Mt.

Private

Shelving Rock Brook

Shelving
Rock Bay

Shelving
Rock Falls

Shelving Rock Rd.

To Hogtown
trailhead

N

Scale in miles

0   .5   1

Shelving Rock Falls Lakeshore Loop (79), Shelving Rock Falls Trail
(unmaintained), West Connector Trail (80), East Connector Trail (81)
Based on Shelving Rock quadrangle, 7.5-min. series, 1966.

era, about 400 A.D. Charcoal from a fireplace excavated near Harris Bay has been dated to 4000 B.C. as documented by staff from the state museum in Albany.

After crossing the bridge, the trail continues along the wooded shoreline, until at 1.25 mi. it takes a sharp switchback L and begins to ascend the side of the hill. (Straight ahead along the shore at this turn are an outhouse and an old campsite in about 100 ft.) This switchback is the first of a series of switchbacks that continue up along the S side of the brook.

At 1.5 mi. the trail levels off in a forest of stately hemlocks, pines and oaks. Staying level, the trail soon swings around to the top of the falls and a nice side lookout over the falls at 1.6 mi. A rugged, unmaintained foot trail leads from the L side of the old carriage pull-off to the bottom of the falls and then down the ravine to the plank bridge.

Warning: Many have been hurt here. The dam at the top of the falls is algae-covered and slippery, and in the winter icy conditions make footing hazardous.

Descending from just W of the pull-off just W of the top of the falls, this rocky, unmaintained trail descends steeply to the base of the falls. This is a nice place to cool your feet in the water and enjoy the view of the falls. The route continues down through the rocky gorge past rushing rocky chasms and swirling pools under the dark, towering hemlocks. The route soon moderates, reaching the Loop Trail by a bridge near Shelving Rock Brook's entrance into the bay at 0.25 mi.

Continuing E on the main trail, on the L are remnants of the old plank bridge that used to span the top of the falls. A crossing is not recommended here now. The trail follows around the edge of an old beaver pond, and then reenters the woods following the pretty brook. The trail is mostly level to its jct. with Shelving Rock Rd. by a bridge at 2.0 mi.

Trail in winter: The trail would be a good ski from E to N (with some tight turns from the falls down to the lake shore), and fine for snowshoeing. This trail is used by snowmobiles. Extra caution is advised around the falls in winter.

Distances: *N trailhead (0 mi.) to jct. with West Connector Trail (80), 0.9 mi. (1.4 km); to Shelving Rock Falls (top), 1.6 mi. (2.6 km); to Shelving Rock Rd., 2.0 mi. (3.2 km). Elevation of Lake George, 320 ft. (98 m); by the road at the bridge, approx. 500 ft. (152 m).*

(80) W Shelving Rock Falls Connector Trails
Map: p. 177

These trails form an angular crisscross in the Shelving Rock Falls area between the brook and the dirt road. They are each rather short, and help to form a variety of shortened loops that also utilize the Shore Loop Trail (79).

Trailhead: *From the Shelving Rock Mt. trailhead (see trail 85) (0 mi.) after a short distance there's an "S" turn in Shelving Rock Rd. Just after that at 0.2 mi. is the trailhead and parking lot on the L. In another 0.2 mi. (0.4 mi. from Shelving Rock Mt. trailhead) is the second entrance, also on the L with a metal barrier gate. The last parking area on the road is just 0.1 mi. past this trail.*

This is a pair of trails from Shelving Rock Rd. that meet by the Loop Trail (78). There is a parking area in between the two entrances, as well as just beyond the second. Starting at the farthest E entrance 0.2 mi. from the Shelving Rock Mt. trailhead (0 mi.), the trail parallels the road for a while and descends at a moderate grade. At 0.2 mi. is the intersection with the other access trail from the R. From this intersection, each leg (straight ahead or L) connects with the Loop Trail (79) in about 250 ft.

From the intersection (0 mi.), turning R to return to the road, the trail follows along a wetland for a distance and climbs gradually. After a switchback, the trail heads across a stream and reaches the road at 0.1 mi. The last parking area is less than 0.1 mi. to the NW.

Distance: *W entrance to jct. with Loop Trail and back to E trailhead, 0.3 mi. (0.5 km).*

(81) E Shelving Rock Falls Connector Trails

Map: p. 177

Trailhead: *From the pine knoll just past the bridge (0.0 mi.), heading W on Shelving Rock Rd., is a pine grove. One entrance is to the L in the pines. A second entrance is by the gate on the L, 0.1 mi. farther, and the third is 0.1 mi. past the Shelving Rock Mt. trailhead (see trail 85) at the gate on the L.*

The trail heads W through the pines, soon coming to a power line. The trail follows the power line and at 0.2 mi. comes to a jct. with another entrance on the R. (The entrance is a bit over 0.1 mi. away to the R on a level trail.)

The main trail descends slightly and then, just before dropping into a deep gully with a stream, reaches a T jct. at 0.3 mi. To the R is another entrance from Shelving Rock Rd. (The entrance is about 200 ft. away on a mostly level trail.) Turning L, the trail parallels the stream, which is down a steep bank to the R. The forest is dark with many tall and stately pines and hemlocks.

At 0.5 mi. the trail reaches the top of the falls on the N side. With the bridge out the only way to reach the other side is by wading, or attempting to cross on a washed-out old beaver dam. Crossing here is NOT recommended. The view from the falls is better from the other side on the Loop Trail (79). It's a nice walk, though, when doing the loop and heading back to the car.

Distance: Total trail distances, 0.6 mi. (1.0 km).

(82) Hogtown Trailhead to Fishbrook Pond via Dacy Clearing and Bumps Pond

Map: E-8

This trail is a major N/S route up the E side of the Shelving Rock trail system. Since many trails intersect along the way, this isn't just a trail to a destination; it's also used in part for a number of other routes in this quadrant. Using this trail as a base, any number of trips of varying duration can be planned that take in mountains or some of the other ponds.

Trailhead: From the intersection of NY 9L and County Rt. 149, drive E 1.6 mi. to the intersection with Buttermilk Falls Rd. Turn L onto Buttermilk Falls Rd. (0 mi.). In 3.2 mi. just after the jct. with Taylor Wood Rd. on the R, the road becomes Sly Pond Rd. and the pavement ends. Continuing straight ahead on Sly Pond Rd., at 8.7 mi. Hogtown Rd. intersects on the R. Continue straight ahead on Shelving Rock Rd. with the dead end sign. At 9.4 mi. is the Hogtown trailhead and parking for the Lake George Trails System. Sign the register here (0.0 mi.).

The trail follows the narrow road N, reaching the Buck Mt. Connector Trail (78) on the L at 0.5 mi. At 0.6 mi. one leg of the Old Farm Rd. (84) branches off to the L. At 1.2 mi. the road passes through a small clearing on the R with a view up to the cliffs on Sleeping Beauty Mt. Soon the road goes through a larger clearing with hitching posts for horses and a jct. with the Shortway Trail (85) on the L (W). The road bends around the foundations of the old Dacy farmhouse. (The Dacy family supplied the Knapps with vegetables and also helped keep the roads clear.)

After a bridge, the Longway Trail (86) cuts off to the L. The road to Dacy Clearing goes R past an old stone dam in a stream. At Dacy

Clearing, 1.6 mi., the trail bears R past a steel gate, following yellow markers, and begins a steady climb uphill. At 2.0 mi. a stream crosses the washed-out road. The trail soon crosses another stream and then levels out.

At 2.2 mi. is the jct. on the R for the Sleeping Beauty Trail (83). This is a more spectacular but longer and more strenuous route to the N end of Bumps Pond. The trail continues to the L, following red markers now. The trail follows the road, now going uphill fairly steeply with few switchbacks, over loose rock. An overlook is reached at 2.4 mi., and another at 2.6 mi. Buck Mt. is to the S, and Lake George to the SW. It's often possible to see ravens and hawks here.

The trail soon begins to level off, and at 2.8 mi. begins a gradual descent, reaching Bumps Pond at 3.1 mi. On the L is the old stone chimney of a former hunting lodge that was part of the Knapp Estate. This is now an informal campsite. The trail soon comes to the jct. with the Bumps Pond Spur Trail (87) on the L at 3.2 mi. The trail curves E around the N shoreline of Bumps Pond, then heads N, reaching the jct. with the N end of the Sleeping Beauty Trail (83) on the R at 3.3 mi.

Continuing straight ahead (N) for Fishbrook Pond, at 3.4 mi. the trail passes an old beaver dam, and soon after an old beaver pond. The road is wet for a while, then levels out at 3.6 mi. and is drier. The trail soon begins its descent toward Fishbrook Pond, reaching a rusted culvert at 4.0 mi.

Before long, Fishbrook Pond is visible through the trees, and at 4.2 mi. there is a turn-off to a pretty point with a fireplace. A lean-to is visible on the N shore. From this point it's possible to walk around either side of the pond.

Heading to the R from the jct. at the point (4.2 mi.), just past the S lean-to at 4.3 mi. there's a rocky outcrop with a nice view of the pond and the lean-to. The outlet is crossed on a bridge at 4.4 mi. Just beyond, an orange-marked snowmobile trail heads off to the R. The end of the trail is reached at the intersection with the Fishbrook

Pond from Lake George Trail (95) and the Lapland Pond Trail (98) at 4.6 mi. The N lean-to is 0.2 mi. W on trail 95. This lean-to is situated at a pretty spot on a rocky shelf that slopes into the pond. Great blue herons may be seen in the shallows at the edge of the pond, and owls can be heard through the night.

Distances: Hogtown trailhead (0 mi.) to Dacy Clearing and jct. with Long-way Trail (86), 1.6 mi.; to jct. with Sleeping Beauty Trail, 2.2 mi.; to Bumps Pond, 3.1 mi.; to N end of Sleeping Beauty Trail, 3.3 mi.; to Fishbrook Pond, 4.2 mi.; to jct. with Fishbrook Pond from Lake George Trail (95) and Lapland Pond Trail (98), 4.6 mi. (7.4 km). Elevation of Hogtown trailhead, 1309 ft. (399 m); pass W of Sleeping Beauty, 2100 ft. (640 m); Bumps Pond, approx. 2020 ft. (616 m); Fishbrook Pond, 1836 ft. (560 m).

(82A) W Fishbrook Pond Trail   Map: E-8

From the jct. at the point on Fishbrook Pond (0.0 mi.), take the L trail past the privy. At 0.1 mi. the trail crosses an inlet stream and at 0.5 mi. it reaches another inlet. At 0.7 mi. the trail ends at the jct. with the Fishbrook Pond from Lake George Trail (95). From here it's possible to make a loop down to Lake George and back to Dacy Clearing, or to work out any number of other possibilities. Turning R (E), it's 0.2 mi. to the lean-to, and 0.4 mi. to the intersection with the E side trail (A).

Distance: From jct. at point on S side of Fishbrook Pond to jct. with trail 95, 0.7 mi. (1.1 km).

(83) Sleeping Beauty   Map: E-8

With all the switchbacks on the trail to the summit, this is a moderate walk to a great destination. To return, either use the ascent route, or continue N to Bumps Pond and return via trail 82 along Bumps Pond to the Hogtown trailhead.

Trailhead: *The beginning of this trail is reached via Fishbrook Pond Trail (82) from the Hogtown trailhead. The Sleeping Beauty Trail cuts off to the R (S) 2.2 mi. N of the Hogtown trail register on trail 82. This trail is marked with yellow markers.*

From the trail jct. (0.0 mi.), after crossing a wet area on logs the trail climbs along the shoulder of a hill at 0.2 mi. At 0.4 it passes a large rock cliff on the L and then soon switchbacks to the R. After another switchback, the trail becomes steeper and more eroded at 0.7 mi. It soon levels off for a short distance and then makes a R turn around a red pine on solid rock.

There is soon a view through the trees, and shortly after at 1.1 mi. the trail reaches a Y jct. The trail R leads to Bumps Pond. The L turn leads to the summit at 1.2 mi. From the top are fine views of Lake George and the SE Adirondacks. A narrow trail follows another ledge to just below the summit for an even broader expanse of view. Visible are Buck Mt. to the S, Shelving Rock Mt. to the W and the Tongue Mt. area to the NW.

To continue on to Bumps Pond, from the Y intersection (1.1 mi.) head N on the moderately-used trail. At 1.4 mi. the trail enters a hemlock grove and soon dips into a wet hollow. After winding uphill through some birches and hemlocks, the trail begins its descent at 1.6 mi. At 2.1 mi. the trail crosses the outlet of Bumps Pond and climbs up a short hill to the T intersection with the Hogtown to Fishbrook Pond Trail (82). From here it's 3.3 mi. S on trail 82 to the Hogtown trailhead, making a total loop length from the Hogtown trailhead of 7.8 mi., including the 0.1 walk to the summit.

Distances: *From S jct. with Hogtown/Fishbrook Trail (82) (0 mi.) to Y jct. near* summit, 1.1 mi.; to summit, 1.2 mi. (1.9 km); via Y jct. to Bumps Pond, 2.1 mi. (3.4 km). From Hogtown trailhead register (0 mi.) to summit of Sleeping Beauty, 3.4 mi. (5.4 km). Elevation at register, 1309 ft. (399 m); at S trailhead jct., approx. 1700 ft (518 m); Sleeping Beauty summit, 2347 ft. (715 m).

(84) Old Farm Road Map: E-8

This is a pleasant old carriage path that is currently used by both horses and hikers. Motorized vehicles are prohibited, except for snowmobiles in the winter. This old road flows gracefully downhill through a bouldery woods with many beech and hemlocks. While it has no real destination, it's a great connector trail for a number of loop possibilities.

Trailhead: There is access to this trail from two points. The E access (84A) is 0.5 mi. N of the Hogtown trailhead on trail 82. The W access (84B) is from the Shelving Rock Rd. 1.25 mi. W from the Hogtown trailhead (see trail 82). There are yellow horse trail markers on 84A and 84B, then blue on the main leg.

(84A) E Old Farm Road Leg Map: E-8

From the jct. with the Hogtown-Fishbrook Pond Trail (82), 0.0 mi., the trail crosses an old stone culvert at 0.2 mi. The path is built up with stonework along the hillside and for almost a half mile travels almost level through the woods. Ground cedar, princess pine, ferns, and beech saplings grow in this pretty woods.

The road rises and falls, generally meandering downhill. At 0.7 mi. it reaches the jct. with the other access leg (84B), coming from the L.

(84B) W Old Farm Road Leg Map: E-8

From the barrier at Shelving Rock Rd. (0.0 mi.), this trail follows another old carriage path. It starts heading uphill, passing by some sizable oaks, a result of the moderating effect of Lake George on the local microclimate. Much rock work was done to stabilize this road many years ago. The trail continues at a moderate grade uphill and passes through a grassy clearing with huge maples and a rock pile on the L, remnants of farming days. The intersection with 84A is reached at 0.6 mi.

From the intersection of 84A and 84B at 0.0 mi., the trail heads in a northerly direction over rolling terrain. As the trail straightens out, look to the R for an old stone wall about 100 ft. in the woods. The trail continues straight for a while through pines and past a couple of old clearings. Soon the trail follows around an S-curve in a mixed hardwoods forest and then continues on a long gradual straightaway.

At 0.7 mi. the trail reaches the intersection with the Shortway Trail (85). To the L it's 1.9 mi. to Shelving Rock Rd., and to the R it's 0.5 mi. to Dacy Clearing.

Continue straight ahead across the intersection, soon going downhill and crossing a brook. The trail curves uphill to the L along the hill, then turns R again after cresting the hill. At 1.1 mi. the trail crosses a small stream where there are several huge old hemlocks. In a short distance, the trail ends at a jct. with the Longway Trail (86) at 1.2 mi. At this point it's 1.0 mi. R to Dacy Clearing, and 1.2 mi. L to the Shelving Rock Mt. trailhead.

Distances: 84A: *From jct. with Hogtown/Fishbrook Pond Trail (0 mi.) to jct. with 84B, 0.7 mi. (1.1 km).* **84B:** *From Shelving Rock Rd. (0 mi.) to jct. with 84A, 0.6 mi. (1 km). From jct. of 84A and 85B (0 mi.) to Shortway Trail (85), 0.7 mi. (1.1 km); to Longway Trail (86), 1.2 mi. (1.9 km). There is minimal elevation change except on trail 84B, which ascends almost 400 ft. (122 m) to jct. with 84A.*

(85) Shortway Trail

Trailhead: This old road starts from the first small clearing of the old Dacy farm (1.4 mi. from the Hogtown trailhead on trail 82). Raspberries are filling in the clearing. It is quite probable this was a farm-to-market road down to boats at the lakeshore. It proceeds to the Shelving Rock Mt. trailhead, 3.0 mi. W on Shelving Rock Rd. from the Hogtown trailhead, which is a good place to spot a car for a return trip to Hogtown trailhead or Dacy Clearing. The choices for backpacking and skiing are extensive.

A trail sign (with no mileage mentioned) and yellow horse trail marker point to the L. Another trail sign above it points back to the Hogtown trailhead on Shelving Rock Rd. and onwards to Dacy Clearing, accompanied by a red horse trail marker.

Walk L at the sign, downhill through the clearing into the wood. You are in for a treat.

At 0.2 mi. the road reaches a lovely glen with a stream on the R and a stone fire circle on the L. Ahead is a barrier with a stop sign. Just beyond it is a bridge over the stream. This is an eastern branch of Shelving Rock Brook below the S slope of Sleeping Beauty Mt.

The road reaches a second bridge as the stream flows L to R, weaving its way downhill. At 0.3 mi. the road crosses a third bridge. Hobblebush flowers float gracefully over the stream in late May. Christmas fern and ostrich fern grow beneath a canopy of white birches, hemlock, beech, maple and hophornbeam.

At 0.5 mi. the road reaches an intersection with the Old Farm Rd. (trail 84). The trail L goes S, then splits W to Shelving Rock Rd. or E to Dacy Clearing Rd. A sign on the R points back the way you came to "Dacy Clearing Short Way." Across a small culvert, a trail coming in on the R has a sign "Dacy Clearing Long Way." Continue downhill, straight ahead.

The grade becomes steeper. At 0.7 mi. the road enters a hemlock glade. At 0.8 mi. it goes along a broad ridge with a stream gurgling at the bottom of the hill to the R. At 0.9 mi. it descends more steeply. As it bends L the stream comes into full view to the R below.

The road cuts across a hillside and then winds around the contour downhill to a sturdy wooden bridge with railings. A stream comes downhill from the L over a 50-ft. expanse of moss-covered solid rock.

Fringed polygala (gaywings) flower in bright pink profusion along here in late May. The small, tubular, tropical-looking flowers with dark green glossy leaves are an especially welcome sign after the long winter. Fringed polygala is on the state list of protected plants.

At 1.1 mi. a lovely gorge with an exquisite rocky chasm below is a great picnic and wading spot (after mosquito season). Just upstream 60 ft. is a series of pleasant cascades.

At 1.3 mi. the road crosses a large wooden bridge. There is a jct. on the L at 1.4 mi. with the Big Bridges Trail (89). The road to the Shelving Rock Mt. trailhead continues straight ahead.

At 1.6 mi. a trail to the R bears a sign for Mt. Erebus and Shelving Rock Mt. (trail 86). This route also leads back (E) to the large clearing at Dacy Clearing.

The road crosses another bridge, on the level, then ascends among mature hardwoods and white pines. More fringed polygala blooms in late May at 1.7 mi., near a large birch cut up along the road. One giant log is propped on two shorter ones to make a perfect bench for lunch, contemplation, nature study or rest.

At 1.8 mi. a sign at an intersection says "Dacy Clearing 2.0 mi." Continue straight. In 100 ft. is another jct. with a road on the R that continues N over Mt. Erebus (trail 88) and a narrower trail W up Shelving Rock Mt. (trail 88A).

At 1.85 mi. a small seasonal stream crosses the road. There is a water pipe on the L. At 2.0 mi. there is a culvert under the road. Now the road is a carpet of golden pine needles with brown pine cones. A stream to the L 4 ft. below the road is another tributary of

Shelving Rock Brook.

At 2.3 mi. at a jct. with the Shelving Rock Mt. Trail (90) a sign says Dacey Clearing 2.3 mi. (Dacy seems to be spelled with or without an "e" on various signs), Shelving Rock Mt. 1.5 mi., Black Mt. Point 4.6 mi., Shelving Rock Road .25 mi. Continue straight ahead. At 2.4 mi. the old road meets Shelving Rock Rd.

Distances: *Small clearing at Dacy Clearing to first intersection with trail 84, 0.5 mi.; to second intersection with trail 89, 1.4 mi.; to intersection with Longway Trail (86), 1.6 mi.; to jct. with trail N (trail 88) over Erebus Mt. and Shelving Rock Mt., 1.8 mi.; to jct. with trail up Shelving Rock Mt. (90), 2.3 mi.; to Shelving Rock Rd., 2.4 mi. (4.0 km). Elevation at Dacy Clearing, 1300 ft. (400 m); at Shelving Rock Rd., 460 ft. (11.7 m).*

(86) Longway Trail   Map: E-8

This is another beautiful "hidden" walk in the Shelving Rock area. Since this route is popular with horseback riders there are places (steep and wet) where horses' hooves have created considerable erosion and quagmires. Nonetheless, it is rather enjoyable to see a group of horseback riders coming through the woods.

Trailhead: *On the NW side of the large clearing at Dacy Clearing a sign, "Stop—barrier ahead," and a horse trail sign direct you to the start of an old road. This is 1.6 mi. from the Hogtown trailhead (trail 82). Two privies are on the L. There is a stop sign on a steel barrier across the entrance to the road, barring vehicles.*

The trail heads NW, gently descending through the woods along a rock-strewn hill on the R. There are light blue horse trail markers. The trail, often filled with rocks, undulates through mixed hardwoods and crosses several very small brooks which feed into Shelving Rock Brook.

At 0.5 mi. a rocky cliff appears to the R, on the S side of Sleeping Beauty Mt. Christmas fern, maidenhair fern, round-leaved hepatica, hobble bush, goldenrod, Dutchman's breeches, white aster, meadow rue and violets all combine to make this a wildflower lover's heaven for three seasons of the year.

The trail continues W underneath the sheer cliffs of Sleeping Beauty to the N. Polypody ferns look like a toupee on top of a huge boulder.

At 0.9 mi. the sky opens up above a small beaver meadow, a haven for birds. The trail crosses a small outlet stream on rocks placed there, then meanders above the little stream gurgling below. In mid-October the forest floor is a carpet of golden, brown and red maple and beech leaves.

At 1.0 mi., at a jct. with the Old Farm Rd. (trail 84), turn R onto a yellow-marked horse trail continuing W to Shelving Rock.

Now the trail goes more steeply downhill. Horses' hooves have churned it into a muddy mire. After another small stream crossing, the trail goes uphill on more solid ground. Mature beeches have fallen to the ground, allowing hundreds of beech saplings to start the race for life and light.

The trail now descends a gentle pitch above a tiny feeder stream for Shelving Rock Brook. Then it crosses the boulder-filled brook on a wooden bridge on top of an old, ambitiously constructed set of stone cribwork. Huge ash trees tower over this glen. The lovely rocky stream winds downhill on the L, now guarded by hemlocks, maple and ash. Yellow horse trail markers direct hikers to a short re-route closer to the stream to avoid a mire. Hikers may ignore the detours marked with surveyor's tape, but horseback riders will want to follow them.

Soon the trail heads down again on a gentle diagonal with a hill to the L. There is a side route marked with yellow horse trail markers and red surveyor's tape. The detour goes over and down a hill to intersect at 1.8 mi. with an old road marked with blue horse trail markers. Three small logs have been placed across the road L.

The Longway Spur Trail (86A) is at R.

A lovely brook heads downhill to the L. This is the northernmost branch of Shelving Rock Brook, coming off Erebus Mt. Two enormous maples have fallen across the old road and stream about 0.1 mi. downstream from this spot. With several attractive cascades here, the intersection is a good spot for a rest and picnic by the brook.

Following on the original trail, one must scramble over the two large fallen trees. The rushing stream gathers strength and flows noisily through a lovely little gorge down to the R, providing another nice spot to explore and rest.

The old trail winds through a dark and beautiful hemlock glen with Shelving Rock Brook merrily flowing down at a steeper angle on the R. The trail and stream flirt with each other, then finally become partners as they pass through a narrow draw. The trail is almost level, thanks to considerable rock work on the R.

The trail crosses a small feeder stream on rocks 300 ft. before the intersection with Shortway Rd. (trail 85) from Dacy Clearing and Shelving Rock Mt. trailhead at 2.5 mi.

Distances: *Dacy Clearing to intersection with Old Farm Rd., 1.0 mi.; to intersection with spur trail to Erebus Mt. Trail, 1.8 mi.; to intersection with Shortway Rd., 2.5 mi. (4.1 km).*

(86A) Longway Spur   Map: E-8

A spur trail R 0.2 mi. to Erebus Mt. Trail (88) goes upstream 100 ft., then crosses the stream on rocks just above a picturesque small waterfall. It continues upstream with blue horse trail markers and the stream on the R. Then it winds around uphill to an intersection with a beautiful old road to Erebus Mt. R (trail 88), marked with red horse trail markers.

(87) Bumps Pond Spur

Map: E-8

Trailhead: The S end connects with the Hogtown trailhead to Fishbrook Pond Trail (82) 3.2 mi. from the Hogtown trailhead. The N end intersects the Erebus Mt. Trail (88) 2.1 mi. from the Shortway Trail (85), and 1.3 mi. from the Lake George to Fishbrook Pond Trail (95).

The trail begins on the W shore of Bumps Pond. Heading through the grasses into the woods, it begins a very gradual climb, passing by an old spring in a short distance. At 0.2 mi. the trail begins to descend along the top of a wooded ridge and then soon reaches a sharp switchback to the R and continues on a moderately steep descent. At 0.4 mi. there is a sharp L switchback, soon followed by another switchback to the R.

The descent moderates and soon levels off to a pleasant walk as the trail winds through the forest. Soon after crossing a stream on a plank bridge, it reaches the jct. with the Erebus Mt. Trail (88) at 0.9 mi.

Distance: Bumps Pond to Erebus Mt. Trail, 0.9 mi. (1.4 km).

(88) Erebus Mt. Trail

Map: E-8

This trail runs in a NE direction centrally across the Shelving Rock trail system and helps connect routes from both sides of the region. In particular, it connects with the Ridge Trail (92) in two spots, more easily linking the shoreline of the Lake George area with the interior trail system. The trail itself is a pretty hike, following the brook that drains the S side of Erebus Mt. (pronounced locally "Air-a-bus" and meaning "dark, unfriendly place close to Hell"). It shows little signs of use, by horses or by people, especially near its summit. While the trail doesn't lead directly to the top of Erebus Mt., those who enjoy a good bushwhack challenge might enjoy exploring the woods above the cliffs near the top of the mountain. When hiking this trail it is important to remember that this is designated as a horse trail and that some wet and muddy areas are not bridged or maintained in the same way a hiking trail is.

Trailhead: *The S end links with the Shortway Trail (85) 0.6 mi. E of the Shelving Rock Mt. trailhead (see trail 85) along Shelving Rock Rd. The N end intersects with the Fishbrook Pond from Lake George Trail (95), 1.6 mi. from the Lakeside Trail (93) and 1.2 mi. from the intersection of trails 82 and 98 at the NE corner of Fishbrook Pond. This trail has red horse trail markers.*

The trail bears L from the Shortway Trail (85) and heads gradually uphill. Almost immediately is the jct. with the First Ridge Spur Trail (88A) on the L.

The Erebus Mt. Trail continues on a constant gradual grade uphill for 0.25 mi. where it levels off briefly, then begins climbing again. The forest along most of this trail is a nice mix of maturing mixed hardwoods and conifers. At 0.4 mi. the trail levels off once again and soon reaches the jct. on the R with the Longway Spur Trail (86A) at 0.6 mi.

The trail soon crosses a streambed (which may be dry), then at 0.7 mi. crosses a stream on a wooden plank bridge. The trail continues to climb at a gradual to moderate grade along the L bank of a pleasant stream that bubbles its way along over rocks and then rests in small pools. Before long, another jct. is reached on the L at 1.3 mi. This is the Second Ridge Spur Trail (88B).

From the jct. the Erebus Mt. Trail soons climbs moderately steeply up around a beautiful series of cascades on the R. After a brief respite, the trail climbs steadily once again along a series of rock ledges on the L, with another set of cascades off to the R. This area has a primeval feel to it. The trail then moderates briefly, crosses a plank bridge over a stream (may be dry), and then at 1.5 mi. crosses over the main stream on some extensive rockwork.

The trail now continues up the R bank of the stream at a gradual grade uphill, soon reaching another plank bridge at 1.7 mi. that recrosses the stream by a rocky and mossy cascade. After the bridge the trail climbs steeply and then continues up on mostly gradual to moderate grades. The trail levels off after passing through some blowdown, and reaches the jct. with the Bumps Pond Spur Trail (87) at 2.1 mi. Bear L here for the Erebus Mt. Trail.

The trail now is mostly level, wandering in and out of a streambed (mostly dry except after a rain) and through some wet and muddy areas. At 2.4 mi. the trail passes by a large rock face on the R and then follows along at the base of these cliffs for a while. It may be possible to catch a glimpse of the upper reaches of these cliffs through some openings in the leaves on the trees. The trail soon begins another gradual to moderate ascent, and at 2.7 mi. reaches a plateau which is the highest point on this trail.

The trail drops and then climbs briefly again before its moderately steep descent over a rocky trail to a jct. with the Fishbrook Pond from Lake George Trail (95) at 3.4 mi.

Trail in winter: *This trail is fine for skiing up to its jct. with spur trail 88B. From there the steeper sections are more suited to snowshoeing, particularly the descent from the top of the trail down to the jct. with trail 95.*

Distances: *Shortway Trail to jct. with trail 86A, 0.6 mi.; to jct. with trail 88B, 1.3 mi.; to jct. with trail 87, 2.1 mi.; to N end and jct. with trail 95, 3.4 mi. (5.4 km). Ascent from Shortway Trail to highest point, approx. 1600 ft. (488 m).*

(88A) First Ridge Spur   Map: D-8

This is the first connecting spur from the Erebus Mt. Trail to the Ridge Trail (92). It bears L about 100 ft. after the Erebus Mt. Trail leaves the Shortway Trail (85). This trail has yellow horse trail markers and orange snowmobile markers. The trail heads across a wet area, then soon ascends along a rocky ledge. It levels off at 0.2 mi., and comes to a wetland at 0.3 mi. It swings around the perimeter of the wetland, then at 0.5 mi. heads W up a moderately steep ascent through a hemlock forest. The trail becomes more gradual for a short distance, then begins a moderate ascent up through a rocky gully with ledges on both sides. At the top of the gully it begins to level, reaching the jct. with the Ridge Trail (92) at 0.7 mi.

Distance: Erebus Mt. Trail to jct. with trail 92, 0.7 mi. (1.1 km). Ascent, approx. 300 ft. (91 m).

(88B) Second Ridge Spur   Map: E-8

Leaving the Erebus Mt. Trail (0.0 mi.), the trail follows blue horse trail markers. The trail first heads W through a predominantly hemlock forest. Soon it swings to the R, then winds back and forth, climbing on gradual to moderate grades. After crossing a wet area, it comes to the jct. with the Ridge Trail (92) at 0.3 mi.

Distance: Erebus Mt. Trail to jct. with trail 92, 0.3 mi. (0.5 km). Ascent, approx. 200 ft. (61 m).

(89) Big Bridges Trail   Map: D-8

Trailhead: This route starts 2.6 mi. W of the Hogtown trailhead parking area off Shelving Rock Rd., just 0.1 mi. W of the bridge over Shelving Rock Brook (see trail 79). This old road is popular with horseback riders, snowmobilers and skiers as well as hikers. It is marked with blue horse trail markers after a barrier with a stop sign.

There is a V-shape entrance to this road on the N side of Shelving

Rock Rd., across from an informal camping area. A sign points E along Shelving Rock Rd. to Hogtown trailhead parking area and W along the road to Shelving Rock Mt. trailhead; however, there may not be a sign here for the destination of this road heading N into the woods. It connects to Shortway Trail to Dacy Clearing (85), and to Longway Trail (86).

The road goes gently uphill, then levels under tall hemlock, ash, maple, white pine and beech. Chanterelle mushrooms may be found here in fall.

In 0.3 mi., after an almost level walk, the road crosses Shelving Rock Brook on a large new wooden bridge under gigantic pines, then a smaller bridge 30 ft. beyond. Now the road curves uphill above the beautiful brook below a towering cliff. Considerable rock work on the L holds the road into the hill above the brook. Another tributary cascades down the cliff before joining the brook.

The road goes more steeply uphill, continuing to follow the brook. The stream here tumbles down through a rocky ravine.

At 0.8 mi. the road crosses a wooden bridge with railing on top of a spectacular old hand-built stone abutment. This is a good place to rest and explore.

At 0.9 mi. the Big Bridges Trail meets Shortway Trail (85) between Dacy Clearing and the trailhead for Shelving Rock Mt. To the R (E) it is 1.4 mi. on Shortway Trail to the small clearing at Dacy Clearing. To the L it is 1.0 mi. to Shelving Rock Rd.

Distances: Shelving Rock Rd. to wooden bridge over Shelving Rock Brook, 0.3 mi.; to intersection with Shortway Trail, 0.9 mi. (1.5 km).

(90) Shelving Rock Mt. from Shortway Trail to Lakeside Trail   Map: D-8

Shelving Rock Mt. is a nice walk with partially obstructed views from the top. There also are some nice views along the way.

Trailhead: Drive 2.6 mi. W along Shelving Rock Rd. from the Hogtown trailhead (see trail 82). Park at the trailhead on the R for Shelving Rock Mt. This is also the trailhead for the Shortway Trail (85). There's a space to park a few cars just off the road. Please note Shelving Rock Rd. is a narrow, winding dirt road. The sides of the road can be soft (especially in spring and early summer), so use care when approaching other vehicles. The trail has blue horse trail markers and orange snowmobile markers.

From the parking lot head uphill following the Shortway Trail (85) past the steel gate. The trail follows the old road uphill above the brook on the R, reaching a jct. at 0.2 mi. on the L. Turn L here (0 mi.) for the start of the Shelving Rock Mt. Trail. The beginning of the trail is almost level under huge white pines for the first 0.3 mi.

The trail soon enters a hemlock glade where stonework holds the roadbed. After a couple of switchbacks, the trail moderates. The trail is now heading in a more N direction. At 0.4 mi. the trail switchbacks L (W). A long steep rocky slope is up to the R with several walled switchbacks ahead. The trail climbs uphill over the switchbacks that get increasingly steeper, reaching the top of them at 0.7 mi.

Now the trail rolls up and down a bit and then heads downhill to a jct. at 0.9 mi (1.1 mi. from the Shelving Rock Mt. trailhead). The R fork (trail 91) heads N to the Lakeside Trail (93) and also leads to the Ridge Trail (92). Continue straight (W) to Shelving Rock summit, now with yellow markers. The trail rises at an easy grade under hemlocks, turning and heading S high above Lake George. At 1.1 mi. the trail makes a switchback to the L, and soon reaches an overlook at 1.3 mi. W to Lake George and Tongue Mt.

At 1.5 mi. (1.7 mi. from the trailhead at Shelving Rock Rd.) the trail reaches the summit that's now overgrown with oak and sumac. S along a narrow trail there's an overlook above the young trees in a grassy clearing. Sleeping Beauty Mt. is to the E, Buck Mt. to the S, and some of the S end of Lake George may be visible. The Knapps had a pavilion on the summit of Shelving Rock Mt. for afternoon tea parties and evening dances.

Distances: Shortway Trail to jct. with trail 91, 0.6 mi.; to summit, 1.5 mi. (2.4 km). Summit elevation, 1130 ft. (344 m). Ascent, approx. 650 ft. (198 m).

(91) Lakeside to Shelving Rock Mt. Trail

Map: D-8

Trailhead: The trail from the top of Shelving Rock Mt. to the Lakeside Trail (93) begins on the Shortway Trail (85) 0.6 mi. from the summit. This jct. is 0.9 mi. from the Shortway Trail trailhead. This is a short, steep descent to the Lake George shoreline. At this writing (April 1994) there is no public access through the Knapp Estate at the S end of the Lakeside Trail, so the only return to Shelving Rock Rd. is by one of the return trails over the ridge of Erebus Mt. and Shelving Rock Mt. Continuing down to the Lakeside Trail gives a lot of flexibility in choosing some nice loops to hike. This trail has red markers.

Heading N from the jct. with trail 90 (0.0 mi.), the trail descends slightly, reaching the closed off jct. on the L in about 200 ft. with a closed trail that leads to private land. The trail soon switchbacks up the ridge to the R, then heads E across the ridge. It soon turns L at a small knoll, then drops into a small col and reaches a jct. on the R at 0.3 mi. with the Ridge Trail (92). The trail bears L through a notch and soon begins a steep descent. After a switchback, the trail descends steeply, moderates a bit, then gets steep again.

At 0.8 mi. the trail descends along a ravine with huge rock walls covered with polypody ferns. Still heading steeply downhill, the trail reaches the Lakeside Trail (93) at 1.0 mi. From this jct., a L turn leads to private land in 0.6 mi. A R turn heads N to Red Rock Bay and Black Mt. Point.

Trail in winter: *The upper parts of this trail are steep for skiing, particularly the descent to Lake George. They would be fine for snowshoeing, but be sure to carry instep crampons for icy conditions.*

Distances: *Shelving Rock Mt. Trail to Lakeside Trail, 1.0 mi. (1.6 km). Summit elevation, 1130 ft. (344 m). Ascent from Lake George to the summit, 780 ft. (238 m).*

(92) Ridge Trail
Map: D-8

This route is a horse trail that follows the ridge line from Shelving Rock Mt. to the W flanks of Erebus Mt., before dropping down to the shoreline of Lake George. The rugged trail traverses mostly through deep, dense hemlock forests, but there are open hardwoods on some of the rocky ledges. The views from the couple of vistas are expansive and unique. The trail appears to be little used, by horses or people. The trail is maintained as a horse trail, so there are no bridges over wet areas or rock work to stabilize some of the loose areas.

A nice route is to head up Shelving Rock Mt. (trail 90), over the Ridge Trail to the Lakeside Trail (93), then S to the Red Rock Bay Trail (94), and return via the Ridge Trail and the First Ridge Spur Trail (88A) and back to the trailhead via the Shortway Trail (85). This sounds complicated, but once on the trails it comes together easily; see the map that accompanies this book. Total elevation gain is about 2300 ft.; distance is about 10 mi. over some very scenic country.

Trailhead: *Access from the Shelving Rock Rd. trailhead (see trail 90) is via the Shortway Trail (85), the Shelving Rock Mt. Trail (90) and the Lakeside* *to Shelving Rock Mt. Trail (91). It is 1.4 mi. from the trailhead on Shelving Rock Rd. to the SW start of the trail. This access is marked with blue horse trail markers and orange snowmobile disks. N access is from the Lakeside Trail (93), 1.2 mi. S of Black Mt. Point, and 2.2 mi. N of the jct. of the Shelving Rock Mt. Trail (91) with the Lakeside Trail. This access is marked with yellow horse trail markers.*

From the jct. at the small col with the red-marked Shelving Rock Mt. Trail (91) (0.0 mi.), the blue-marked horse trail heads E and switchbacks up the small ridge. Once on the ridge line, there is a rocky outcrop to the L from which there are some views of Northwest Bay and the Tongue Mt. area, partially obstructed by treetops.

The trail continues along the ridge, then soon takes a R turn to the ridge top. It bears L along the flat, wooded ridge top, then heads more N again. At 0.3 mi. the trail crosses the first of three wet spots in a nice hemlock forest. The trail here, as in much of the way along the top, is in a deep forest. If not for the wind blowing across the ridge it would be easy to imagine the trail was following a secluded ravine.

At 0.5 mi. the trail passes to the N of a rock shelf, then soon turns L, and switchbacks down into a small col, reaching a jct. at 0.8 mi. with a connector trail of the Erebus Mt. Trail (88A) to the R. It's 1.2 mi. back to the Shelving Rock Rd. trailhead via this connector and the Shortway Trail (85). Continuing straight ahead (NE), the main trail climbs and then switchbacks up the ridge, then follows the ridge for a while. At 1.0 mi. the trail makes a sharp switchback R, heading SW along the side of the ridge.

It soon swings around S and then E, and comes to some open hardwoods on top of a small cliff. First there's a view through the trees, then at 1.2 mi. the trail comes to an open ledge just off the trail that's covered with lichens, caribou moss, and grasses. There are great views from the ledge that overlooks the Shelving Rock Brook basin. To the E is Sleeping Beauty Mt., to the S is Buck Mt.,

SW Lake George and Shelving Rock Mt.; and NW is the Tongue Mt. area. Crane Mt. is in the distance beyond other mountains surrounding Lake George. Ravens often frequent this spot, floating on the thermals not far from the cliff.

The trail heads up over ledges with more vistas, then heads N back into the woods. The trail is mostly level, passing a couple of wet spots, and wanders up and down through the hemlock forest. At 1.7 mi., a jct. with the Red Rock Bay Trail (94) is reached in a wet area. There's a sign pointing L for the lakeshore, 0.8 mi. ADK's measurement showed it to be 1.36 mi. instead.

Heading straight ahead (N), the main trail soon swings R (E) and then S. It winds around uphill to the ridge top heading NE, reaching a wooded rocky ridge at 2.0 mi. After one has walked in the hemlocks for so long, the open hardwoods here are like a breath of fresh air.

After following the ridge a short distance, the trail circles around a wet area, climbs over the ridge top and descends along the SE side of the ridge. At 2.2 mi. is the jct. with the Second Ridge Spur Trail to the Erebus Mt. Trail (88B). The snowmobile trail cuts to the R here, along with the blue-marked horse trail.

Head L for the Ridge Trail and up the rocky section that leads into the small ravine, now following yellow horse trail markers. At the head of the ravine is a sign for the trail to make a sharp L. From here the trail is mostly downhill to the lake along the NW side of the ridge. The trail descends gradually at first, then at 2.5 mi. begins a moderately steep descent with The Narrows of Lake George visible through the trees on the L.

At 2.75 mi. the trail goes down around a rocky ledge where there's a sign for a vista to the L. A side trail leads to a small cliff in about 250 ft., with superb views of The Narrows with all the islands, the Bolton Landing area, Shelving Rock Mt. and this ridge, Tongue Mt., and numerous mountains in the distance. The trail rolls up and down a bit, then continues its descent on gradual to moderately steep grades, with a couple of steep sections.

Soon the trail follows and crosses a couple of small streams (may be dry in late summer). At 3.6 mi. the trail crosses a larger stream, levels off through the evergreens for a short distance, and then swings L down around a rocky outcrop. There's a sign at 3.75 mi. with an arrow pointing to the R. Before long the trail comes into a section of open hardwoods, with a few huge old oak trees towering overhead.

The lake is visible through the trees, and the trail descends to meet up with the Lakeside Trail (93) at 3.9 mi. Just beyond to the L there's a tent platform and campsite (reservations required) on a small rocky point. It's a great place to enjoy the panorama up and down Lake George.

Trail in winter: Not recommended as a ski trail. It makes a great snowshoe trail. With the leaves off the trees there are some better views, but not many. Instep crampons should be taken along for possible icy sections.

Distances: Shelving Rock Mt. Trail (0.0 mi.) to jct. with First Ridge Spur Trail, 0.8 mi.; to next jct. with Red Rock Bay Trail, 1.7 mi.; to jct. with Second Ridge Spur Trail, 2.2 mi.; to Lakeside Trail, 3.9 mi. (6.2 km). Highest elevation along the trail, approx. 1550 ft. (472 m); elevation at jct. with Shelving Rock Mt. Trail, approx. 700 ft. (213 m); Lake George elevation, 320 ft. (98 m).

(93) Lakeside Trail to Black Mt. Point

Map: D-8

At one time, the Knapp Estate consisted of 9500 acres and 75 miles of roads and trails. The people who built these roads and trails left a wonderful legacy for hiking. To learn more history of this area, read *Sweet Peas and a White Bridge* by Elsa Steinbeck (North Country Books, 1974), filled with anecdotes about the summer hotel visitors and staff, local characters and customs. Also of interest is *From Then Til Now* by Fred Stiles (Washington County Historical Society, 1978). The original estate house on a lower slope of Shelving Rock Mt. burned in 1917. Today the family owns about 75 acres with several camps on Pearl Point. Be sure to respect the boundaries of their land. The state owns the remainder of the land, including Black Mt., Erebus Mt., Shelving Rock Mt., Sleeping Beauty Mt. and seven ponds (all with trail access and described in this section). Hiking is possible on most of the network of roads that remains.

At this writing (1994), there is no public access through the Knapp Estate. Access to the S end of this trail is via the Shelving Rock Mt. Trail (90). It is also accessible by boat at one of 20 campsites along Lake George or two picnic areas, all of which have docks. Seven other trails also connect to this road, providing options for hikes of various lengths: from Shelving Rock Mt. via trails 90 and 91, two from Erebus Mt. (trails 92 and 94), from Fishbrook Pond (trail 95), and from the Pike Brook Rd. trailhead (trails 96 and 97).

Camping at one of the state campsites along the lake requires reservations, and there's a nightly fee. In winter there is good skiing along the road and also on the lake. Shelving Rock Rd. is plowed in winter as far as the gate to the Knapp Estate.

From the private land boundary at the S end of the trail (0.0 mi.), the trail heads NE, following the shoreline. At 0.1 mi. there is a point on the L. At 0.2 mi. there is a spring by the shore on the L with a dock for boaters to obtain spring water. At 0.4 mi. the road is on a bluff by a point looking down into a lovely cove. At 0.6 mi. a trail on the R leads steeply up to an intersection with the road up Shelving Rock Mt. (trail 91). Watch Island is offshore on the L. Red trail markers are infrequent, but that is no problem since the roadway is easy to follow.

Now the road goes uphill, levels off and then goes downhill. At 1.0 mi. it passes a lovely low point that would be a good picnic spot. Now the road is level again, passing a point that forms the S boundary of Red Rock Bay. The road descends again a short distance, coming almost level with the bay.

The road reaches Commission Point at 1.2 mi., with hemlocks, a stone picnic pavilion, grills and picnic tables spread along the S shore with six docks on the N shore. Overnight mooring from dusk to 9 a.m. has a fee (although boats may dock here overnight only if the campsites are full). Dogs are prohibited. There is a view S to Shelving Rock Mt., Pearl Point and several islands, and directly W to Fork Island and Tongue Mt. (see above). In spring and fall this is a peaceful spot with the lake empty of motorboats and the tourists gone.

The road goes uphill from Red Rock Bay, rolls up and down, then at 1.5 mi. levels out by the lake. To the L there is a dock on the N side of a point. This is the first of 20 state campsites along this road. A stream goes through a culvert under the road. To the R is a dock on the S side of a point.

At 1.6 mi. the road passes a springhouse in the woods to the R. A pipe from the springhouse goes under the road, then ends in mid-air, giving a source of water. Soon the road arrives above the second dock. There are two picnic tables, two grills, a stone fireplace and two privies here. At 1.7 mi. there is another dock with several picnic tables, grills, fireplace and four privies, then two more docks.

At 1.8 mi. the road bends L. The Red Rock Bay Trail with yellow horse trail markers (trail 94) goes uphill to the R to the Ridge Trail (92). Red horse trail markers indicate a little-used trail to the R. Keep on the road, which still bends L.

The road passes a R turn, then arrives at a T jct. It bears R onto a rocky bluff with a rope on a cable between two white pines above the water of Paradise Bay at 1.9 mi. There might be a dozen tame mallard ducks eager for a handout. The water has a green-blue tint here.

At 2.0 mi. the road meets another T jct. to complete a short loop. Turning L, at 2.1 mi. the road passes an abandoned road on the R. At 2.3 mi. the road arrives at the lake again, after an inland walk, at a tent platform, picnic table, fireplace, dock and privy. At 2.4 mi. there is a similar campsite, also with tent platform. After a third campsite, the road goes gently uphill, passing another campsite almost out of sight on a point at 2.5 mi. At 2.6 mi. the road passes another tent platform, another campsite without a platform, a dock in a cove within 50 ft. of the road, then another tent platform campsite. At 2.7 mi. the Ridge Trail (92) goes R uphill almost directly opposite a path lined with stones to a point with a tent platform campsite. (The trail leading uphill goes up the W side of Erebus Mt. and along a ridge to Shelving Rock Mt. These trails seem too steep and rocky for horses.) At 2.8 mi. there are two more campsites on another point, with another campsite a short way beyond.

At 3.1 mi. another trail on the R leads to Fishbrook Pond (trail 95). There is another campsite on the R, and at 3.2 mi. a campsite on the lake, followed by two more campsites.

At 3.3 mi. the road crosses a rock streambed (sometimes dry) and arrives at Black Mt. Point with a stone picnic shelter, many picnic tables and privies in a grassy area. At 3.4 mi. there is another picnic area on a more northern point. On the N side are five docks. The Lakeside Trail ends at 3.5 mi. where the Black Mt. Trail (96) heads uphill.

Distances: *From boundary with private land to trail up Shelving Rock Mt., 0.6 mi.; to Commission Point picnic area, 1.2 mi; to Red Rock Bay Trail, 1.8 mi.; to jct. with Ridge Trail, 2.7 mi.; to trail to Fishbrook Pond, 3.1 mi.; to Black Mt. Point picnic area, 3.3 mi. (5.3 km); to trail up Black Mt., 3.5 mi. (5.6 km). Elevation of Lake George, 320 ft. (98 m).*

(94) Red Rock Bay to Ridge Trail

Map: E-8

This trail is marked as a horse trail, but is a fine hiking trail as it climbs switchbacks up the rugged W flank of Erebus Mt. to meet the

Ridge Trail (92). A nice outlook at the top of a small cliff part way up looks over the central Lake George region. The trail is sparsely marked, but not too difficult to follow. At its terminus with the Ridge Trail a DEC sign states the distance to the lake to be 0.8 mi. ADK's measurement found this instead to be 1.36 mi.

Trailhead: *This trail begins on the Lakeside Trail (93) 1.3 mi. NE of its jct. with the Shelving Rock Mt. Trail (91), and 1.5 mi. S of Black Mt. Point. The other terminus is on the Ridge Trail (92), 1.7 mi. from the Shelving Rock Mt. Trail (90) and 3.1 mi. from the Shelving Rock Mt. trailhead. This trail is marked with yellow horse trail markers.*

From the jct. with the Lakeside Trail (93), the trail heads uphill in a SE direction, and soon switchbacks up the hillside at a gradual to moderately steep angle. At 0.2 mi. the rocky trail heads up, over and around some rocky ledges; then, after using a small streambed, heads up and L across the hill. The sparsely marked trail soon turns L and then R up through a rocky gully and then winds across a level area to the side of the hill. This is a quite rugged horse trail, parts of it being more reminiscent of High Peaks trails than gentle horse trails.

The trail soon begins a gradual ascent heading S along the hillside. It becomes moderately steep along some ledges on the L, then begins a series of switchbacks, some of them fairly steep. At 0.5 mi. the trail follows along a cliff, first with views through the trees, and then with a fine panorama from a rocky ledge (50 ft. from the trail) of The Narrows, Tongue Mt. and the Shelving Rock Mt. area. Just beyond this lookout is a rock knoll about 100 ft. off the trail with even more expansive views.

After climbing briefly, the trail levels out among some hemlocks and then wanders around and across a small stream. At a R turn the trail begins climbing up on a moderate grade. It ascends a rocky area at 0.8 mi and continues a gradual ascent heading SW along the hillside. The trail soon turns L at a sharp switchback, now heading NE. After more switchbacks, the trail once again heads SW on a gradual to moderate grade.

At 1.1 mi., the trail follows along a ledge on the L, on a gradual grade through a deep hemlock forest. After leveling off at 1.25 mi., the trail begins a very gradual descent to its jct. with the Ridge Trail at a wet area at 1.4 mi.

Trail in winter: *This is not recommended as a ski route, but would be good for snowshoeing. It would be wise to have along instep or full crampons for the potentially icy sections.*

Distances: *Lakeside Trail to lookout, 0.5 mi.; to jct. with the Ridge Trail, 1.4 mi. (2.2 km). Ascent, approx. 900 ft. (275 m).*

(95) Fishbrook Pond from Lake George   Map: E-7

This is a nice connector trail, connecting the Lakeside Trail (93) with the midpoint of the trail system that runs up the E side from Hogtown to Pike Brook Rd. (trails 82 and 98). It also caps off more loop possibilities from both the N and the S. The trail gains about 1600 ft. in elevation from the lake shore to the pond, so it's not to be taken lightly, but it adds some real diversity to the possibilities in the region.

Trailhead: *The W terminus is at a jct. with the Lakeside Trail (93) 2.5 mi. N of the Shelving Rock Mt. Trail jct. (91). This is 0.2 mi. S of the Black Mt. Point picnic area and 0.4 mi. S of the jct. with the Black Mt. Trail (93). The E end is at the trail intersection at the NE corner of Fishbrook Pond. This point is 4.6 mi. N of the Hogtown trailhead via trail 82, and 4.0 mi S of the*

There are two beginnings to this trail where it intersects with the Lakeside Trail (92) (0 mi.). They are a short distance apart. These spurs join together after a distance of 0.1 mi. The N spur is the official trail. This trail climbs steadily at a fairly steep grade up along a brook that drains the N side of Erebus Mt.

The trail soon reaches switchbacks and an outlook at 0.4 mi. and continues up the ravine with the stream and a steep drop off on the L. At 0.5 mi, bear L where it looks like an old logging road might lead off to the R. After climbing steeply along the ravine, the trail begins to moderate somewhat as it swings away from the stream. The woods is a mix of hardwood saplings interspersed with huge old trees.

At 1.6 mi. there is a jct. with the Erebus Mt. Trail (88) which comes in from the R. Head straight ahead for Fishbrook Pond. The trail is now level with occasional wet spots. It passes a beautiful white ash just before reaching a ridge on the L that rises up from the N end of Fishbrook Pond. The trail continues through an open hardwood forest, passing by a considerable amount of beaver handiwork, and at 2.2 mi. reaches the jct. with the W trail around Fishbrook Pond (trail 82A).

Continue straight ahead following the red markers. At 2.6 mi. the trail reaches the N lean-to on Fishbrook Pond. This lean-to is a great place to camp or just view the pond and the wildlife from the ledge that slopes into the water in front of the lean-to. On the main trail it's just a short distance E to the intersection at 2.8 mi. with the Hogtown trail on the E side of Fishbrook Pond (trail 82) and the Lapland Pond Trail (98). The jct. for Greenland Pond (trail 100) is about 250 ft. to the N on trail 95.

Trail in winter: *This is a steep trail and can be icy in spots: a great* *snowshoeing trail, but not a recommended ski route.*

Distances: *Lakeside Trail (93) (0.0 mi.) to Erebus Mt. Trail, 1.6 mi.; to jct. with W side trail (trail 82A) at Fishbrook Pond, 2.2 mi.; to intersection at NE corner of Fishbrook Pond, 2.8 mi. (4.5 km). Elevation at beginning of trail, approx. 340 ft. (104 m); at height of pass, approx. 1940 ft. (591 m); Fishbrook Pond, 1836 ft. (560 m).*

(96) Black Mt. Point to Black Mt. Map: E-7

Black Mt., on the E side of Lake George, is the highest mountain in the Lake George area. From the top of Black Mt. are some of the finest views in the Lake George region, and this trail from the shoreline of Lake George is the most spectacular way to climb to the top. It is the lesser used of the two trails up Black Mt., but definitely the more interesting of the two. Leaving the shoreline at one of the wildest remaining areas of the lake, and then climbing past waterfalls and over open rock ledges on the way to the summit, this trail gives a feel of what it may have been like when this region was a summer home for Native Americans in the region hundreds of years ago.

Trailhead: *This trail begins at the N end of the Lakeside Trail (93) at Black Mt. Point. Black Mt. Point is accessible by boat, or by one of the many trails that come from S in the Shelving Rock area. This trail is also accessible from the summit of Black Mt. via the trail from Pike Brook Rd. (trail 97). This is marked with red markers.*

At the jct. with the Lakeside Trail (93) (0.0 mi.) at Black Mt. Point, the trail heads E steeply uphill. At 0.3 mi., it crosses an expanse of bedrock, then soon moderates as it meanders through a forest of tall hemlocks. A brook down to the L comes from Black Mt. Pond.

The trail soon crosses the brook and climbs again until at 0.6 mi. it levels off briefly and bends L. At 0.7 climbing begins again, past a small gorge on the L. Then it bends R away from the gorge and to the E. A short detour off the trail to the gorge will bring you to a number of pretty cascades and flumes just out of sight of the trail.

At 0.8 mi. the route makes a switchback L, not far from some more rushing water. Soon the trail is back along another gorge along the stream on the L, and at 1.1 mi. the cascades in the stream are once again visible from the trail.

The trail soon bends R away from the stream, heading up over bare rock. At 1.3 mi. the trail climbs steeply along a huge rock filled with moss, lichens and ferns on the L. It soon crosses a stream, then briefly levels off. At 1.6 mi. it crosses a stream on a wooden bridge, just below a small waterfall. The jct. with the Black Mt. Ponds Trail (99) is reached at 1.8 mi. To the R are Black Mt. Ponds and Lapland Pond; to the L is the summit of Black Mt.

Heading L, the trail climbs to 2.0 mi. where it passes a huge rock wall on the R and then comes to a rocky outcrop with a nice view. Just off the trail there's a rock ledge that overlooks Black Mt. Pond and Round Pond. The trail levels off briefly, then climbs up several switchbacks with some nice views, reaching a side trail on the R at 2.6 mi. This trail leads to a grassy clearing and ledges with a great view to the S of Lake George and many of the islands. Below are Black Mt. Pond, Round Pond and Lapland Pond farther E.

The main trail soon passes a slanting rock wall, then heads over bare rock and reaches the closed fire tower at the summit at 2.8 mi. Here it meets the trail from Pike Brook Rd. (trail 97).

Trail in winter: This route would be a great snowshoe trip with a good snow-fall. Access is the problem since Black Mt. Point is reached only across Lake George, or from the Shelving Rock Mt. trailhead (see trails 90, 91). A nice route that would involve part of this trail would be to come in from the E on trail 97 and descend from the summit on this trail to the Black Mt. Ponds Trail (99), returning to the Pike Brook trailhead via Black Mt. Ponds and the Lapland Pond Trail (98). Be sure to have instep crampons for icy conditions.

Distances: From Black Mt. Point jct. with Lakeside Trail (93) (0.0 mi.) to jct. with Black Mt. Ponds Trail, 1.8 mi.; to summit, 2.8 mi. (4.5 km). Elevation, 2646 ft. (807 m). Ascent from Lake George, approx. 2300 ft. (701 m).

(97) Black Mt. from the East   Map: F-7

Black Mt., on the E side of Lake George, is the highest mountain in the Lake George area. Since this trail, from Pike Brook Rd., starts at 1600 ft., it is a climb of only 1046 ft. to the summit at 2646 ft. The ascent from the shoreline of Lake George on the W trail is much steeper (see trail 96).

Trailhead: From NY 22, turn W at the sign for Huletts Landing and drive 2.7 mi. to a L turn onto Pike Brook Rd. At 0.8 mi. is the trailhead parking lot and register for Black Mt.

From the parking lot (0.0 mi.), the route, an old road, avoids another old road to the R at 0.2 mi. Following red trail markers, at 0.5 mi. the road reaches an old farmhouse and barn. It turns R here and goes up behind the farm. At 0.7 mi. the road crosses a wet place.

At 1.0 mi. the road reaches a jct. (The trail L goes to Lapland Pond, Millman Pond and Fishbrook Pond [trail 98]). Black Mt. is straight ahead. The road has been gently uphill and almost level to this point.

At 1.3 mi. the road divides. Go L. At 1.4 mi. the trail crosses a wet place. It soon crosses a lovely brook tumbling across shelving rocks and at 1.6 mi. crosses the brook at another jct., where a snowmobile trail joins the trail and veers off again. The trail goes L along the stream. It becomes steep, going up a small rock staircase. At 1.7 mi. it goes up bare rock next to the stream. Now the trail is washed out. At 2.0 mi. it follows a small streambed. Then it cuts R away from the stream.

At 2.1 mi. the trail becomes very steep in a fern-filled glen. At 2.2 mi. avoid a R turn for a snowmobile trail. The trail divides again. These forks rejoin; the L fork enters a clearing with huge open rock. Ahead are the ranger's cabin, toolshed and woodshed. At 2.5 mi. the trail reaches the closed tower. There is a view the length of Lake George, except for The Narrows, which is obstructed by the W shoulder of the mountain.

Sugarloaf Mt., directly NE, has a transmitter tower on top. Elephant Mt. to the N obstructs a view of Huletts Landing. Bluff Point is the first point in view on the E shore, with Sabbath Day Point across on the W shore.

Trail in winter: *This is a nice snowshoe trail with some fairly steep climbing near the top. Instep crampons are recommended for icy sections.*

Distances: *Pike Brook Rd. trailhead to jct., 1.0 mi.; to summit, 2.5 mi. (4.3 km). Ascent, 1046 ft. (337 m). Elevation, 2646 ft. (854 m).*

(98) Lapland Pond Trail

Map: F-7

This is a great hiking trail that connects the Pike Brook Rd. trailhead and the Black Mt. area with the NE corner of the Shelving Rock carriage paths SW of Fishbrook Pond. It also takes in three ponds in the NE corner (Lapland, Millman and Fishbrook), and connects with the trails to the others in this quadrant (Black Mt. Ponds and Greenland Pond). Within just a few miles there are a half dozen lean-tos, several ponds, some great hiking potential, and some great fishing, too.

Trailhead: The N end of this trail is at the jct. 1.0 mi. SW of the Pike Brook trailhead on the Black Mt. from the East Trail (97). S access is from the NE corner of Fishbrook Pond at the jct. with the Hogtown Trail trailhead (82), the Fishbrook/Lake George Trail (95).

From the jct. with the Black Mt. from the East Trail (0.0 mi.), the trail heads S following blue markers. The trail goes along the pond on the R until crossing a wooden bridge next to a beaver dam at 0.2 mi. Because of backwaters caused by industrious beavers, the routes in this area may change somewhat from time to time. At 0.5 mi. the trail passes a tiny pond, then soon crosses a stream on a log bridge. This section can be pretty wet.

At 0.8 mi. the trail starts heading downhill and at 0.9 mi. reaches the spur for the Lapland Pond lean-to on the N shore. A side trail leads L (SE) over the stream and along the pond about 250 yds. to a nice lean-to on a point above the pond. From the point, a giant rock slopes into the water. Ducks and herons feed in the shallows around the pond. This would be a great pond to paddle in a small ultralight canoe.

The main trail proceeds from the jct. past a "Motor Vehicles Prohibited" sign, and at 1.0 mi. crosses an inlet to Lapland Pond. After emerging from a grove of hemlocks, at 1.1 mi. it meets the Black Mt. Ponds Trail (99). The trail heads L to Millman Pond, now following yellow markers.

The trail soon becomes a narrow little-used footpath, crosses a couple of inlet streams, and then heads uphill at 1.2 mi., arriving at the end of a marshy section of the pond at 1.4 mi. Here the trail turns L, following the marsh, and soon crosses a brook on stones. It crosses a wet area and then heads uphill to a T jct. with a wide snowmobile trail at 1.6 mi. (The snowmobile trail L heads E and eventually comes out on lower Pike Brook Rd.) It would be good to look behind you here to note this turnoff for your return trip. Look for the trail markers, and listen for the rushing of the stream.

After turning R, the trail heads uphill with the stream on the R. The trail crosses the stream below a nice 4-ft. waterfall. Here a snowmobile trail goes straight and the foot trail turns L. Continuing uphill, with the stream on the R, the trail soon crosses the stream and goes up along the side of a hill. It comes to a flume on the outlet of Millman Pond at 1.8 mi. Soon the trail goes uphill, reaching a crest at 1.9 mi., then heads down toward Millman Pond. At 2.0 mi. the trail crosses an inlet stream on a bridge, with a bog on the L. It turns abruptly R and shortly comes to a lean-to on the E side of the pond at 2.1 mi. This is situated on a bluff that overlooks the pond.

Heading S, the trail reaches the end of the pond at 2.2 mi., then turns L and uphill following a stream and snowmobile markers. At a wet place the snowmobile trail and the hiking trail divide. They soon rejoin after crossing a stream at 2.4 mi., and then make a sharp L. The trail heads downhill with the stream on the L, flanked by a steep hillside. The trail rolls up and down a little, then climbs again and reaches the top of a pass at 2.8 mi.

Now the trail heads downhill to Fishbrook Pond, crosses a stream, then turns L and keeps heading downhill, first coming to the Greenland Pond Trail (100) on the L, and then, in approx. 250 ft., an intersection with the Fishbrook/Lake George Trail (95) to the R (W) and the trail to Hogtown trailhead via Bumps Pond (82) straight ahead. An unmaintained trail heads L (E) from this jct. There's a lean-to to the R at the N end of Fishbrook Pond, another along trail 82 at the S end of Fishbrook Pond, and yet another 1.2 mi. away on the E shore of Greenland Pond.

Distances: *Black Mt. Trail to lean-to spur trail on Lapland Pond, 0.9 mi.; to jct. with Black Mt. Ponds Trail, 1.1 mi.; to Millman Pond lean-to, 2.1 mi.; to intersection at NE corner of Fishbrook Pond, 3.0 mi. (4.8 km). Elevation of*

Lapland Pond, 1731 ft. (528 m); Millman Pond, approx. 1860 ft. (567 m); Fishbrook Pond, 1836 ft. (560 m).

(99) Black Mt. Ponds Trail

Map: F-7

This is a short connector trail between the Black Mt. Trail (96), and the Lapland Pond Trail (98) that not only helps form some interesting loops, but is also a good trail to hike. There's a lean-to on Black Mt. Pond, and the trail passes through some nice woods and beaver work. For those who walk slowly and take the time to observe all the signs, there's the possibility of seeing a good bit of wildlife in the area.

Trailhead: *The W end is 1.8 mi. E of Black Mt. Point and 1.0 mi. S of Black Mt. summit on trail 96. The jct. with trail 98 on the E end is 2.2 mi. SW of the Pike Brook Rd. trailhead, and 1.9 mi. N of Fishbrook Pond. The trail is marked with yellow markers.*

The trail begins on the Black Mt. Trail (0.0 mi.). Heading E, at 0.2 mi. the trail follows a rise with Black Mt. Pond below to the R, and soon reaches the edge of the pond. Across a stream and up a short steep hill is the lean-to just off the trail. There's a nice view of the pond from the lean-to.

The main trail follows along the edge of the pond, then at 0.4 mi. heads up a hill and back into a hemlock woods. At 0.6 mi. it goes down a short steep hill to an inlet to Round Pond. It crosses another inlet at 0.7 mi. and soon there's a view of Round Pond and the beaver activity there. The trail continues back in the woods, reaching the jct. with the Lapland Pond trail at 1.0 mi.

Distances: *Black Mt. Trail to lean-to side trail 0.25 mi.; to Round Pond,*

0.8 mi.; to jct. with Lapland Pond Trail, 1.0 mi. (1.6 km). Elevation of Black Mt. Pond, approx. 1700 ft. (518 m).

(100) Greenland Pond

Map: F-8

While this trail is short but sweet, any public route to get to it is at least 4 mi. long. Greenland Pond, though, is well worth the visit. It's a pretty little pond, with a lean-to situated on the E shore, a nice place to camp and fish.

Trailhead: *The trail begins at the intersection of trails at the NE corner of Fishbrook Pond. The Hogtown trailhead is 4.6 mi. to the S on trail 82, and the Pike Brook Rd. trailhead is 4.0 mi. to the N via trails 97 and 98. Black Mt. Point is 2.8 mi. to the W via trails 95 (2.8 mi.) and 93 (0.2 mi.). The trail is marked with red markers.*

From the intersection at the NE corner of Fishbrook Pond (0.0 mi.), the trail heads E over some potentially wet areas. At 0.3 mi. a stream is crossed on stones, and the trail begins heading downhill. It soon crosses the stream again, and then turns L and continues downhill. After passing a pretty set of falls at 0.5 mi., at 0.7 mi. the trail crosses another stream and then comes to Greenland Pond.

The trail follows along the SW shore of the pond, crosses a couple of inlets, and then at 1.0 mi. crosses a larger inlet. The trail continues around the S end of the pond, and crosses the outlet on a bridge. There is a jct. here; an unmarked trail S leads to private land in a short distance. The red-marked trail heads N a short distance up the E shore of the pond, reaching the lean-to at 1.2 mi.

Distances: *Fishbrook Pond to Greenland Pond lean-to, 1.2 mi. (1.9 km). Elevation of Greenland Pond, approx. 1600 ft. (488 m); of Fishbrook Pond, 1836 ft. (560 m).*

Appendix I

Glossary of Terms

Bivouac   Camping in the open with improvised shelter or none at all.

Bushwhacking To make one's way through bushes or undergrowth without the aid of a formal trail.

Cairn   A pile of stones to mark a summit or route.

Chimney   A steep, narrow cleft or gully in the face of a mountain, usually by which it may be ascended.

Cobble   A small stony peak on the side of a mountain.

Col   A pass between two adjacent peaks.

Corduroy   A road, trail or bridge formed by logs laid side by side transversely to facilitate crossing swampy areas.

Couloir   A deep gorge or gully on a hillside.

Cripplebush   Thick, stunted growth at higher elevations.

Dike   A band of different colored rock, usually with straight, well-defined sides. Formed when igneous rock is intruded into the existing rock. Dikes can manifest themselves either as gullies, if the dike rock is softer, or as ridges.

Duff   Partly decayed vegetable matter on the forest floor. It can burn easily. Burning duff has started many forest fires.

Lean-to	A three-sided shelter with an overhanging roof on the open side.
Lumber Road	A crude road constructed for the purpose of hauling logs.
Tote Road	A better road constructed in connection with logging operations and used for hauling supplies to a lumber camp, etc. Often built with corduroy, many of these roads are still evident after 80 years and are often used as the route for present-day trails.

Firetower on Poke-O-Moonshine Mt.

Appendix II

Table of Short Hikes

To help those looking for some of the easier routes in the Eastern Region of the Adirondacks, the following table lists hikes to destinations with distances of less than 2.5 mi. (one way). These are listed from shortest to longest for each section of this guide. This table should help those unfamiliar with the region to locate the easier hikes and worthwhile destinations, almost all of which are suitable for hiking with children. (See the section on Hiking with Children in the Introduction of this guide.)

The name and number of each of these trails are given, along with a brief note as to the hiking terrain to help in quickly choosing an appropriate hike. Most of these hikes are over level to moderate terrain. Please bear in mind though, when selecting a hike, that within this selected group of hikes, there can be quite a difference in terrain between, for example, the hikes to the top of Shelving Rock Mt., and along Lake George to Shelving Rock Falls.

Mi.	Objective	Trail Name & Number	Notes on Terrain
		NORTHERN SECTION	
0.4	Belfry Mt summit and tower	Belfry Mt. (16)	Moderate grade
0.8	Island hike	Nomad Trail (2)	Access by boat
1.3	Island hike	Royal Savage Trail (3)	Access by boat
1.2	Summit views	Poke-O-Moonshine (4)	Steep sections

Mi.	Objective	Trail Name & Number	Notes on Terrain
1.6	Woods walk	Morehouse Bridge to Boquet (17)	Mostly level
1.9	View from cliffs on Lake Champlain	Snake Den Lookout (9)	Mostly level
2.3	Blueberry Cobbles	Bald Peak (19)	Steep for 0.5 mi.
2.5	International summit view	Lyon Mt. (5)	Mostly steep climbing

HAMMOND POND WILD FOREST SECTION

Mi.	Objective	Trail Name & Number	Notes on Terrain
0.3	Pretty setting	Arnold Pond (30)	Steep climb
0.6	Woods walk to a pretty pond	Challis Pond (26)	Easy hike
1.2	Enjoyable walk to 2 ponds	Howard and Munson Ponds (24)	Some climbing
2.2	Views of the Pharaoh Lake Wilderness	Peaked Hill Pond and Peaked Hill (29)	Access by boat; some climbing up to Peaked Hill

PHARAOH LAKE WILDERNESS SECTION

Mi.	Objective	Trail Name & Number	Notes on Terrain
0.5	Nice small pond	Gull Pond (56)	Easy hike
1.2	Schroon Lake views	Severance Mt. (58)	Moderate climb
1.7	Some fine Lake George views	Cooks Mt. (59)	Some steep climbing
1.7	Views of Pharaoh Mt. over the pond	Spectacle Pond (55)	An easy climb
2.3	Fine views of the SE Adirondack Mt. area	Treadway Mt. (46)	Moderate climb from the Putnam Pond shoreline (access by boat)

Mi.	Objective	Trail Name & Number	Notes on Terrain

NORTHWESTERN LAKE GEORGE WILD FOREST SECTION

Mi.	Objective	Trail Name & Number	Notes on Terrain
1.4	Nature trail	Charles Lathrop Pack Demonstration Forest Nature Trail (70)	Easy hike
1.4	Riverside walk	Parks & Recreation Nature Trail (71)	Easy hike
1.6	Two pretty ponds	Long & Island Ponds (63)	Easy woods walk mostly on old roads
1.7	Lake George views	Deer Leap (66)	Moderate hike at N end of Tongue Mt. Range

SOUTHEASTERN LAKE GEORGE WILD FOREST REGION

Mi.	Objective	Trail Name & Number	Notes on Terrain
0.8	Pleasant walk to a beautiful pond	Inman Pond (75)	Easy hike
0.9	Great walk along a cascading brook	Big Bridges Trail (89)	Easy hike
1.7	View of Lake George	Prospect Mt. (72)	Steep hike
1.7	Lake George views	Shelving Rock Mt. (90)	Moderate climbing
1.8	Expansive views to the E, S, & W	Sleeping Beauty (83)	Some steep climbing (distance to the summit from Dacy Clearing)
2.0	Shoreline views and a beautiful waterfall	Shelving Rock Falls Lake Loop (79)	A short section of moderate climbing
2.3	360° views	Buck Mt. from Hogtown (77)	Some steep climbing
2.4	Attractive woods walk	Shortway Trail (85)	Gradual grade
2.5	Exceptional views	Black Mt. from the East (97)	Some steep sections, great views from rock ledges (fire tower is **closed**)

Appendix III

Opportunities in the Eastern Region for Physically Impaired Recreationists

The following is a list of outing opportunities in the Eastern Adirondack region for people who are physically impaired. Because there are many types of physical challenges, users of these trails must carefully select those that are suitable for the particular individuals or group that will use them. **These trails and access points do not conform to formal accessibility standards and are subject to changes in weather conditions.**

Most people enjoy the out-of-doors in part because of the challenges found there. Those who lead trips must carefully consider the capabilities of the individuals in their party and the degree of challenge they desire. This is particularly important for leaders of the physically impaired. Leaders must plan these trips carefully and be thoroughly familiar with the routes to be taken.

Scenic Vistas

There are many vistas throughout the Adirondacks. Some of the more outstanding ones in the Eastern Adirondacks are listed below.

Prospect Mt. 5.5 mi. on a four-lane highway from the S end of Lake George village to the parking lot, then take "viewmobiles" to the summit. Fine views of Lake George, the Adirondacks and Vermont mts.

Top Of The World. Exit 21 off I-87, Northway, Drive 6 mi. NE off

NY 9 on NY 9L to the sign; steep drive to the top. Beautiful Lake George overlook.

Federal Hill Rd. and Coolidge Hill Rd., Bolton Landing. Fine views of Lake George.

Riverbank Rd. The hill just W of NY 9N, N of Bolton Landing, has exceptional views of Lake George and the surrounding mountains.

NY 8 Rest Area. On the S side of the highway approx. 8 mi. E of the town of Brant Lake. Views looking W to the SE Adirondack Mts.

Hague on Lake George. Beautiful views of the N Lake George area.

Mt. Defiance. Drive to the top of the mountain S of Ticonderoga. (Follow the signs from downtown.) Views of the S Champlain Valley.

Ferry Ride from Essex, NY to Charlotte, VT. A real treat and a beautiful panorama of the Adirondacks.

Lakeshore Rd. between Westport and Essex. Lake Champlain views and mountain views.

Middle Rd. S of Willsboro. Views from the Champlain Valley farming country.

Willsboro Point N of Willsboro. Fine views of Lake Champlain and the mountains.

Trail Access

Valcour Island (trail 1). Accessible by boat.

Split Rock Mt. area (trail 9). Trail follows old roads.

Mill, Murrey, & Russett Ponds (trails 13, 14, 15). Easy access to pretty waters.

Crane Pond and Crane Pond Rd. (trail 36). Interior access to Crane Pond via the access road.

Cooks Mt. (trail 59). Observe wildlife habitat along an old road on the first section of the trail.

Charles Lathrop Pack Demonstration Forest Nature Trail (trail 70). Approx. 2 mi. N of Warrensburg.

Warren Co. Parks and Recreation Nature Trail (trail 71). Approx. 2.5 mi. NW of Warrensburg on River Rd.

Shelving Rock Falls, Shelving Rock Mt., and Hogtown Trailhead (trails 79, 80, 81, 82, 84, 85, 86, 89, 90). This region contains many old carriage paths of varying degrees of difficulty. The interconnecting paths offer a range of tours for a variety of abilities.

Lakeside Trail to Black Mt. Point (trail 93). Beautiful trail along the Lake George shoreline following an old carriage path. Accessible by boat.

Boating Access

Peru Dock, Clinton Co. On US 9, 1.5 mi. N of the hamlet of Valcour. Parking for 50 cars and trailers. Hard-surface ramp.

Port Douglas, Essex Co. On Co. Rt. 16, 3 mi. SE of Keeseville. Hard-surface ramp. Parking for 20 cars and trailers.

Willsboro Bay, Essex Co. On Co. Rt. 27 on E side of bay, 3 mi. N of Willsboro. Hard-surface ramp. Parking for 100 cars and trailers.

Westport, Essex Co. On NY 22 in Westport. Hard-surface ramp. Parking for 35 cars and trailers.

Port Henry, Essex Co. Off NY 9N in Port Henry. Hard-surface ramp. Parking for 45 cars and trailers.

Crown Point Reservation, Essex Co. On Bridge Rd., off US 9N, 9 mi. N of Crown Point. Parking for 10 cars and trailers. Hard-surface ramp.

Ticonderoga, Essex Co. On NY 74 at Ticonderoga Ferry. Hard-surface ramp. Parking for 80 cars and trailers.

Putnam Pond Campground, Essex Co. Off NY 74, 6 mi. W of Ticonderoga. Parking for 10 cars and trailers. Hard-surface ramp.

Paradox Lake Campground, Essex Co. On NY 74, 2 mi. E of Severance. Parking for 25 cars and trailers. Hard-surface ramp.

Schroon Lake, Eagle Point Campground, Warren Co. On US 9, 2 mi. N of Pottersville. Parking for 4 cars. Hand launching.

Horicon, Warren Co. Off US 9, just N of Pottersville on Co. Rt. 62. Hard-surface launching ramp. Parking for 49 cars and trailers.

Brant Lake, Warren Co. On NY 8, 1 mi. NE of hamlet of Brant Lake. Beach launch. Parking for 11 cars and trailers.

Mossy Point, Essex Co. On Black Point Rd., 2 mi. N of Ticonderoga on E shore of Lake George. Hard-surface ramp. Parking for 110 cars and trailers.

Lake George, Rogers Rock Campground, Warren Co. On NY 9N, 3 mi. N of Hague. Concrete ramp. Parking for 24 cars and trailers.

Northwest Bay Brook, Warren Co. On NY 9N, 4 mi. N of Bolton Landing. Hand launching. Parking for 15 cars.

Million Dollar Beach, Warren Co. On Beach Rd. in the village of Lake George. Hard-surface ramp. Parking for 200 cars and trailers. **Closed during the summer** from the week before Memorial Day to the week after Labor Day. Underpass clearance 7 ft. maximum.

The Department of Environmental Conservation (DEC) produces a brochure, "Opening the Outdoors to People with Disabilities," available from the DEC, 50 Wolf Rd., Albany, NY 12233.

DEC also provides a free permit for physically impaired people who want to take a motor vehicle onto a normally restricted access road in Wild Forest areas. Allow three to four weeks' lead time for obtaining this permit. There is no restriction on the use of motorized wheelchairs (as long as they are the kind used in the home) in Wilderness areas. Consult DEC at the above address for further information.

Appendix IV

Lean-tos in the Eastern Region

The following is a listing of all lean-tos within the area covered by this guidebook. They are listed according to the guidebook sections, with information on USGS map and location. Unlisted sections did not have any lean-tos at time of publication. As Unit Management Plans (UMP) are completed, relocation, removals or additional lean-tos may alter this listing.

Shelter	USGS Map	Location
NORTHERN SECTION		
Poke-o-Moonshine	Ausable Forks	0.85 mi. from trailhead; 65 yds S of ranger cabin
HAMMOND POND WILD FOREST SECTION		
Moose Mt. Pond		on W shore
Eagle Lake	Paradox	On Crown Pt. Bay, also picnic area w/beach, 6 tables, 2 stone fireplaces, reached by boat only
PHARAOH LAKE WILDERNESS SECTION		
Pharaoh 1 & 2	Paradox	On SE shore
Pharaoh 3	Paradox	On E shore
Pharo (Pharaoh lean-to #4)	Paradox	On N shore at Split Rock Bay

Shelter	USGS Map	Location
Pharaoh Lake 5	Paradox	On a point on W shore
Pharaoh Lake 6	Paradox	On SW shore
Tubmill Marsh	Paradox	On a rise N of marsh
Oxshoe Pond	Paradox	On W shore

PHARAOH LAKE WILDERNESS SECTION

Grizzle Ocean	Paradox	On N shore
Berrymill Pond	Paradox	On N shore
Rock Pond	Paradox	On E shore
Little Rock Pond	Paradox	Facing wetland N of pond
Lilypad Pond	Paradox	On N shore

NW LAKE GEORGE WILD FOREST SECTION

Five Mile Mt.	Silver Bay	On N side of mt.
Fifth Peak	Silver Bay	On E side of peak 2.7 mi. from Clay Meadow

SE LAKE GEORGE WILD FOREST SECTION

Fishbrook Pond 1	Shelving Rock	On S shore
Fishbrook Pond 2	Shelving Rock	On N shore
Black Mt. Pond	Shelving Rock	On N shore
Lapland Pond	Shelving Rock	On E shore 0.1 mi. from main trail
Millman Pond	Shelving Rock	On E shore
Greenland Pond	Shelving Rock	On E shore

Appendix V

State Campgrounds in the Eastern Region

Public campgrounds have been established by the DEC at many attractive spots throughout the state. Listed below, going gnerally N to S, are those campgrounds which might be useful as bases of operations for hiking in the Eastern Adirondacks region. A complete listing of all campgrounds is contained in a brochure of the New York State Forest Preserve Public Campgrounds titled "Come Back Next Summer." This brochure is available from the DEC, 50 Wolf Rd., Albany, NY 12233.

Point Au Roche State Park. Off US 9 near Beekmantown on Lake Champlain. Presently under development and will have campsites in the future.

Valcour Island. Accessible by boat from the Peru Boat Launch site on US 9.

Cumberland Bay. 1 mi. N of Plattsburgh on NY 314.

Ausable Point. US 9, 12 mi. S of Plattsburgh.

Poke-o-Moonshine. US 9, 6 mi. S of Keeseville.

Lincoln Pond. 6 mi. S of Elizabethtown on Co. Rt. 7.

Sharp Bridge. US 9, 15 mi. N of Schroon Lake in the Town of North Hudson.

Crown Point Reservation. On Lake Champlain off NY 9N, 8 mi. N of Crown Point.

Paradox Lake. On NY 74, 2 mi. E of Severance.

Putnam Pond. Off NY 74, 6 mi. W of Ticonderoga.

Rogers Rock. On Lake George off NY 9N, 4 mi. N of Hague.

Eagle Point. On Schroon Lake, US 9, 2 mi. N of Pottersville.

Hearthstone Point. NY 9N, 2 mi. N of Lake George village.

Lake George Battleground. US 9, 0.2 mi. S of Lake George village.

Luzerne. NY 9N, 8 mi. SW of Lake George village.

Fishing licenses may be purchased at campgrounds or from town clerks.

For information on the islands in Lake George or on the E shore of the lake, or on Valcour Island in Lake Champlain, write for this brochure: "Island Camping," Public Information and Publications Unit, NYS DEC, 50 Wolf Road, Albany, NY 12233. For a complete listing of all campgrounds in the New York State Forest Preserve, send for the brochure "Come Back Next Summer" from the same address. This and other helpful brochures are available at regional DEC offices or tourist information centers.

Index

Note: Lakes are listed under their names instead of under "Lake."

Notes

Notes

Notes

The Adirondack Mountain Club, Inc.
RR 3, Box 3055
Lake George, N.Y. 12845-9522
(518) 668-4447

BOOKS

85 Acres: A Field Guide to the Adirondack Alpine Summits
Classic Adirondack Ski Tours
Adirondack Canoe Waters: North Flow
Adirondack Canoe Waters: South & West Flow
The Adirondack Mt. Club Canoe Guide to Western & Central New York State
Winterwise: A Backpacker's Guide
Climbing in the Adirondacks
Guide to Adirondack Trails: High Peaks Region
Guide to Adirondack Trails: Northern Region
Guide to Adirondack Trails: Central Region
Guide to Adirondack Trails: Northville–Placid Trail
Guide to Adironadack Trails: West–Central Region
Guide to Adirondack Trails: Southern Region
Guide to Catskill Trails
An Adirondack Sampler, Day Hikes for All Seasons
An Adirondack Sampler II, Backpacking Trips
Geology of the Adirondack High Peaks Region
The Adirondack Reader
Adirondack Pilgrimage
Our Wilderness: How the People of New York Found, Changed, and
Preserved the Adirondacks
Adirondack Wildguide (distributed by ADK)

MAPS

Trails of the Adirondack High Peaks Region
Trails of the Northern Region
Trails of the Central Region
Northville-Placid Trail
Trails of the West-Central Region
Trails of the Eastern Region
Trails of the Southern Region

Price list available on request.

Backdoor to Backcountry

ADKers choose from friendly outings, for those just getting started with local chapters, to Adirondack backpacks and international treks. Learn gradually through chapter outings or attend one of our schools, workshops, or other programs. A sampling includes:

- Alpine Flora
- Ice Climbing
- Rock Climbing
- Basic Canoeing
- Bicycle Touring
- Cross-country Skiing

- Mountain Photography
- Winter Mountaineering
- Birds of the Adirondacks
- Geology of the High Peaks
  ... and so much more!

For more information about the Adirondacks or about ADK:

ADK's Information Center & Headquarters
RR3, Box 3055, Lake George, NY 12845-9522
(518) 668-4447
Exit 21 off I-87 ("the Northway"), 9N South

6/15–Columbus Day:
Mon.–Sat., 8:30 a.m.–5:00 p.m.

Tues. after Columbus Day–6/14:
Mon.–Fri.. 8:30 a.m.–4:30 p.m.

For more information about our lodges:

ADK Lodges
Box 867, Lake Placid, NY 12946
(518) 523-3441   9 a.m.–7:00 p.m.

Join a Chapter

Three-quarters of ADK members belong to a local chapter. Those not wishing to join a particular chapter may join ADK as members-at-large.

Chapter membership brings you the fun of outings and social activities or the reward of working on trails, conservation, and education projects at the local level. You can still participate in all regular Club activities and receive all Club benefits.

Adirondak Loj	North Elba
Albany	Albany
Algonquin	Plattsburgh
Black River	Watertown
Cold River	Long Lake
Connecticut Valley	Hartford
Finger Lakes	Ithaca–Elmira
Genesee Valley	Rochester
Glens Falls	Glens Falls
Hurricane Mountain	Keene
Iroquois	Utica
Keene Valley	Keene Valley
Knickerbocker	New York City and vicinity
Lake Placid	Lake Placid
Laurentian	Canton-Potsdam
Long Island	Long Island
Mid-Hudson	Poughkeepsie
Mohican	Westchester and Putnam counties, NY/Fairfield Co., CT
New York	Metropolitan Area*
Niagara Frontier	Buffalo
North Jersey	Bergen County
North Woods	Saranac Lake–Tupper Lake
Onondaga	Syracuse
Penn's Woods	Harrisburg, PA
Ramapo	Rockland & Orange counties
Schenectady	Schenectady
Shatagee Woods	Malone
Susquehanna	Oneonta

*Special requirements apply

Adirondack
ADK
Mountain Club

Membership
To Join:

Call **1-800-395-8080** (Visa or Mastercard)
or send this form with payment to
Adirondack Mountain Club
RR3, Box 3055
Lake George, NY 12845-9522.

Check Membership Level:

☐ Life	$1,000*
☐ Forest Preserve	$250*
☐ Patron	$125*
☐ Supporting	$75*
☐ Contributing	$50*
☐ Family	$40*
☐ Adult	$35
☐ Senior Family	$30*
☐ Senior (65+)	$25
☐ Junior (under 18)	$20
☐ Student (18+, full time)	$20

School _____

Includes associate/family members

Name _____
Address _____
City _____ State _____ Zip _____
Home Telephone ( ) _____

☐ I want to join as a member-at-large.
☐ I want to join as a _____ Chapter member.

List spouse & children under 18 with birthdates:

Spouse _____
Child _____ Birthdate _____
Child _____ Birthdate _____

Bill my: ☐ VISA ☐ MASTERCARD Exp. date _____
☐☐☐☐☐☐☐☐☐☐☐☐☐☐☐☐

_____
Signature (required for charge)

ADK is a non-profit, tax-exempt organization. Membership fees are tax deductible, as allowed by law. Please allow 6-8 weeks for receipt of first issue of **Adirondac** or the **ADK Newsletter.**

Membership Rewards

- **Discovery:**
  ADK can broaden your horizons by introducing you to new places, recreational activities, and interests.

- **Enjoyment:**
  Being outdoors more and loving it more.

- **People:**
  Meeting others and sharing the fun.

- *Adirondac* Magazine and **ADK Newsletter:**
  Eight times a year.

- **Member Discounts:**
  20% off on guidebooks, maps, and other publications; 10% off on lodge stays; reduced rates for educational programs.

- **Satisfaction:**
  Knowing you're doing your part and that future generations will enjoy the wilderness as you do.

Adirondack **ADK** Mountain Club   **Conservation** **Recreation** **Education**